A Smuggler's Guide to Good Manners

A Smuggler's Guide to Good Manners

A True Story Of Terrifying Seas, Double-Dealing,
And Love Across Three Oceans

Kenny Ranen

Cover Art by Tracey Fedor

ISBN-13: 9780692884331
ISBN-10: 0692884335
Library of Congress Control Number: 2017908572
No Cure No Pay, Carmen, ID

Table of Contents

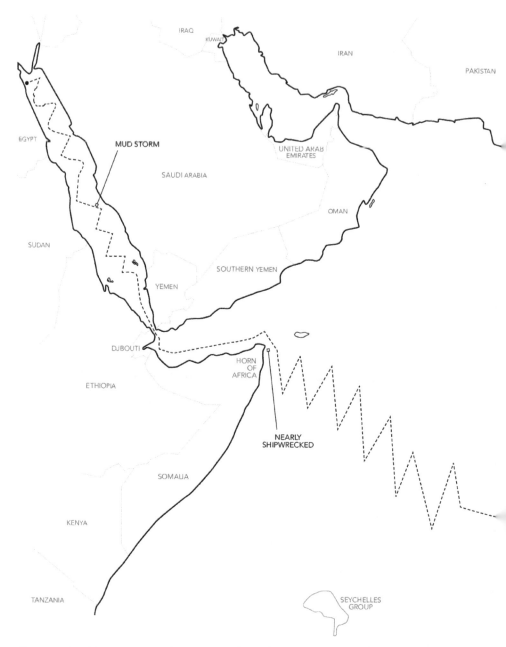

Sara's Route through the Indian Ocean
From Thialand to the Red Sea

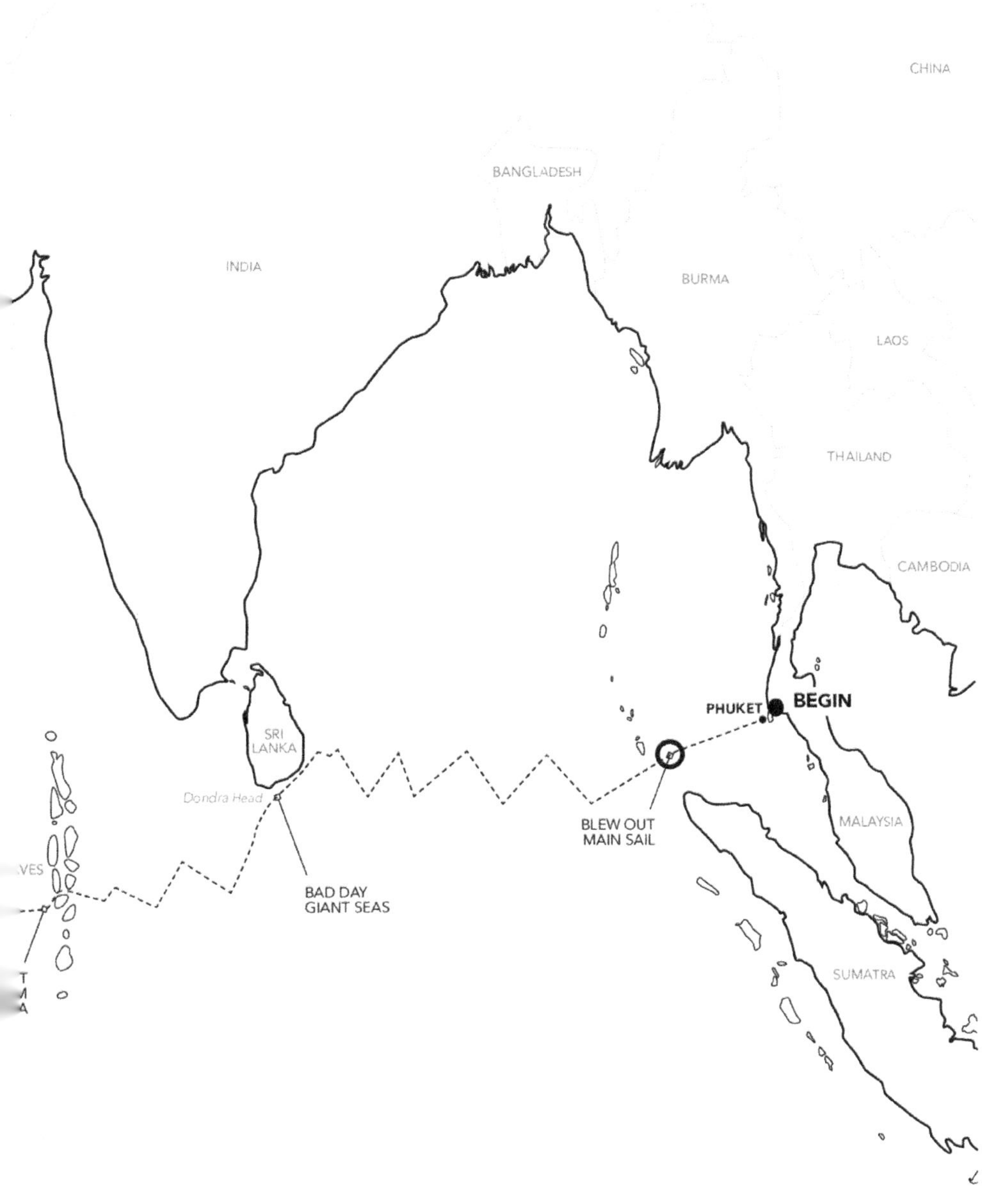
CHINA
BANGLADESH
INDIA
BURMA
LAOS
THAILAND
CAMBODIA
PHUKET
BEGIN
SRI LANKA
Dondra Head
BLEW OUT MAIN SAIL
BAD DAY GIANT SEAS
MALAYSIA
SUMATRA

Forward

OF SMUGGLING, AMERICANS have always been of two minds. John Hancock's family armada of sailing vessels ran contraband blatantly. The British busted him twice but both times local support around Boston got the charges dropped.

In the 19th century all classes smuggled, and the nature of the contraband determined one's position on the issue. Silks and perfume at one end and slaves at the other. The early twentieth century saw rumrunners morph into respected industry magnates as prohibition ended. Beginning in the 1960's the global demand for narcotics outsourced this ancient misconduct to anyone with a taste for adrenaline and a big score.

Kenny Ranen, my best friend from middle school in Atlanta in the early 1960's disappeared for fifty years. He had been a wild and audacious boy, dismissive of the racist views of our peers and our parents. Before he was old enough to drive he was hanging out at the Royal Peacock nightclub on Auburn Avenue, befriending artists like Otis Redding. When Ike and Tina had an open date, Kenny called all the white Frat houses at Emory and Georgia Tech and found them work. Soon Kenny was a white high school kid, booking an unknown Otis Redding at high School proms.

Meanwhile I had moved up North in high school and began to lose touch with Kenny. After graduation, I was in college in Maryland, and heard Kenny had dropped out of the University of Georgia in his freshman year and the following year dropped out of San Francisco State to "Climb Rocks."

I didn't know what climbing rocks meant, and after that Kenny Ranen disappeared. Turns out his summers were spent climbing out of Camp 4 and hanging out with Jim Bridwell, Michael Covington and Dean Ketcham. Winters, he was sewing mountain gear at First Lead in Telluride, working on the crew that built the mountain's first chairlift, and then he was gone. No house, no address, no phone, living on sailboats, and in the boatyards of the world for 28 years.

A *Smuggler's Guide to Good Manners* is an five year slice of those 28 years, on the sailing vessel *Sara,* in the waters of the Indian Ocean, and in the jails of Spain. A sea story. A love story. A tale polished while rolling antifouling in faraway boatyards and told in port bars where seafarers drank and waited for good weather.

Kenny was working in a boatyard in Michigan, when he called me in October of 2015. He soon quit his job and showed up at my house in January to finish this book. He brought the ship's logs and charts, a few old photos, and endless stories from the days when he was sailing ten to twenty thousand miles a year without GPS, and without a care, notwithstanding sharks, pirates, monsoon storms, medical emergencies at sea, and the Guardia Civil.

Mark Mendel 2016

PART 1 – Welcome Aboard, 1961-89

C H A P T E R   1

Almerimar, Spain, 1989

I SLID BACK the hatch, climbed the companionway ladder to the cockpit, and a blast of sandy, dry wind punched me in the face. The Mistral had been blowing hard, straight off the Sahara desert for three days. It was February on the Costa Del Sol and the winter sun offered little warmth. I looked up through the haze of wind-borne sand at a fuzzy, brown sun and clearly understood how after nine days of Mistral, Vincent van Gogh could cut off his own ear.

Sara was moored alongside the boatyard quay in a little-known out-of-the-way yacht harbor called Almerimar on the Mediterranean coast of Spain, right in the heart of Andalusia, where the Moors invaded Europe and established an Arabic stronghold that lasted a thousand years. That's a long time. A millennium. Typically Europe changes the invaders, and not the other way around, but this is that part of Spain that resisted Europe, Dark-eyed Flamenco dancers, wrought iron, crumbling stucco, and Granada, the Moors summer palace in the Sierra Nevada.

Almerimar was a high-end luxury resort that just never took off. It was too far from an airport, didn't have the great beaches, or the gaudy, new-money timeshare action of nearby Southern Costa Del Sol. The Almerimar developers eventually sold the condos off cheaply to Spanish families who came down on holidays.

The first-class marina was empty, with a few cruising sailboats scattered around the floating docks. It did have a decent bar, with a cook who put out a fresh, elegant tapa with every beer. It was one of those sleepy little ports that I kept filed away in my memory for times when I might need to lay low, and right about then I really needed to lay low.

We were there to lick our wounds after months of beating into vicious Indian Ocean seas, more of the same up the Red Sea, and then (in case that wasn't enough), another 2000 miles of nonstop Mediterranean winter storms.

Sara, my 46 foot, classic racing yacht, was still startlingly beautiful: a two-masted, sleek white hull, with dark green canvas, and a teak cockpit. She was dead in the water. Nevertheless, appearances are everything. So despite the stressed and broken equipment, she had to look every bit the fast, custom-built deep-ocean racer she was.

I'd had a busy morning, five knuckle-busting hours detaching hoses, fittings, and frozen engine parts, getting ready for the yard crane driver to pick the engine out of the boat and put it on the shore. Aside from cursing rusted bolts, I hadn't spoken a word since last night at the bar.

My stomach was growling so loud it was scaring off the gulls and I started wondering if Paul and Annie had any of their usual gourmet leftovers. So, after slipping into my All Stars and grabbing a bottle of red wine, I jumped to the quay and walked across the dusty shipyard to their boat.

Paul and Annie were the closest thing to friends I had in the marina. Maybe it was because they were the only other live-aboard sailors there, but, now that I think about it, thirty years later, it was because they'd sought my company. For sailors, they were pretty cosmopolitan, in a Euro-trash sort of way, and I did enjoy their company, even though I didn't trust them.

Paul was an ex-KGB Russian emigrant, one of many ex-Soviets drifting into Europe as the Russian "republic" was falling to pieces. He asked too many questions and talked too much about things that are better left unsaid.

He confided that they had a load of Moroccan hash onboard they needed to get out of Spain, because he knew that we had come from Thailand, but I just kept quiet about business details. He even gave me a chunk of hash the size of a bar of soap, hoping his calling card would open a dialogue about smuggling. I threw it away. I couldn't think of why a smuggler would set us up, but why take chances?

Their 38 foot sailing boat was out of the water and their ancient Renault 16 was parked just next to it, so I rapped on the hull and hailed the boat as I climbed up the ladder. "Ahoy, Paul and Annie. Up for freeloaders?" Annie called out in her low, gravelly voice, with a hint of Belgian accent, "Come below, Ranen, I've got cold chicken for lunch."

Paul was sitting at the salon table, drinking a glass of wine, rolling a spliff. "Are you worried about coming into the boatyard?" Paul asked. "People in our line of work don't like having their boat out of commission. You can't leave if things get hot. We were in the yard when I was arrested in Palma."

There it was again, always pushing for information. Ignoring his line I said, "As soon as I get the engine pulled out tomorrow morning they'll lift me out of the water." I tried to change the subject, "Here's some of that wine I found in the village. It's not Rioja but it is a really good wine."

"Ranen!" Annie called out insistently. "You better get over to your boat. There are police all around *Sara.*"

I instantly shot up on deck.

One look at the scene around my boat paralyzed me with fear. Dark-green Land Rovers and Guardia Civil in dark-green military uniforms were all around the quay next to *Sara.* They looked kind of ridiculous, in their little pillbox, patent-leather hats that were too small for heads, until you remembered that the Guardia Civil had held all of Spain in an iron grip since the 1930's. Franco had created the organization as his own private army and secret police, and the fascist bastards still held the nation captive, even ten years after his death.

By my side, Paul whispered to himself, "Christos, it's the Spanish KGB."

The first rush of adrenalin cleared my mind and slowed down time. I felt completely calm and hyper focused. Running away was not an option I had ever considered. I had weathered situations like this before, by projecting a totally non-criminal image. Front is everything.

I memorized the scene and stepped over the life lines, climbed down the ladder, and slowly walked toward *Sara* through the rows of boats propped up in the yard. This was a stage, and I was playing the wealthy, young owner of a sailing yacht on my world cruise.

I strode up to the one plain-clothed Guardia. The plain-clothes cop is always the one in charge. "Can I help you?" I demanded, polite, but a little arrogant.

"Is this your boat?"

"Yes it is."

He showed me some papers, "I am Capitán Ramirez and I have authority to search. We have a dog."

I stepped aboard before they could tell me not to, followed by Ramirez, three uniformed men and a German Shepherd. In this situation it is really important to exercise as much control as possible and try to keep them all under your eye. All it takes is a little planted contraband for the Guardia Civil to gain a new, beautiful sailing yacht.

They all awkwardly descended the main companionway. Ramirez muttered, "Smells like honey down here." The dog hated the steep ladder and was nervous in the orderly, confined space. I always kept the cabin spotlessly clean and the varnish perfect. Police are likely to respect a beautiful yacht that is clearly a wealthy person's home.

They methodically went through every locker, opened every container in the galley, and looked under the floorboards. However, it was the dog that they were relying on, and the dog was not interested. The dog handler led him throughout the cabin and forced him to sniff everywhere, but still the dog seemed bored. Appearing to stay out of their way, I casually leaned against the companionway ladder concealing the view of the entrance to the crawl space that led to the aft[1] cabin.

---

1 **Aft** The back of the boat behind the mast as opposed to forward. Fore and aft.

After an hour, the dog handler was cursing the dog, and the whole group began to argue in rapid-fire Spanish. They argued all the way to the pier and were still arguing when one of the cops pointed at the back of the boat, "Qué es eso?"

Ramirez asked, pointing at the aft-cabin window, "Why did we not search there?"

I shrugged.

They trooped back and again entered the boat with the dog, bumping into each other while filing into the small aft cabin, and my rising anxiety started to redline. All of the action was now right next to the sealed, hollow bulkhead where sixty kilos of prime, Thai buds were hidden away in their bees-wax packages.

Sitting in the cockpit, I watched Ramirez carefully go through all the lockers, and just as he was about to climb the ladder to leave he lifted the bottom step, and my heart sank into my stomach. He picked up and showed me the pickle jar that held the weed I had kept out to smoke on the trip.

I could see Ramirez was asking me something, but I couldn't hear him, my ears seemed to be stuffed with cotton. Barely aware of what was going on around me, my thoughts flickered like a silent movie, trying to separate the possibilities from the probabilities. They had only found the smoking stash, which was usually well hidden. Clearly, Ramirez suspected the stash was the tip of the iceberg and enough to make a case for distribution, or an excuse to impound, or tear apart the boat. This was serious trouble and every decision, every move I made right now, would decide how much worse it was going to get.

I regained focus and just caught the end of what Ramirez was saying, "Please get your passport. You are coming with us."

I jumped back aboard the boat and down the companionway stairs, picked up the electronic organizer, grabbed a pencil, and pressed the pin that erased all the information. It was a bit of cutting-edge technology I had found in Singapore and bought for just this situation. Every phone number and contact was now safe from Interpol's database.

I grabbed a down vest and picked up my wallet and passport off the chart desk. As I climbed back to the cockpit I pulled out the joint in my pocket and swallowed it, closed up the boat, then stepped over to the quay.

Flanked by two thugs in green, I walked to Ramirez's Land Rover.

Sitting alone in the backseat I realized *Sara* was unlocked with the engine compartment closed but not sealed. I was on my way to jail in a foreign country, for who knew how long, and the only people who knew that I had been arrested were a couple of sketchy con men. My partner, Arianna, who was in London staying with friends, had no way of knowing that we were in yet another perilous situation.

The sun was setting as they turned up the road that headed into the mountains. We drove to Berja, a small village about an hour inland, that I am sure had not changed in 300 years. Aside from a few old cars and dim electric lights behind the windows of an ancient cottage, I saw no sign of modern technology.

Ramirez walked me into a small, stone building that must have served as the Guardia station during the Franco years of fascist terror. It still stank from the sweat of terrified leftists who had been brought to this hidden village in the Sierra Nevada to be tortured by Franco's gangsters during the Spanish Civil War.

In twenty years as an outlaw, I had been in some tight spots, but this was as bad as it gets. The forces of evil had me locked up where they held all the cards. I didn't speak the language, and, as far as I knew, Spain still had no constitution.

Oh shit, I thought.

That joint I ate is starting to get me high.

Paranoia is creeping in through the chinks in the walls.

Last thing I need, for fuck sake.

We walked around the scarred wooden counter and an older, uniformed guard opened the heavy wooden door to the lock-up.

I walked in.

He closed the door behind me.

CHAPTER 2

Ranen from Atlanta, June 1961

ALL THE FOCUS of the adrenalin was gone.

It had been a long, stressful day and the weed I had eaten was fueling the cacophony of voices in my head. I must have actually started answering them out loud, because someone spoke to me from a dark corner of that windowless cell with moldy stucco walls and a concrete floor.

My eyes adjusted to the dim light provided by the barred opening in the door. There were three upper and lower bunks in one corner and a toilet against the opposite wall. A couple men, sitting on a bunk, shared a smoke.

One of the voices in my confused, worried head was saying, *Look! So what, they only found a little more than the legal limit of weed, there's another sixty kilos hidden in the sealed compartment that they didn't find. Are they going to go back?* Another voice replied, *Stop playing out scenarios and calm down. You can get out of this.*

But I was plenty scared, and all I could do was think about how the hell a Jewish kid from Atlanta, Georgia, ended up being an ocean-going outlaw.

A pristine memory surfaced of a deserted highway crossroads, in the middle of the night, eight hours out of Atlanta. I was fourteen, alone, with just the clothes on my back, hitchhiking to New York City. Not running away--I just wanted to be out on the road and to see New York on my own.

I had to be home by Sunday, at four in the afternoon, or my mother would know I hadn't spent the weekend with Scott at Lake Lanier.

My last ride had dropped me in North Carolina, somewhere just west of Cape Hatteras. In 1961 cell phones didn't exist and neither did the interstate. I was standing by the side of a two-lane blacktop, in the intermittent glare of a blinking, yellow caution light, hoping to thumb a ride. Damp summer air diffused the light so every time it blinked the air pixelated in yellow... in a way I would recognize five years later on my first acid trip.

I felt extra alive out on the road. This delicious cocktail of freedom from my suburban life, mixed with the danger of a kid alone on the road, was just the stuff of the Rudyard Kipling stories I used to read. Even at that age, my complete faith in my ability to know if I was in danger gave me the confidence to do this sort of thing. It was just something I always knew. It was a gift, like being able to throw and hit a baseball, which I never could do.

The huge, live oaks were starting to give me the creeps out there in the Carolina night. A coonhound howled a solo in the metallic buzz of the cicada symphony, when a pair of headlights appeared out of the dark. A big semi pulled up, stopped, and a door swung open.

A face like the grill of a Mac truck appeared. "Kid, I don't know what the hell you're doin' out heah, but git on in," the truck driver said, as he cleared the packets of Slim Jims off the seat.

"Where y'all headed?" he asked, shifting up through an endless succession of gears.

"I've got to be in New York City by tomorrow morning," I answered.

"Well, you're in luck," he replied. "'Cuz I'm headed straight to the Fulton Fish Market right down in Lower Manhattan. Tell you what kid, if ya' help me unload I'll buy ya' the best breakfast that can be had in this heah country."

The morning sun on my face woke me as we pulled into New York. At six in the morning, the Fulton Fish Market was a hive of activity, sprawling out of the open buildings into the streets and under the bridges. Everywhere I walked the air buzzed with shouting and haggling in six different languages.

I helped sling boxes of fresh flounder out the back of the semi to market laborers, 'till eight that morning. The driver had me hose out the trailer while he haggled over the price of the fish. After the truck was parked and locked, we made our way through the bustling crowd of chefs and retailers buying fresh fish from the stalls in the street.

True to his word, that driver bought me the best breakfast of my life at the worker's café right there in the market. We ate huge plates of homemade corned beef hash and eggs, followed by a cup of coffee with a shot of whiskey. It was heady stuff working with grown men who accepted my presence, without question, as another worker.

The driver, Earl Daniels, gave me a ride all the way back to the turn-off for Cape Hatteras, where his family owned fishing boats and the packing plant. He kept himself awake by telling stories about Europe in World War II and bad storms off Cape Hatteras in the winter.

Finally, Earl stopped in at a big truck stop for fuel, and found me a ride back to Atlanta while he was at it. He handed me five dollars and said, "You're okay, kid. Thanks for the help."

PART 2 – *Sara* and Beach Rat, 1984

CHAPTER 3

Leaving Djibouti

IT WAS ALREADY baking at 6:30 in the morning in the Port of Djibouti, Africa.

The stink of sewage and rotting garbage from the refugee camps followed us with the breeze as we motored past a French destroyer moored at the end of the seawall. I was on the foredeck getting the big, number one genoa[2] out of the long, zippered sail-bag lashed to the rail right up forward. The mainsail was up and my mate and old friend, Beach Rat, was at the wheel motoring us out of the harbor.

As we passed the seawall the breeze freshened. I clipped the sail to the stay[3], tied the sheets on, danced barefooted up the rough, burning-hot deck, and started pulling the halyard[4] hand over hand as fast as I could get it up. The shackles rang as they passed up the stainless steel rigging.

As soon as I felt the resistance of the wind starting to fill the sail, I got three fast wraps on the winch and started cranking. The equatorial sun beat hot on my back as I sweated the big sail up until the halyard wire vibrated bar-tight.

Leaning back against the mast, I caught my breath while I coiled the supple Dacron line. The sails were blinding white against a blue sky desaturated by the blazing sun.

---

2 **Genoa** (or jenny) Large forward sail that, when raised, overlaps and may completely conceal the mainsail. Larger surface area means greater thrust, and the overlap makes it more efficient and aerodynamic. In conjunction with the mainsail, the genoa creates lift, like the wing of a plane, literally *pulling* the boat forward.

3 **Stay** Stainless steel cable that supports the mast fore and aft. In this case the forestay, to which the forward sails are attached by shackles.

4 **Halyard** The line or cable used to hoist a sail.

In the cockpit, Beach was furiously cranking in the genoa sheet. When the green yarn streamers hanging from the sail came up in line, he stowed the winch handle then reached for the switch, and killed the engine.

The immediate silence was almost loud.

As the sails started to draw and the boat picked up speed, *Sara* heeled over and rose to a swell marching down the Gulf of Oman, from the Indian Ocean. She paused for a moment at the top of the wave, then plunged down into the trough, landing with a crash as the recently stowed equipment found its best resting place.

I was thirty-six years old and I didn't owe anybody anything. I was owner and master of the exquisite sailing yacht *Sara*, a 46 foot yawl in perfect condition. She was my home, my only occupation and replacement for *Misty*, the 30 foot custom-built sailing boat I had lived aboard for eleven years.

Business was good. I was headed for the Indian Ocean. I needed a bigger boat.

Sailmaker Rick had spotted *Sara*, covered in vines, in a South Florida boatyard. He, myself, and a couple other outlaw sailors spent the next two years (and a small fortune) refitting her for long-distance, nonstop smuggling. We had replaced everything but the mast and the elegant teak interior. All state of the art.

That was two and a half years ago.

For the past month, Beach Rat and I had been waiting in Djibouti, a godforsaken, African desert port. Waiting for word that never came, to pick up a thousand pounds of Afghani hashish. Unfortunately, the Russian Army stood between us and the hashish, and, as it turned out, the soldiers had gotten their hands on it and sent it all back to Russia anyways.

We had traveled some 7,000 nautical miles to do this, our dream voyage, nonstop from Pakistan to Canada via the Cape of Storms. We could certainly use *Sara*'s share of the profit if everything had come together. Instead, we wrote the whole thing off to bad juju and left the refugees, flies, and smell of Djibouti behind. Big disappointment.

As usual, a dialog was running in my restless mind, *What the hell do you want, Ranen? You have the finest sailing boat ever, you aren't broke and the whole Indian Ocean… wait a minute… all of the* world's *oceans are in front of you. You just have to find somewhere to regroup and figure out what to do next.*

"Beach Rat, turn us down the coast. I'll set the self-steering vane[5]."

Beach and I could have been brothers, most people thought we were. Both of us were small and wiry with sun-bleached, longish, curly hair. I doubt we had a pound of fat between us. Climbing overhangs, skiing big peaks, body surfing Steamer Lane, we were fine tuned machines.

We had an understanding. I would sort out the gigs it took to pay for everything, give him one-quarter share of any profits, and buy him a ticket home whenever he wanted to leave. So far he was still onboard.

Beach Rat and I went way back. He moved to Atlanta from Bay Area, California, in the tenth grade. The South was so backward then that anyone from California must be a surfer, hence the nick-name Beach. It didn't matter that there was no beach or surfing anywhere near where he came from.

He was also really small for his age so he became Beach Rat.

Although we didn't go to the same school he knew my "hot sister," so we knew about each other. Beach and I were prominent among those Buckhead kids who danced on the edge of the law.

We ended up in the same dorm our first year at the University of Georgia and became good friends. That school was so conservative in 1966 that everything we did was inappropriate, and we only lasted one semester. We wanted out.

I got lost in Europe, Morocco then San Francisco, and Beach ended up in the Army.

---

5 **Self-Steering Wind Vane** A completely independent mechanical system that steers the boat on a wind-based course. Once set up the boat will steer itself.

Later, when I was living in a Lake Tahoe junkyard garage apartment, he appeared one day, just released from the Army because of a badly broken leg. A lucky fall from a truck on his fourth day in Vietnam.

Beach Rat just tended to show up in my life. We weren't always in the same place but somehow we were always in the same orbit. This time had lasted longer than most, I think, because this voyage was way off the grid. *Sara* was sailing along the coast of Somalia and we were just getting started.

"Keep us a mile off, Beach. There's a coral reef along this whole coast. We should have fresh fish this leg, so have an eye on the fishing line. Fish and chips sure are talkin' to me."

Beach grunted. He was that guy, that reticent person who said nothing.

Three days later, I was down below, sitting at the navigation station studying the East Coast of Africa on an inadequate chart. We were headed for the Western Indian Ocean and I hadn't anticipated needing detailed charts to find a harbor in East Africa. But now I needed to find a good anchorage in Kenya.

Being capable of making things happen, when "Plan A" goes south, comes with the job description of a smuggler, and I was born to do this job. I could study a chart and intuitively know where to lie low, wait, and kill time. Usually in style.

It seems like I was always waiting for something. Waiting for word to move, waiting for parts, waiting for an inspiration.

Lou Reed said it:

He's never early.
He's always late.
First thing you learn is
You always have to wait.

Smuggling was something I did for the money to support the lifestyle. All of this was about the lifestyle, traveling the world and taking my house with me.

When you arrive by sea with the right boat you have instant status. You can move through any level of society. Women are attracted to the romance, men to the adventure, and everyone to the freedom.

Unlike most smugglers, I didn't care about being rich or powerful. When I had enough money to refit, provision, and a bit to travel with, I'd stop working until I was broke. I used the pocket method of accounting. When my pockets were nearly empty it was time to go to work. My rule was, like a gambler, I would always keep a little out to buy into the next game.

I kept an edge of the chart weighed down with a large, brilliant clamshell we used as an ashtray when we weren't at sea. No toke until the anchor's down. *We have to put in somewhere. Lamu it is.*

"We're headed for a little town in Kenya called Lamu," I called up to Beach Rat who was on watch. "I have no idea what it's going to be like. This book on Africa says it's the legendary home of Sinbad the Sailor. The course is 87° then we turn south after we pass the Horn of Africa."

"Okay, 87° it is. There are a lot of ships but they're all pretty far offshore."

I wondered about that. The most direct route to the Indian Ocean shipping lanes was right where we were. Ships don't go off the rhumb line, the direct course, for no reason. I had another close look for underwater obstructions but we were at least a mile off the reef on my chosen course.

"Keep a close watch, Beach. I've got a bad feeling about this place. I'm going to start some bread then get some sleep. Don't let me oversleep."

Beach Rat woke me around midnight local time with a cup of coffee then went into the aft cabin to get his head down.

I kneaded the bread, cut it in half, put the dough in pans, and then put them in the oven to bake. All the while stopping to go up on deck to have a look around for ships, and check the course and sails.

An hour later I turned off the gas, left the bread to cool, made a fish sandwich from the tuna we caught the day before, then went out on

deck to eat and watch the moonless night sky. The stars were remark-
ably bright. With no ambient light and no air pollution, for a couple
thousand miles in every direction, the universe is right in your face.

I don't know how long I was daydreaming and looking at the stars
moving over my head, until I realized I had been hearing something
out there in the dark. I stood up on the cabin top and listened more
closely. It was an engine and it was getting closer.

"Beach Rat, wake up. Get up here!" I shouted down the
companionway.

He popped out of the aft cabin hatch rubbing his eyes, "Jesus,
Ranen, I just got to sleep."

"Listen man. Do you hear something? Like a motor? Not a ship
engine, more like a small, diesel fishing boat. There's no one living on
this coast. The only boats in these waters are pirates!"

"Yeah man, I hear it."

Beach stood on the deck, out of the dim, red glow of the compass
light, and peered into the dark of the hot, moonless night. He plugged
in the 10,000 candlepower searchlight while I rushed below to get
the shotgun and rifle. I passed Beach the shotgun, stepped over the
cockpit coaming to steady myself on the mizzenmast[6] against the rolling of the boat, and positioned myself so as not to be blinded by the
powerful light when Beach turned it on.

The beam of light reached out over the nearly calm sea to illumi-
nate an old, converted Arab sailing dhow motoring towards us 100
meters away.

I locked and loaded the stainless Mini-14 and the quiet night
exploded as I fired fifteen high-velocity bullets into the dhow. With
both boats rolling in the waves, aiming was difficult, no idea what or
who I was hitting.

The dhow's crew started yelling, desperately steering their boat
away from the light and the gunfire.

---

6 **Mizzenmast** The mast immediately aft of the main-mast. Typically shorter than the
fore-mast.

"Jesus Christ, Ranen!" Beach shouted over the aftershock. "Did you hit anyone?"

"I don't know!" I shouted back, adrenaline pumping. "Didn't you see their guns? They're sure as hell not fishing. Now they'll have something to do besides following us. They can plug the holes I put into their hull. They won't ever screw with us again! Hell! I won't put up with anybody screwing with us, not in the Caribbean and certainly not in this hellhole! Good work with the light, Beach, you blinded the guy at the tiller!"

"Shit man! They didn't know what hit them!"

"Turn on the deck lights for a few seconds so they can see us clearly. I want them to remember that we are not to be messed with. There are plenty of other vessels coming by here that don't shoot back. Screw these guys. Now they'll know who we are."

I went to the aft rail, still shaking as I adjusted the wind vane self-steering, turning the boat to port and away from the pirates. Beach sheeted in the sails to pick up speed and get the hell out of there.

The dhow disappeared into the dark night.

"God Ranen, that was fucking weird." Beach Rat muttered as he nervously paced and periodically peered into the darkness. "Did they shoot at us?"

I didn't answer.

"So? Did they shoot at us?"

"Hell no! I didn't give 'em a chance! As soon as I saw the guns, I started shooting. Would you rather I'd waited until they killed you? After all, you were the obvious target, you were the one holding the light."

"Do you think you hit anyone?"

"No idea. Shit, it's freaky to shoot at people. I can't tell you how freaky it is."

"So much for sleeping," Beach said, jumping down into the galley. "Crazy shit."

CHAPTER 4

Sinbad's Home Port

FIVE DAYS LATER, I was lying in a bunk reading a tattered Louis L'Amour novel for the tenth time, when the cabin filled with the surprising and unmistakable scent of frangipani.

After months of sailing along desert coasts the scent of flowers permeated my very soul and inspired a huge rush of excitement. There was no doubt in my mind that this was good juju. I had a strong feeling that I was entering a new phase of my life.

Beach called down, "Hey Ranen, I think we're here. There are five or ten native fishing boats out here, but I can't really see the anchorage or the harbor."

Our chart was for the entire east coast of Africa, with no detail of the harbors, so we followed a fishing boat into the mouth of an estuary. There were low-lying islands with pure white sand beaches to starboard. In fact, the entire harbor was comprised of large islands in a delta.

Beach Rat was steering down the channel and I was checking out the land through the binoculars. As we entered the harbor there was a hilly island to port with a single-story hotel nestled in the sand dunes, sport motorboats pulled onto the beach, and a small dock jutting out into the channel.

"I'm pretty sure those buildings are some kind of hotel or club. Definitely the only first-world looking facility in this harbor, so they've got to have a bar. I'm sure that's going to be our hang-out, and we'll anchor across this channel over there, near that empty beach, but first we have to find customs and clear in. I'll go put up the quarantine flag."

An hour later we pulled up to the stone quay in the town of Lamu, flying the yellow Quarantine Ensign to show we hadn't cleared in yet. I had sewn up a Kenya flag from nylon scraps I kept for just that purpose. My Kenyan colors flew directly beneath the Q (for quarantine) flag.

I was shaved and dressed in my arrival uniform: navy blue shorts, white cotton shirt, deck shoes, and my long hair tucked neatly beneath a clean North Sails baseball cap. I had the boat papers, our passports, and a fifth of Johnny Walker Black Label scotch in a nylon briefcase. Scotch whiskey is the universal lubricant for the squeaky entering ceremony conducted by third-world customs officials.

Only the captain is permitted ashore until the "Q" flag comes down, and it only comes down after you have officially entered the country. All foreign vessels, from supertankers to tiny yachts, have to follow these age-old maritime customs.

When I stepped ashore the stone quay seemed to be undulating, an effect you feel sometimes when you have been at sea for a while. It's weird, but it only lasts a few minutes. The air was fragrant with flowers and spices, I was totally exhilarated to be ashore in this exotic, ancient port, and I wondered if anyone was going to call me *bwana*.

All the women were wearing full Muslim garb, covered head to toe, and I don't know why but that was a shock to me. As I swaggered through the narrow lanes of the town I caught the eye of a young Swahili woman in full *Bui Bui* regalia and I swear she winked at me out of the corner of her veil.

Eventually, I found what passed as a government official, who didn't speak any English... until I produced the expensive whiskey. At that moment he acquired excellent English, quickly filled out the papers and stamped six-month visas in our passports.

Walking back to the boat, I realized how much this coast had been infused by the Arab culture. The Sultan of Oman had traded for slaves on this coast hundreds of years before Christ. The *lingua franca* of East Africa, Swahili, is a combination of Bantu and Arabic, and was devised by the Sultan as an easy-to-learn common-language to make commerce possible on a continent where every local tribe spoke a different language.

Of course, I didn't know that then. All I knew was that I better pick up some Swahili if I wanted to get anything done here.

By the time I got back to the boat I had a gang of kids and one old man in tow. While Beach took down the "Q" flag, I got out a plastic sack full of of non-organic garbage we had saved since Djibouti, gave it to the old man with a dollar and gestured that it was trash. He gestured his thanks in return, and promptly emptied the sack into the outgoing tide, then carefully folded up the plastic sack as he walked away.

"Welcome to Africa," I said.

Beach Rat let out a peal of laughter as he threw the lines aboard, pushed us off, then jumped to the deck.

At the wheel motoring us out into the channel, I shouted, "All fucking right, let's go get a drink at that hotel." Beach was already unpacking the inflatable speedboat. I guess he was ready for a drink and anything but another night watch. We dropped the anchor in 2 meters of clear water over white sand.

Beach Rat was at the winch and I was down in the forward cabin guiding the 25 hp outboard out the forward hatch. "Easy there, just a few more feet and she's out." The inflatable sport boat was alongside and ready to go and Beach dropped the engine on the transom, neat as can be.

We came speeding up to the beach in front of the hotel on Shela Island in our orange hot rod dinghy. Beach Rat and I were looking and feeling good. The intimidation of starting all over again in the Indian Ocean was gone. We may have been playing in a new arena, but the pirate encounter showed me that it wasn't so different here than in other venues I had played.

I knew that our arrival had not gone unnoticed when we passed the hotel. Few sailing boats cruise the African East coast, especially this close to Somalia, so we were probably the first to arrive in a long time, and *Sara* was not just any sailingboat. She was always the hottest vessel anyplace we tied her up. An Italian woman at a party on a big yacht in Gibraltar once said, "Your Barca is a verrry sexy." And sexy she was. They say image is everything, and our act was a study in image. We were broadcasting the shining image of a couple of fly young men sailing up to a remote African island resort in an exquisite boat. That was our LPL, "latest pack of lies." It wouldn't do at all to tell anyone what we really were up to. My method was to be who I wanted people to believe I was, and generally they did believe.

As I drove us up onto the beach, Rat jumped out and dropped the anchor so the boat wouldn't float away at high tide. I was out of the boat in an instant and we walked barefooted up to what was surely a bar. And what a bar it was…

The Peponi bar remains to this day at the top of my "favorite bars of the world" list. As we walked across the veranda, I felt at once that this was our kind of place. I swear that bar was a living thing. The barroom was bright with white washed walls, a polished concrete floor, an 8 stool carved and polished wooden bar and a few tables and chairs. The bartender was a very dignified African dressed in spotless whites, both shirt and sarong (called *kikoi* in Kenya).

From behind me an upper class British accent said, "So. Where have you chaps come in from?" I turned for my first meeting with Lars Korschen, the man who was and forever will be an East African institution, and would become a great friend and ally to *Sara* and her crew. Lars was a fair, fit looking, handsome young man in his early thirties, dressed in a pressed white *kikoi* and a short-sleeved cotton shirt with a collar.

"Hey. I'm Ranen and this is Beach Rat McAndrews. We left Djibouti 17 days ago on that sailing boat anchored across the harbor and we really need some drinks with lots of ice… and a dinner. I for one am tired of the cuisine on Sailing Vessel *Sara*. Can we pay in U.S. Dollars?" I answered.

"Let's start with the drinks, shall we? Welcome to the Peponi Hotel. You can call me Lars." He turned to the bartender. "Charles, we'll have three Old Pals, *taffadhali.*"

"*Ndio, Bwana.*" Answered the bartender.

Lars and I drank the house specialty, Old Pals: vodka, tonic, and bitters with sugar around the rim. Beach Rat, who never drank spirits, had his usual cold beer. Lars ran the whole scene down to us, while plying us for stories. He was one of those rare individuals who are good communicators, could tell stories and entertain, but was also a good listener and a shrewd judge of character. A man who was a great sport, as well as sportsman. Water skiing, sport fishing for billfish, or cruising this wild coast on a dhow, he was up for anything outdoors, the perfect person to run a famous hotel in one of the more remote places on earth.

Lars was my favorite kind of person. This was my kind of place. We had sailed halfway around the world to come home.

We had our drinks and then feeling really high, moved into the restaurant where we tucked into a fresh seafood feast. Beach Rat had prawns cooked in a spicy *piri piri* sauce over coconut rice and I had the chili lime ginger crab followed by tuna carpaccio. Coffee out on the veranda served Arabic style and brewed with ginger, then hours more in that bar on the coast of East Africa some 50 miles from Somalia.

That night at the bar was an eye opener to say the least. Almost immediately I could see that Shela Island and the Peponi Hotel was one of those places that wealthy world travelers know about, and the Peponi bar was one of the favored watering holes in Africa. While Beach Rat and I were eating our four-course dinner, the bar started to fill and was comfortably full until we returned to *Sara* around one in the morning.

We had left North America mid summer and had arrived in Kenya at the beginning of "The Season" in Lamu. Actually, there are two seasons in Equatorial Africa, the rainy season and not the rainy season. No one goes on holiday to the coast during the rainy, malaria season.

The Peponi bar and restaurant is the focal point of social life in Shela, a tiny ancient village of tall whitewashed stone houses built into what was once part of the sand dunes. There are no cars or roads on Shela Island, just narrow lanes with bougainvillea hedges winding up through the hills. There is a small village square with a lovely mosque complete with tower and the ever-present call to prayers. The houses are built in Arabic style with hardwood posts and beams and polished concrete floors. Most all have roof apartments with open rooms and verandas. All of the fresh water in Shela is rainwater runoff from roofs and verandas captured in cisterns during the rainy season.

Many of the houses were owned by white Kenyan settlers who used them on holidays during the dry season. When the owners weren't using them, they rented the house, a flat, or the roof garden apartment to visitors. Each house had its set of servants: cook, handyman, and maids. Guests never had to leave Shela to take the shuttle boat to Lamu for supplies. Reality seemed far away. I suspect that Lars or his mother handled many of the rentals, because it seemed as if the Korschens were orchestrating the entire scene in Shela. No doubt, this was one of the great scenes on the world circuit, and it was well managed.

CHAPTER 5

Land of the Lotus Eaters

FOR THE MOMENT the Afghani hashish trip was off, and I knew that I had to get something else organized. I figured that I could keep the dealers paying my expenses in the hope that the pipeline out of Afghanistan might open again, but I also knew without a doubt they would eventually lose interest. The gold chain and fast lifestyle crowd has a short attention span and are hooked on fast money. Waiting is not their strong suit. A year of expenses was the best I could hope for. It was time to cut them loose. They threw a party in the Indian Ocean and I was the only one who showed up. Now I'm sitting in a harbor on the other side of the world with dwindling funds, no contacts, and a forty-six foot supermodel to support.

My lifestyle and personality were perfectly matched with this career if you could call it a career. Making new friends and contacts, gathering information, and networking were all hard-wired into my personality. For years I had been sailing into foreign countries finding safe resources, getting things wired then leaving in one piece with a cargo of some kind or another... all in short order. I needed a paying job and this was Africa, a continent full of third world governments, and the perfect place to run refugees, grow weed, or smuggle gold or diamonds. There had to be something I could organize here on "the dark continent." This was virgin territory for someone like me, but right then I was just having a good time and making the most out of our being the interesting "new guys in town." Arriving on *Sara* was our ticket into what was a pretty sophisticated club.

In that first night at the bar we were awarded full membership to the inner circle of the Kenya cool elite. We also got our first taste of the local weed called *bhangi,* an introduction to African politics in general, and details on the latest political situation in six countries. I was drinking, but as usual not so much that I couldn't keep up with the banter.

Beach Rat was the perfect foil for my personality. I was the Pisces with the Aquarius rising and he was the double Virgo. I was always over the top and he was solid and quiet. That night Beach drank a lot and laughed a lot but said very little. I drank a little, laughed and talked too much, but was careful about maintaining our LPL, latest pack of lies. Lars may have added two and two about us but he wasn't shouting four.

One evening soon after our arrival, Beach Rat and I were at the Peponi veranda for sundowners and the always popular bullshit session. I was entertaining a group of young guys at the bar with sailing stories and tales of life at sea. The guys were a mixed bag of twenty to thirty year olds, a couple of rich Italian renegades drying out on the Kenya coast, some British sons of wealthy upcountry ranchers, a Swedish aid worker down from Uganda, and a couple of serious hash highway travelers on their way to Bali. I was encouraging these guys to tell their stories as well and I was picking up a lot of precious information that I would need to get started in this new ocean. They all had first hand information straight from the source. Even the gossip, especially the gossip, was great stuff for my crash course on what was happening in East Africa. I needed to connect, and this was the place to do that, to connect.

"So Ranen, you see some *squali grandi en la mer profundo*?"

"Sharks? Yeah, well normally you don't see much out there in the deep water, but on the Atlantic crossing on our way here, we stumbled onto a really creepy scene. Beach was motoring on a hot calm day a hundred miles northeast of Bermuda. I jumped up from a sweaty sleep and came up on deck when the engine slowed. Beach Rat said, "Look over there, there's a half sunken ship or something!" It was an overcast gray day and there wasn't any wind, but there was an oily looking swell running. Rat motored toward something big rolling in the swell. Lemme tell ya, it's pretty creepy running up onto something big out there, mid Atlantic. Then as we got closer the smell hit us… rotten flesh. It was the decomposing body of a dead blue whale, twice the size of our boat."

Alberto said, "What abouta the Squali?"

"Wait wait. I'm getting to the wild part.

"So, Beach was just pointing at a fast moving grey, five-foot scimitar slicing through the water. It was a horror show. That scimitar was the tailfin of a monstrous Great White shark. The fin was speeding toward the whale and when it hit, the huge whale body shuddered and the shark's tailfin swept back and forth, propelling the biting jaws deeper into the whale.

"There were at least a dozen of those vicious monsters ripping into the whale, and those were the ones we could see. All those days at sea we were feeling comfortably alone in the middle of the Atlantic Ocean, but, in fact, we weren't alone. There were monsters sharing our world. Listen. In the old days of wooden sailing ships, sailors didn't learn to swim and after seeing those sharks devouring their dinner, I understood why.

"I was feeling a little shaky when Beach motored away from that nightmare as fast as he could. I was so freaked that none of the photos I took were even focused. Remind me next time you come by the boat, I'll get out the photos."

Alberto asked, "Thees a really happen?"

"Yeah man. Ask Beach Rat he saw it first."

Alberto looked over at Beach. Beach shrugged and said, "I'm a body surfer man. I find it easier not to think about sharks."

"Che cazzo!" Exclaimed Chicco, my favorite young Italian. "Why you no take us with you on *Sara* nexa time you and Beach go down the coast? Umberto maka the best zuppa di pesce and maybe he the best *pescatore* as well."

I had Chicco the handsome and charming young heroin addict and his friend Alberto, his equally handsome pal, on board often. Umberto usually came around with them.

I would have loved to have Umberto as crew. He was the mechanic in residence at the Peponi that season. Umberto, who was one of the amazing characters that Lars had working at the hotel, could fix anything. The Africans called him *fundi,* which means craftsman. He was also a master chef and a skilled spear fisherman. Lars lured talented and interesting staff to the Peponi with the prospect of good food, lodging and a great time in a magical place.

I had pulled into the one place in all of Africa where I could feel the pulse of the entire Eastern half of the continent. It was the perfect spot to gather intelligence without anyone noticing. Was it luck? I don't think so. I seemed to have an instinct for finding the right place at the right time, Haight Ashbury in '67, Telluride in '71, Jamaica in '76, and Ibiza/Formentera on and off all of those years. I collected happening scenes.

"Jambo sana, chaps! Ahoy and all that. Up for some waterskiing?" I sat up and stuck my head out the hatch. The early morning equatorial sun blinded me but I could make out a speed boat hovering off the port bow. At the wheel Lars called out, "One ski or two?" "I'll take a slalom," I croaked. "Just a sec, I'll grab my life vest." Jerome Jamisson threw out the rope as I dived into the chill water, "Just the ticket for an early wakeup, what?"

An hour later we were having fresh papaya with lime, strong coffee with a shot of cheap Kenya rum and a big spliff with the ski boat tied up behind *Sara.* Jerome had been chopping lines of coke on a polished slice of agate. "Care for a line?" "None for me. I'm way too hyper already, but thanks," I answered. I passed the coke to Rat who would always try a little of anything. Jerome was going on about some hippy traveler who he had lured into some dirty sex scene the night before. He was the heir to some small industrial fortune and was a classic wastrel. The weed, the coffee and the rum were flying around in my head and there was a freaky dialog running with it as well. *Whoa this guy feels dark. Watch this guy Ranen, he's a nasty piece of work.* Jerome's features were exaggerated with thick lips, buggy eyes and his supercilious manner only added to the vampire effect. *Watch what you say Ranen, this is a demon. Holy fuck is this real? Lars looks okay.*

So it went. The party flowed and time passed unnoticed and ignored. November came and with it the colonials started showing up from Nairobi and the upcountry ranches. The younger generation colonials were called Kenya Cowboys and Cowgirls. Lars' brother Nils was the ultimate Kenya cowboy. Nils was younger and spoke white African accented English. The accent sounded like a softer smoother version of a New Zealand accent with an echo of Dutch thrown in.

The Cowboys were party animals but they were all bush wise. They were European but they were also African. We partied up and down the coast with them from Mombasa to Kiwayu on the Somali border. It was sex, drugs and rock and roll, except we weren't getting much sex. Those cowgirls were a pretty closed bunch 'till they got to know someone.

Willy and Mike were a couple of good looking cowboys who had a native ocean going dhow. The *Munira* was old with no engine but they sailed the coast and camped and fished and took friends and tourists for trips to deserted inlets in and out of Lamu. When I first met them they had some really beautiful girls with them, three real stars.

"Beach Rat check out this boat headed in." We were having coffee in the cockpit, listening to Stevie Ray Vaughn full blast under the huge green awning. A month had gone by, or more… who knew? It must have been a long time because that awning took forever to put up and even longer to take down. We only put it up if we were staying awhile. In a rare moment of loquacity Beach commented, "Look at those bodies." He handed me the binoculars and said, "Check out the blonde, she's unreal!"

That was my first look at Carol, who had arrived at the Peponi by dhow. She was a vision framed in the round field of my binoculars.

A long legged blonde in a bikini, zero makeup with unmanageable hair and she moved like a gymnast. Carol was the catering manager of the Peponi during the years that *Sara* was on the Kenya coast. She was the first Kenya cowgirl that I met and I was impressed. She was totally at ease camping on an untamed coast or running a four star hotel. Carol was naturally graceful and elegant but somehow managed to escape the arrogance that often comes with that package.

There was never a spark between Carol and I, but these Kenyan women were a new species and I was intrigued. For the first time in years I was thinking about having a woman in my life, but there were major problems with me hooking up with a woman.

Any woman who sailed with me had to be able to endure the hardship of long, difficult ocean passages, days of hard (sometimes dangerous) work, and the lack of comforts of modern life like hot showers and refrigeration. Then there were the couple of weeks or months in some dirty, very male shipyard. Yet she had to be completely at ease with the wealthy yachting crowd, and be able to keep her head when cruising the social fast lane or pirate infested waters. And she had to put up with me. I was a lot of things but grounded wasn't one of them.

Nevertheless, I had found over the years that I was better off with a woman partner. Aside from the standard reasons that men and women live together, the profile of a couple cruising on a sailing boat was easy for any kind of government agent to accept without ringing any alarm bells. No doubt, an attractive couple cruising on a fancy yacht look more like innocent tourists than a couple of guys up to who knows what.

There was another less obvious reason. In a tight situation, I knew from real experience, that a woman will pull the trigger, while a man will take a crucial moment to think about it. Years before, my girlfriend had shot a Colombian who attacked me. I have no doubt that she saved my life. I believe that women have an evolutionary bias to go into immediate action when their family or nest is threatened. And if there was one thing I knew, I knew people.

The other two beautiful bikinied girls on the *Munira* that day were the sisters from California, Phoebe and Daisy Vreeland. They had come overland to Kenya from Egypt by way of Sudan, passing through some of the wildest, most dangerous places on the planet. They worked with Ethiopian refugees for Save The Children in Southern Sudan. Then they were sent to Darfur. These were not your average Hollywood girls.

Christmas came and went, the New Year came and went, Nils was awarded the *umbwa* (dog) trophy and Phoebe hooked up with Chicco. Sometime in February Beach Rat was frying some fresh snapper he had speared out on the reef while I stared at the Indian Ocean chart thinking how to make some decent money. As he flipped the fillets, he turned and said, "Let's get out of here. Everybody is leaving for rainy season and I don't want to be here for it either. The reef is over fished and it's too hard to travel inland from here. If we were down near Mombasa we could take the train to Nairobi or even buy a Land Rover and do some safaris. I'd like to see that desert up near Ethiopia. Carol said it's really wild up around Lake Turkana."

"I've been thinking the same thing Beach, especially about having a vehicle. Easy knows a local called Karim from Mombasa that can hook us up with a tribe that grows weed up near Lake Victoria. I'm thinking that with your expertise and those seeds you've got from your crop in Maui, we could grow a crop worth a cargo and improve the lot of a poor tribe. Shit, it might be a lot of fun. Anyway, we need to haul the boat out of the water to antifoul the bottom. There's some kind of boatyard down in Kilifi. Let's leave tomorrow."

Easy was a tall dark good looking American expatriate hustler on the "hash highway" who we met when he was briefly in Lamu. Easy lived and scammed between Bali, Porto Seguro, Brazil, and Kenya. Like most hustlers, Easy was quick witted and entertaining with a slippery feel. Morality was not Easy's highest priority, but contacts were his game and we needed his services. Growing weed was only one

possibility. I had an idea that there were a lot of white Africans in unstable nations, like Zimbabwe, who needed an exit strategy that didn't involve airports. He knew a lot of people and everything that was going on in white Kenya. It all seemed to fit because Easy had a house on the beach right near Kilifi.

CHAPTER 6

Lots of African Hands

"A<small>CCORDING TO MY</small> dead reckoning this is Kilifi, but I'll be fucked if I can see the ferry or anything that looks like Kilifi Creek. I'm gonna jump in the dinghy and have a look around that bluff. If that's it then I'll find the way through the reef. Throw some of those weighted buoys in the raft will ya," I called from the bow.

Thirty minutes later I steered *Sara* as we motored over brightly colored coral under two meters of crystal clear water. Beach Rat was at the bow with a long boat hook picking up the buoys I had dropped to mark the undulating safe passage through the reef. "Looks like good fishing. Wonder if there're any women here?" he mused in a loud voice.

We passed into the deeper murky water of Kilifi Creek and continued north along the inside of the barrier reef until we passed the bluff and the Kilifi Creek Harbor revealed itself. The entrance was framed by a hundred foot bluff on each side of the creek, which was a couple of football fields wide. The land here was lush and green with tasteful houses in the trees on the bluffs peppered by garden paths that led down to docks on the creek. We passed the ferry landings with bustling kiosks, selling food and African craftwork. Rat dropped the anchor further up the harbor where there were a couple of sailing boats and some modern sport fishing boats anchored. The boatyard consisted of a concrete ramp, a collection of sheds and open pole barns, and a dock that you could pull into at spring high tide so the boat would be high and dry for six or eight hours a day.

Beach Rat and I were poking around the yard checking out the facility, if you could call it that. From behind us an upper class British voice said, "I know the Bowman well, I raced one in the Capetown to Rio race seven years ago." We turned to see a tall white gentleman in his mid seventies.

I offered my hand, "Hello. We've come to see if it is possible to haul her out to repair the rudder and do the anti-fouling. This is Beach McAndrews, I'm Ranen and that is my Bowman 46, *Sara*. Do you have any grinders here? I'd like to take her down to the gel coat."

"No. We do not have any grinders but we do have lots of African hands." He said as he made a polishing motion with his hand. "And… I am Richard Desborough Malcom Mason.

"I believe we can haul her out, however, she is going to be right at the limit of our equipment."

"What equipment?" I asked. "I don't see any kind of lift. She weighs something like 16 tons."

Well, it turned out that Mason had built a cradle on a cart that had eight or so little steel wheels. On the day we hauled her out, he had the whole African village from the adjacent sisal plantation on hand with four locally made two-inch sisal ropes that were fastened to the cart. Dicky Mason stood at the top of the ramp giving orders in Swahili. They lowered the cart down the ramp into the water at maximum high tide that month. I motored *Sara* slowly into place, then dove down with a snorkel and mask to position the supports. When I surfaced and gave the signal all 40 of the villagers, men, women and children started hauling on the ropes. The whole rig was questionable and I was plenty nervous. I looked over at Beach Rat who shrugged and crossed his fingers, as the cart carrying my sailing yacht lurched out of the water and up the ramp. Near the top, the boat started to move way too slowly. Beach and I squeezed into a place on the rope and put our backs into the effort. When we finally had the boat blocked in position, I looked down at my bleeding hands and thought how incongruous Sailing Yacht *Sara* looked being hauled out of the water by an entire African village. What amazed me even more was that I felt that it was normal.

During the time *Sara* was in Kilifi I got to know some of Mason's story. He came to Kenya in the early days of colonial settlement. My guess was that he had caused trouble for his family in England and was packed off to Africa to be Lord Delamer's horse trainer and to organize the racecourse in Nairobi. By the time I met him he had Leukemia, but was in remission as a result of being treated by a well-known *muganga* (witch doctor). What I know of Bwana Mason's story comes from bits and pieces of his witty reminisces and random comments on events and people throughout his time in British East Africa. He had had a large successful farm up country, but lost it when the liberal British government gave back the land to the Kikuyu after the Mau Mau revolt. He took the meager compensation for a lifetime's work and started the little boatyard where he built himself a 40 foot fiberglass cruising boat.

Mason and I were generations apart and aside from speaking a common language, we shared no cultural common ground. Yet, we became good friends. We must have appeared an odd pair, the short, loud, hyper, American and the tall soft-spoken distinguished English colonial. We lived vicariously through each other's stories. Bwana Mason was dying and I was his chance to live a life he had dreamed of but was now denied him. I was fascinated by his history and he enjoyed my commitment to the sailing vagabond lifestyle. As far as the smuggler part of Ranen that I didn't talk about, well… he may have figured it out but never said anything.

Although it was my decision to be a smuggler, there was a series of life circumstances and choices that led to being able to make that decision. Smuggling was the job that financed an addictive rolling stone lifestyle and in my mind, this dynamic lifestyle had it all. I would go to a new place, get in with the locals, then while it was still good, I would take my floating life to the next port, country, or continent. The whole lifestyle automatically excluded me from the petty gossip and societal prejudices found in all societies. It also had the advantage of keeping me quite a few steps ahead of any legal problems associated with getting known by the government. Eight months was pretty much my limit of stay anywhere.

Then there was the state of being unreachable. There is a huge attraction to being in the middle of the ocean where no one can call or visit…out there in the middle of the Earth's biggest wilderness. All the stupid responsibilities that society imposes are gone. No neighbors, no police, no guilt, and no thought of all those things. Consciously rejecting the prescribed lifestyle means you can choose which responsibilities you *will* accept. Real freedom, what a concept!

More importantly, smuggling was a job that paid the bills without compromising the lifestyle, and compromise was not something I was willing to do in those days. Anyway, neither the job nor the lifestyle permitted compromise.

Whatever the complexities that led to my being there at that moment, I saw myself as a kind of people's hero. An anti-hero living outside the law but within a kind of hippie moral code derived from my Haight Ashbury background and reading too many comic books. I was arrogant in those days, yet at the same time I was also pretty insecure. I'd had a bunch of long-term relationships that had all ended in disaster. I also had quite a bit of anger stored up that I would pull out when needed, and even worse, sometimes when I didn't. Somehow though, with all my neurotic insecurities I was pretty much comfortable with whom I was, and Bwana Mason was entertained by my impulsive nature and my voyaging lifestyle.

Beach and I worked our asses off to get the rudder repaired and get *Sara's* underwater hull antifouled before the next month's maximum high tide. Bwana Mason had it together. He knew how to work with fiberglass and he organized the right materials. He was our repair guru and he was as good as his word about getting the hull sanded. His "African hands" sanded and painted the bottom with antifouling so full of poisonous cupric oxide and tin that no barnacles would even think of growing on it… that is, if a barnacle could think. No way you could buy this paint in any first world boatyard. It was way too toxic.

Somehow all the whites that live in Africa know what all the other whites are doing. There are few secrets. I think this is because the favorite spectator sport for the *watu* is watching white people. And the *watu* love gossip. In fact, I once asked one of the guys in the boatyard what the *watu* thought of wazungu (white people, literally means traveler). He said, "Bwana Ranen, *Mungu* put white people on earth to entertain the African." Basically, they think we are funny and, I suppose, foolish.

Once the hard work was done and *Sara* was back in the anchorage, the word got around that *Sara* was open to visitors. Since Mason's boatyard/marina was right at the ferry on the highway between Mombasa and Malindi, we had lots of friends stopping by and sometimes staying for a day or two. We were often dragged to parties in Malindi where we met an Italian who sold us a really nice older four door Land Rover. All the Land Rovers in Kenya had the name of the organization, ranch or company stenciled on the doors so we stenciled *"Boogie Mingi"* (Swahili for a lot of boogie) on our door in red paint, at which point we became mobile.

After that Beach Rat and I were everywhere, chatting up German aid workers in Nakuru, hanging out at the Hurlingham Hotel in Nairobi, and generally drinking at all the *Wazungu* watering holes in East Africa. We were 35, had some money, and all of East Africa was ours to explore. By then we were connected to the Kenyan scene and *Boogie Mingi* was a regular at every party. It was at a party at Lake Naivasha that I had a long talk with Phoebe Vreeland, one of the California sisters who had shown up in Lamu. She was tired of drifting around and we needed some help on *Sara,* and since I was always a sucker for a long legged beautiful girl there were three of us driving back to the coast.

Phoebe fit right in even though she knew nothing about boats. Having a female aboard just balanced things out. One day she came onboard and called out, "Ranen! I brought you a present! This is Lucia. Lucia this is our Captain, Ranen." I looked up from the pump I was rebuilding to see a very hot Italian tourist in a very brief bikini. That was pure Phoebe. Phoebe brought presents.

When I came back from Nairobi with malaria, Phoebe saw me through the high fevers and the wild waking dreams. Phoebe was our friend and our ambassador. For various reasons, *Sara* plus Phoebe equaled credibility in that sleepy colonial African backwater.

Sara had a lot of visitors during her year in Kilifi. We were an easy stop for all the European expats and the Kenya cowboys on their way to Malindi. There were a couple of small tourist hotels with bars. The occasional cruising boat (usually Italian or Australian) would pass through, giving us new and interesting people to interact and party with. Our lifestyle was the ultimate in world travel. Yet, always I was on the lookout for a clue to what *Sara's* next cargo might be.

PART 3 — Arianna, 1985-6

CHAPTER 7

The Meeting

PHOEBE POURED THE coffee, "You guys need to find someone to replace me, someone who doesn't get seasick as soon as you put up the first sail." She had gotten some invitations to visit upcountry but first she was going down to Lamu to visit Chicco. "So let's get it together boys. I can't leave until you guys get a nanny." The look on her face, as she poured the coffee, said everything about how hard it was to talk about leaving.

We sipped our coffee in depressed silence. We all knew it was time to move on. Phoebe was leaving and I needed to start the process of leaving the land of the Lotus Eaters, and the first thing to do was to find a new crew member to replace Phoebe. I jumped up from my seat at the nav station. "Let's print help wanted posters! We can get them posted all over East Africa. We'll give them to everyone in Nairobi who's going on safari, up country, or to Tanzania or Zimbabwe. Phoebe, you can take a bunch down to Lamu to post. Grab a pen and write this down."

Sailing Vessel Sara Accepting Applications For Cook/ Trollop
Applicants must be:
Between the ages of 21-50
Streetable and sophisticated
English speaking preferable
Knowledge of boats helpful
Sense of humor essential

Must be willing and able to travel
Low wage with excellent fringe

Contact Captain Ranen – Swinford Boatyard Kilifi, Kenya

I looked over at Phoebe. She shot me a wry look. "Cook Trollop?"

"What?" I threw up my hands. "It says sense of humor essential. We need a woman who can live on a boat with no toilet, for Christ sake."

Arianna's Journal:
THIS IS WHERE IT STARTED

I arrived back at my parent's house in Nairobi from spending 6 weeks in the Chalbi Desert near the Ethiopian border. I had been working in the wardrobe department for a production company filming We Are the Children, and was riding back to Kenya on the back of my boyfriend Mike's motorbike when we skidded on an oil spill on a roundabout and I ended up with some serious road rash. Mike was a bit confused about life and himself so he decided to go back and live with his folks.

So I found myself unattached and whilst I was debating where I should go and what I should do next, Carrie Gammon, a great friend of mine, popped round and said "Arianna, I have the perfect job for you. I know these wild guys, Ranen and Beach, who have a yacht and are looking for someone. Look, here's a copy of their ad."

A couple of other people, including a family friend Peter Beard, an old family friend, who also saw the ad, said that it was right up my alley. So I called!

I had this feeling before I met Ranen that whatever this job was about, it was going to be dangerous and exciting; and was resolved to follow my instincts.

Beach was cleaning a snapper for dinner. I climbed aboard and tied up the dinghy. "Guess what man? I just got a call from some cowgirl in Nairobi. She saw the flyer and liked it. We're going to Nairobi tomorrow to meet her. Her name is Arianna and she's a friend of Carrie's. Mwenge answered the phone. He said she speaks perfect Swahili. I wonder what she's like. Let's go over to Easy's. Maybe he knows her."

We jumped in the Land Rover and drove over to Easy's rented house on the beach and found Easy rolling a joint on the veranda. "Just in time, gentlemen, I was just about to administer the appetite stimulator." We sat down and Beach pulled cold Tuskers out of various pockets and passed them around. We sat quietly drinking our beers and passing around the joint which smelled vaguely of opium. The sunset over the Indian Ocean that day painted the towering thunder-heads a vivid mix of dark reds and luminous grays and silvers.

I dragged my consciousness out of the clouds and asked Easy, "Do you know a friend of Carrie's named Arianna? She answered the ad."

"Yeah. I know her. She's cool. When I was in Nairobi last week staying at Carrie and Elson's she came by on her bicycle. She has a boyfriend named Mike, I wonder if they're finished?"

I didn't push it, but I got the feeling that Easy was jealous or pro-tective or something. "Well, tomorrow we're going to stop in Nairobi to meet her on our way up to Homa Bay."

We met at the Norfolk hotel, Ranen was wearing his Suncloud rose tinted shades, navy blue short shorts, and a t-shirt. He had that air about him that was humorous but serious, and explained that he and his friend were exploring the world and were look-ing for someone to cook and help out, but more importantly someone that was on for adventure. I was sold, and made my decision there and then that I would take this opportunity.

My instinct told me that whatever he was up to, I wanted in, and felt ready for anything ahead. I was ready to leave, but then realized my road rash had to heal first so we postponed for a week or so until I healed. So plans were made and I packed up my life, and left for the coast.

The lobby of the Norfolk had been, from the time it was built, the classic meeting spot in East Africa. Teddy Roosevelt's famous African safari left from this spot in 1909. You just couldn't miss Arianna Bell. She was an exotic young woman, unique in that crowd of tourists and African travelers: shoulder length thick, straight dark hair that seemed to jump out of her head, huge dark, almost black eyes in a round face, and long legs barely concealed by a Kanga (African sarong) folded into a mini skirt. Her smile was brilliantly white, broadcasting from a dark featured face. As I was to discover later she was a woman who could cause traffic accidents.

"Hey," I said. "I guess you're Arianna?"

"I am."

It was an awkward first interview, standing in the bustling hotel lobby. This striking, poised, and very young creature looked me right in the eyes. She had a gentle self-confidence that spoke of experience rare in someone that young.

Arianna had the curves of a 1950's movie star. *Not my type*, I thought, but then I wasn't looking for a girlfriend. I was looking for a female crew member who could and *would* cook in a storm, or work by day in a commercial boatyard, then scour off the third world filth, and by night metamorphose into a mysterious, sparkling sea gypsy who could navigate the glitterati fast lane.

"Well," I said. "Do you know what this is about?"

"Not really."

"Well, we're just sailing around the world. Actually, not around the world but ON the world. Well, the earth."

"Sounds good to me."

Months later we laughed about that strained meeting and I would sing to her the words to a George Thorogood song:

I went up to the window
I said gimme a ticket, please.
She said where to mister?
I said that's all right by me.

I can remember all of these details but I didn't get a real sense of *who* she was. However cool and alternative, Arianna was from an English colonial culture and personified English reserve. She was, and probably still is, a guarded person. Kind, but guarded. Still, she seemed keen to go and we needed someone to help, so we agreed to meet at the coast as soon as she got things "sorted" in Nairobi.

CHAPTER 8

Wakitchwa Ya Enkebe

MEANWHILE BEACH AND I needed to get up to Homa Bay to harvest whatever was left of our weed in the field… One last drive to Lake Victoria.

Months back, I had approached Easy to get his Kenya fixer, Karim, to find us a place to grow some weed for a cargo. Growing bhang was legal or at least not illegal in Kenya. It was sold in the Nairobi market for Christ's sake. I figured with Beach Rat's growing experience, his Mowie Wowie seeds, better fertilizer, and irrigation we could pull it off.

Karim found a Luo village with a woman chief who was willing to work with us. Then Easy and Karim rode up to Lake Victoria in *Boogie Mingi* with Beach Rat and me to get the project started. Within the month, Beach had his seeds planted in a sunny plot watered by an irrigation system that pumped water up from the lake. When the chief and her advisors saw it all in place, she immediately offered Beach a cozy mud hut with two young wives, if he would live there. He politely declined. The girls all anointed themselves daily with rancid animal grease.

As the crop started to mature and it was time to pull out the males, Beach found that every plant was a hermaphrodite. He didn't see this coming and he didn't know why. So being the detail oriented personality that he was, he went to the agriculture agent at the American Embassy. After a lot of research at the USAID library he discovered that the difference between the longest day of the year and the shortest was something like a few minutes at the equator where we were growing. Our marijuana plants couldn't tell when to select their sex by the lengthening days, so in their confusion, produced both sexes on each plant to make sure they could pollinate. This was important because the female buds were the part of the plant that had the choice resin. These plants just couldn't produce those buds because they were confused about their sexuality.

The weed wasn't export quality but it was a really good smoke. It just didn't look good; not the fat sticky buds Euro pot smokers were used to seeing. After all that work, someone was sure as hell going to smoke this shit. We needed a stash and all of our pals in Lamu and Malindi would love this new Kenyan *bhangi*.

But first we had to score some containers to pack it in. The next day Beach tracked down a place that manufactured containers for the coffee and tea packers. We bought 20 one-gallon tins, the kind that paint comes in.

By ten we were on the road to the lake. We got to the village by three. The villagers had already harvested the plants and sent them by truck to the Nairobi market. Grown from Rat's Maui Wowi seeds, weed that good had never hit the Nairobi market. Our village was about to become the first middle class Luo village in Kenya. Later that year, I was told by a Swedish aid worker that those in the aid community who had heard about our growing venture thought it was a classic successful aid project. We insured the future economy of the village with a sustainable crop without disturbing the tribe's culture, so I guess it wasn't a total waste of our time.

Beach Rat's Luo crew had set aside the plants he had picked out for us. We spent what was left of the day cleaning and packing the weed into tins, creating what would become the legendary "Wakitchwa Ya Enkebe" (canned heads).

I arrived at Malindi airport, Ranen was there to meet me and we drove to the Kilifi to find beautiful Sara peacefully anchored in the bay. She was slender, sleek, welcoming, and perfect. There were two cabins, one double bunk in the forepeak, and one single and one double bunk in the aft cabin. In between was a galley to port, a navigation station to starboard, then the main salon, serving as a sitting and dining room. There was one head, but mostly the bucket and chuck-it method was used. The head was only used when in port and close quarters. Ranen believed that heads were dangerous, with too much maintenance required, so best to keep them shut off.

Every day was busy and exciting, not only with swimming around the bay, but varnishing food tins in preparation for the sea voyage, a very long and tedious task. However, it depended on how one perceived such chores, and, as for myself, it was a task that was incredibly therapeutic. I needed to do this, to spend hours and days fulfilling my soul. The fear, insecurity, and hatred just wasn't there, I had no one to talk to or prove a point to. The days were spent preparing the boat for a voyage.

I put Arianna in the aft cabin with Beach Rat. As crew accommodations go, the aft cabin was pretty good. Two comfortable bunks, one double and one single with sheets and blankets, plenty of cubby space for clothes and personal gear and a convenient companionway hatch to the cockpit as well as a kind of tunnel passageway past the engine room to the main cabin.

As first mate, the task of introducing new crew to life aboard, fell to Rat. He taught her how to tie knots and which knots were used for what. He taught her the proper nautical names of things… windows are called port lights and the ones that open are called ports, the door and stairway to the cabin is called the companionway, the list goes on and on. The rigging list alone is intimidating, but in the middle of a storm with the wind howling and the force of the sea putting tremendous pressure on crew and equipment, instant communication is crucial.

Operating funds were getting low. My backers for the hashish scam out of Asia had become federal fugitives back in the States, so we needed to get *Sara* ready to do some long distance nonstop sailing.

Yet, here we were, one of the very few long distance smuggling boats in the Indian Ocean Basin where there is very little law, apart from the law of the jungle. I had it in mind to do something as close to a sure-thing as existed in the world of contraband. A trip to Thailand or Burma was my best bet. The best, most expensive weed in the world came from there.

A wild Kung Fu captain, named Steve, in Djibouti, had told us about Phuket, an island off the coast of Thailand in the Andaman Sea. "You're gonna end up there at some point. It has protected anchorages, boatyards, and only serious cruisers go there because of the pirates operating in the Andaman and the Malacca Straights. The doctors from Stanford circumnavigating the world on their sabbatical don't consider Phuket a safe stop, so you won't have to deal with nosey straight yachtsmen."

Phuket sounded pretty good and Steve was still in contact with some of the boats in Phuket through the ham radio net, "I'll make sure those guys keep an eye out for you."

It was interesting to know that there was a kind of smuggler's network in SE Asia like there was in the Caribbean and Atlantic. Having a ready-made network of expats would make finding contacts to get a cargo much easier.

Early on, Ranen asked, "So you haven't asked where we are going?" I said, "Okay, where are we going?" "Well we can either go to South America or Thailand." So I said either way is fine by me! The plan was that I wouldn't earn any money, but there would be plenty of adventure, and he would pay for my ticket home once we got to our final destination. I was ready to leave and wasn't concerned whether or not I had a return ticket, or any further plans for the future.

One day, Ranen and Beach said they had to go and sort out an aid project. So we got in the Land Rover and delivered, every ten kilometers off the main road, sparkling silver paint tins full of the prime buds that they had grown with some tribe up near Homa Bay. They were a present to the local tribe, and I am sure many more babies were born the next year. It was soon after, that Ranen kind of explained what I could be getting myself into, I felt all was okay and happy to go along with whatever they were doing.

The three of us spent at least four hours a day working on the boat or outfitting for the upcoming voyage. One morning, soon after Arianna arrived, I was reinforcing the inflatable dinghy transom and Beach and Arianna were sorting out gear and old cans of food we had stored in a shed in the boatyard.

Arianna called over to me, "What do you want to do with these silver paint tins?"

Beach stood up and said, "It looks like it's time to finish our aid project. I wouldn't mind going to Malindi for a beer or three."

Two one-gallon cans of weed were all we needed for the boat stash. Nils had come through on his way to Lamu by road and took a few cans of buds and we had given quite a few to friends in Mombasa and Kilifi, but we still had twelve or so left.

Rat and Arianna loaded the shiny cans into *Boogie Mingi* and we set out for the drive to Malindi. On the way we stopped every couple of miles and left a can by the side of the road. We spent the day driving around Malindi stopping at friends' houses, getting high, eating Italian food, and leaving shiny tin presents. I climbed over the life lines at 3:00 a.m. feeling a lot like Santa after a long night of delivering presents and drinking whiskey-spiked eggnog.

The weeks passed like continuous sets of waves rolling onto a desert coast, as the three of us worked at tasks. The lists grew longer and as we got deeper into refitting we realized how much needed repair or replacement. We spent a couple of days disassembling, scraping, polishing and greasing the gears and drums of *Sara's* winches, until the slightest push sent them spinning with the musical chatter of ratchets clicking like a dialed in Tour de France racing bike. The three of us piled twenty fathoms of rusty chain and two anchors into *Boogie Mingi* and drove it up to Nairobi to have it all sand blasted and galvanized. Engine, pumps and fuel tanks had to be cleaned and repaired or rebuilt, there was no end to it.

Still, we managed to go diving or fishing for dinner and Arianna turned out to be a gifted and creative cook. She had a way of combining unlikely ingredients that turned our dinners into feasts. I can still taste her fresh tuna simmered in fresh mangoes and hot peppers served over brown rice. Every morning she sent Safari, our night watchman, to the ferry to buy fresh *mandazi* (African doughnuts) for us to have with morning chai. Come to think about it, she even got us into drinking chai.

The three of us became a regular feature there on the British East African coast. When we came speeding through the coastal villages the *watu* would jump up and shout *"Boogie Mingi, Boogie Mingi "* Working, shopping, drinking or getting high the crew did everything together.

Arianna was eager to learn. She soaked up everything Beach and I taught her and she took ownership of any project we gave her. Arianna was barely 21 but somehow she commanded respect, and her brilliant smile and infectious laugh could turn around even my dark Pisces moods.

CHAPTER 9

Mombasa Harbour

As the equatorial hot rainy season came to a close in September I started thinking about sailing again. My backers in the States were now long gone and since money was no longer coming in and the boat had come together as well as possible on the East coast of Africa, I was getting restless, becoming nervous, and felt the time had come to get moving.

"Wow! It's been a long time since we've sailed this vessel. Seriously, I don't think I remember how to navigate, Arianna's never even sailed on *Sara*, and we really need to shake this boat down before we jump off toward the void."

"So where are we going, Ranen? And when? We're going to need another cooler for beer." Beach was making damn sure we had his provisions covered.

"We'll need provisions. I've been working on a list based on the old lists in the provisions book," Arianna's safari and hotel management experience was proving to be another of her hidden assets. "I'm sure we can take over the kitchen at the Tamarind restaurant in Mombasa after they close at night. It will be helpful to have a proper restaurant kitchen to make granola and do some canning. I've known the owners for yonks. It's right on the harbor with a nice dock in a lovely, quiet and safe part of town. We'll need to be in Mombasa to do the provisioning for wherever we are going and it will be a lot of fun to be anchored in Mombasa. We can go everywhere in our tender, didn't you say it was time to sell the Land Rover?" Three days later we dropped our mooring in Kilifi said goodbye the Bwana Mason, and sailed down to Mombasa.

Kenny and I were starting to have feelings for one another. I am not sure exactly when, but it was happening. I could tell by the way I kept catching him looking at me while we worked. And I was starting to think about him differently. He had this perfect body, all that sun bleached curly hair and his self confidence just wrapped around me.

We set sail and arrived in Mombasa port and anchored off a small yacht club. Kenny and Beach had to go back to Nairobi and sort out logistics or who knows what. I never asked.

I was left with Sara for at least a week on my own. What an honour. I spent most days doing boat chores and in the afternoon there was always time for a daily cool off at the Tamarind bar.

After my second day there I had collected my laundry from the yacht club and was about to drive back to the boat when a boatman asked for a lift to another anchored boat, so I said sure. I then saw a huge police boat patrolling and asked what it was doing out there. The boatman said he heard someone had drowned. I thought to myself, yuck. I certainly don't want to bump into a dead body. I dropped the chap off, then carried on to Sara. As I was approaching the boat, in the corner of my eye I could see the small club dinghy coming my way with cops on board.

I tied up the dingy, climbed on board, quickly chucked the laundry bag over our stash place. They came along side. I was polite and asked, "What can I do for you?"

They said it was a confidential matter and needed to be discussed in private on board the boat. I was still thinking about the dead body, so without thinking, I let them on board. They showed their IDs from, drug squad, CID, police, and said they had a warrant to search the boat for drugs. I was gob smacked, but knew I had to stay calm. I wasn't experienced enough to know the police had no right to board a foreign vessel etcetera…

I said, "Okay come aboard and search if you want." It was midday, the hatches were closed and it was very muggy and beastly hot down below, so I immediately closed the hatches to make it hotter. They were all pretty fat and had a hard time making their way down the narrow stairs. The men were desperately searching through Sara's medical cabinets and personal cupboards as a speed boat went by and the boat began to rock from side to side. Two of the officers sat down sweating, and one asked in African sing song English, "Why are you not sweating?" I answered, "I have nothing to be nervous about." One of them said, "I am feeling a bit dizzy," so I told them they were becoming sea sick and suggested they jump off board immediately before they start to vomit! So the dinghy was called over and they took off, no drugs to be found!

For the next four days or so, I was being harassed wherever I went by another officer, a sergeant. I couldn't get rid of these pests. They were constantly interrogating me, about anything they could think of.

Then one evening I received a message from the sleazy Indian owner of the yacht club, who was a wealthy lawyer in Mombasa, saying that he was there if I needed help. That's kind of when I twigged that maybe he had something to do with all these cops. At this point, I called Kenny and asked him to come back ASAP. I didn't feel safe anymore. This was getting to be too much.

Beach Rat and I were staying at the Hurlingham Hotel in Nairobi picking up some anchor chain we had galvanized and making some calls to try to squeeze some funds out of some of my former investors. The calls were largely unsuccessful but it was fun visiting with friends who were in town. All the cool younger crowd in Kenya stayed at this hotel and everyone drank at the hotel bar. Beach chased pretty aid workers and I drank pink gins and ate their BLT sandwiches made with gammon, a British version of bacon with almost no fat.

I picked up a message at the front desk from Arianna. It simply said come back ASAP! We were on the road ten minutes later. That same night back on *Sara* Arianna filled us in.

I was beyond furious. I had never met the lawyer who owned the "club" but there was a huge Indian population in Africa. The Indians had long ago established themselves throughout the British Empire. They owned most of the shops, grocery stores, and small businesses. This guy had a reputation as a man who saw himself as a character in an American soap opera. He saw himself as a rich ladies man.

"That fucking sleazy worm thinks he can threaten my crew then trade help for sex? That's what's going on here. He knew I was gone and thought he saw an opportunity to screw a frightened girl. Well, Arianna's not frightened and I'm **not** gonna let this go.

"First thing in the morning we're going to the CID to sort this out. These assholes came aboard an American registered vessel without permission from the U.S. Government. Roll one up Arianna. Otherwise I'll never get to sleep."

The next morning Arianna and I took a taxi to the Mombasa CID headquarters. I found the commander's office and walked in, "I don't know if you are aware of what your officers have been doing, but let me tell you that a group of your men came aboard and searched my American registered vessel without my permission and without notifying the American embassy. Not only that but they went below and intimidated a young woman member of my crew. One of your sergeants has been harassing her since the incident and I'm thinking that you don't know anything about it. Now I am asking you what you are going to do about these problems we have had with your men? I don't want to have to go to my embassy." I could see that he was pissed off that his guys were doing something behind his back and was impatient to get us out of there so he could jump on them.

"I will tell you what I am going to do. I am going to call for a car and driver to take you and this young woman to your boat. I want you both to forget about all of this. I am sorry that my officers have bothered you. You will not see them again because they are being re-assigned to duty at Lake Turkana in the NFD (Northern Frontier District)."

When we got back to the boat we moved down the harbor and dropped the anchor swimming distance from the Tamarind Restaurant dock.

About that time, we told everyone we knew that we wanted to sell *Boogie Mingi* but although I put a really low price on her no one came forward. I knew that a lot of people wanted that car. I had had the engine rebuilt and everything else was in good working order; then it occurred to me that everyone was waiting for the moment we were ready to leave so that we would have to give it away.

One day the three of us were having a couple of beers at the Castle Hotel bar, the favorite watering hole for all the locals and expats in Mombasa. Seems I remember that we had shared a joint of *bhangi* with a little opium on the way to town. I stood up on my chair and banged my mug on the table. In my Captain Ranen shouting-over-a-hurricane voice, I made an announcement. "All of you cheap bastards who want *Boogie Mingi* for nothing are invited to a party next Sunday on the cliffs by Easy's house in Kilifi. There will be lots of beer and a barbeque. At three o'clock if no one has bought the Land Rover I am going to roll it off the cliff onto the rocks. Cheers and thanks." Two days later we sold *Boogie Mingi* to one of the Italians from Malindi.

The weeks before and just after Christmas were really busy. As much as we had already accomplished, the list seemed to keep growing. We had done all the major repairs and maintenance, now we were down to provisioning. I never left for a voyage without six months of food on board. When one of the myriad of disasters that can cripple your boat at sea happens, you need to have enough food and water to survive until you can sort things out. Really, the whole survival issue was always a rationalization for spending time and money shopping for great food.

Living onboard at sea is hard enough, so that having plenty of good food is essential to a quality lifestyle. Furthermore you don't sail properly if you aren't eating well.

A hot meal in a storm is often the best cure for seasickness and demoralization. Seasickness doesn't always present as nausea, sometimes it presents as lethargy or depression and even when motion sickness is not an issue, sailing in bad weather burns up a lot of calories. When the boat is crashing through waves or rolling in a big swell, doing anything requires a lot of physical effort to stop yourself from crashing across the cabin or being thrown overboard. So a high calorie meal or canned milk in your coffee or tea is more than just an indulgence.

We lived by lists: how many pounds of dry beans, rounds of local cheese, canned chicken, pepper, and oatmeal were to be packed in exactly what part of the cabin? We scoured the country for provisions, coffee, tea, quality canned fish, rice, honey, sugar, beans and of course the ingredients for granola. Strange, but although coffee was a big export crop, seemingly no one really drank coffee in Kenya. Ground coffee just did not exist, we could only find really crap instant. Arianna continued to step up. One day, three big, waxed rounds of European, cow's milk cheese were delivered by someone coming to the coast from an upcountry ranch. She laid drying fruit on palm mats in the hot sun then took everything below at night before the dew fell. The sweet smell of papaya and mango rose above the salt air.

Medical supplies of morphine, sutures, five varieties of penicillin, bandages, and splints were carefully organized with the thermometer, scalpels, stethoscope, catheters, and other instruments, all packed neatly in clearly labeled containers in the head. Beach and I cleaned the guns and bought ammunition. We cleaned the foul weather suits and re-rigged nets to the bunks for sleeping in stormy weather. We made trips inland for shackles, paint, fishing line, and sailcloth thread. An entire day was spent making Ranen's super strong trolling rigs for fishing in the deep ocean. These were made by crimping a hundred feet of flexible stainless steel multi-strand cable to a lead weighted large size double hook, then lashing on strips of yellow and white spinnaker cloth to disguise the hooks. These were my never fail rigs for the only fresh protein available at sea: tuna, wahoo, barracuda, sailfish, mahi, and marlin.

Arianna and I took over the big fancy Tamarind kitchen for three nights to cook up twenty-five pounds of granola cereal, nut snacks, and to package the dried fruit and dried fish.

December is high tourist season in Kenya, but it also starts the season when all the expats come to the coast. It's the serious party season for all the bored white Kenyans who need to connect to their "Euro Roots." Whatever... We were there and the three of us were going to make the most of everywhere we found ourselves. It was all part of the "Kung Fu Yachting" lifestyle. Living in Mombasa Harbour was a lot of fun.

We did all of our shopping in our hot rod orange dinghy, from groceries to opium. Rat and I liked to add a little opium in our spliffs, so we navigated the narrow twisty streets of the ancient port, the Medina section of Mombasa, to find a Somali looking Muslim who sold opium. We were getting Mombasa wired to find everything we needed and even most of what we wanted.

And then it was the day before the New Year. The Tamarind was having a big New Year's Eve party on the huge dhow they used for big, day trip parties. We had *Sara* looking quite *maridadi*. The varnish, brass, and stainless were gleaming and the decks were clean and bright. All the sails were stowed in their green canvas covers and bags all lashed neatly on the booms and rails. She was anchored fifty meters off the quay where the party dhow was moored alongside. The three of us were the envy of every white person to see *Sara* shimmering like a mirage in that exotic harbor. Our plan was to dress in our best party clothes, but wear pirate make-up and carry cutlasses (machetes) then board the party dhow during dinner.

We had a smoke of our mixture and went over to the dhow during dessert, around 11 o'clock. Even in the eighties the tourists knew that this was a pirate coast, so we were guaranteed the tourists would be shocked. Some even genuinely frightened. We tied the orange launch alongside and came shouting over the rail. There were plenty locals on board for the party who knew us, and they got into the act. Arianna was grabbing drinks out of guest's hands yelling for "GROG!! Ye hear!" We ate food off their plates threatening them with death by cutlass. It turned out that everyone was already completely hammered, so our arrival kicked the party from out of control to pandemonium just as the New Year arrived. Beach grabbed a bottle of French Champagne and we slipped away back to *Sara*. We made it to the cockpit. Beach threw me the bottle and I opened it without spilling a drop. We were laughing like hyenas and Beach was hysterical about all the kisses he stole from tourist women, some of which were returned with gusto in front of their husbands. The Rat finished his glass of wine and tumbled straight into his aft cabin bunk.

Arianna and I hadn't drunk as much as Beach Rat so the bubbling dry wine was going straight to our heads. There was a bright moon and the noise of the party was moving away as the dhow moved down the harbour to continue its tour. Soon it was just Arianna, myself, and the moon. I was standing leaning against the main hatch when I had a shocking realization of how lovely Arianna was. Maybe I just never allowed myself to really look at her, but I was seeing her clearly now. I leaned over to touch her with my fingertip. It was an electric moment. I said quietly, "You know I've never touched you before."

"No. We haven't ever touched."

And then I kissed her, a light dry kiss that was like a butterfly. Each successive kiss was a greater level of exploration. I touched her face and kissed her eyes. Her smell and taste drove me higher. We wouldn't, couldn't break contact for what was hours. It seemed as if we were on a rocket ride to another universe, a black hole of passion. We were the only thing that existed until the red smear in the sky declared that we had returned from wherever our passion had taken us. How remarkable it was to become close friends and to develop mutual respect;

then be blasted to the stars to become lovers. It was powerful medicine and a different Ranen returned to Earth > Mombasa > *Sara.*

No doubt Beach Rat would surely be pleased to have his cabin back, since Arianna would be bunking up in the forepeak with me. Nothing was discussed. Ever. Life just continued. Nobody missed a step. Gentle good morning sex then a late New Year's breakfast of fish curry, eggs, and a Bloody Mary. There was something about this unexpected love that lightened up my existence.

One bright equatorial morning a few days later, I was sitting in the cockpit savoring morning coffee and toast under the huge dark green awning and watching a family of monkeys chase each other through the trees along the cliffs. Beach Rat popped out of the aft cabin hatch and said, "Listen Ranen, I need to go back to Santa Cruz. I haven't been laid in way too long and I am seriously missing body surfing Steamer Lane, the Catalyst Bar, and my redheaded girlfriend. When I called from Nairobi, she said that Granite Construction was hiring and she was tired of hanging around waiting for me to show up. If you get the ticket and give up some traveling money, we'll be cool. I've got ten grand from our last paying job buried in her yard."

All of this came all in one breath out of nowhere. Sure, we had an arrangement, but I'll admit I was a little shocked, and even a little hurt.

"And, how long is our luck gonna hold anyways?" Beach blurted out.

I thought about that, then replied, "Well, have you noticed anything about our luck lately?" We both chuckled a little over that. It *was* funny, but the chuckle was a little forced maybe, tasted bitter. "We *have* been gone a long time," I reluctantly admitted. "I honestly thought we would have been sailing north from the Cape of Good Hope with a load of hash over a year ago but I guess that was a bit naïve."

"Arianna's pretty good, you should be okay. I waited to see how she was going to work out." This was a high compliment coming from Rat, a man of few words, and even fewer compliments.

"When do you want to go?"

"Let's see when we can get me on a flight through Amsterdam. I wouldn't mind spending a few nights with Annika, the red head, on the way home. Maybe she'll be the attendant on my flight."

"God, you really are obsessed with *red bush*." And just like that, after two years, Beach and I were parted... over *red bush*.

Ranen and Arianna with David and Fiona on Sara in Thailand 1987

Date	UTC	LOG	N.Lat	E.Long	Comment
20.7	1814		5.4.25	18.02	
	2037		5°06	75°56.25	
	2050	67	4°57'.82	79°51'.19	CREW
	2154	74	4°50.75	79°04.5	Z-ZIK
	2344	85	4°40.15	79°46.19	
21	0049	91	4°34'	79.45	
	0133	97	4°28'.94	79°44.14	the boat sails on turn
			4°02'.71	79°43'.51	by herself
	0306	2318	4°08.72	79.32.28	
	0633	220	4°07.10	79°34.75	
	0818	227	4.01	79°.33	CREW takes over
	0838	231	3.56	79°.31	AGAIN
	1118	237	3°49'.51	79°28'.49	
	1228	240	3°46.46	79°26.94	waypoint 3 honour
	1319		3°41.64	79°21'.72	12°N 58°E AFRICA
	1445	243	3°02.184	79°02.416	
		250	3°34.53	79°01.736	
		253	3°28.71	79°17.22	
	2129	256	3°26.45	79'45.5	
	2259	257	3°23'.74	79°14'.330	
	0110	260	3°20.73	79°10.88	
	0701	289	2°55'.23	79°01'.53	
	0733	291.5	2°49.81	76°05'.197	
	0846	297.5	2°43.81	74°01'.33	
	1034	307.5	3.34	78.39'	

Date	UTC	LOG	E.Long	N.Lat	Comment
20.7	1108	310	2°31'	78°59.75	track-go west
	1256	318.6	2°26.5	78°52.2	
	1528	327	2°21.59	78°51.60	
	1730	339	2°19.86	78°44.75	
	1918	340	2°18	78°.38	
	2206	349.5	2°11.26	78°28'19	
	2258	353.5	2°07.78	78°22.611	
21	0125	360	2°0.41	78°22.86	MOTORING WEST
	0316	366	1°59	78°31	
	0520	374	1°52.7	78°.31	
	0708	882	1°55.05	78°02.87	
	0745	384	1°53.13	77°59.14	
	0800	390	1°53.48	72°51.40	
	0950	392	1°51.07	77°41.76	ROELLE is powered best
	1045	395	1°51.43	77°41.4	this super gold medal at
	1137	398.5	1°55	77°41	1988 galley olympics
	1305	404.5	1°56	77°33.5	(penal teddy protests)
	1355	408	1°56'16	77°29.34	white through parslaywim
	1453	412	1°56.75	77°24.17	no olympics Gold medal
	1544	415.5	1°57.40	77°19.77	sneaked rough back to
	1703	420	1°58.30'	77°12'	Roelle.
	1855	430	1°59.52	78°.02	
	1930	432	1°60	78°59	still Motoring 275
	2055	439	2°.5'	76°58.5	no current
	2116	441	2°.6	76°48.2	
	2129	442	2°00'.77	76°47.30	
	2316	445	2°02'.00	76°37.10	

Sara's ships log from on the days we were ill from food poisoning.

(Top) Arianna in the boat yard in Almerimar 1989
(Bottom) Steering mid-Atlantic 1991

(Top) Beach and Phoebe's gift (Lucia) on Sara 1985
(Bottom) Phoebe with Arianna on her second day on Sara 1985

Kenny Ranen

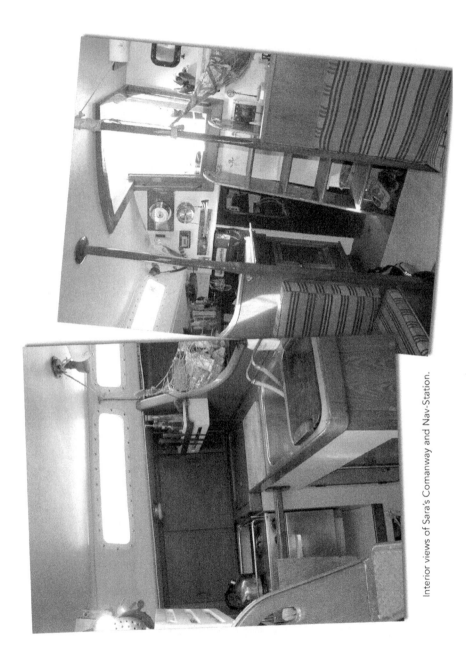

Interior views of Sara's Comanway and Nav-Station.

(Top) Beach and Phoebe's gift (Lucia) on Sara 1985
(Bottom) Phoebe with Arianna on her second day on Sara 1985

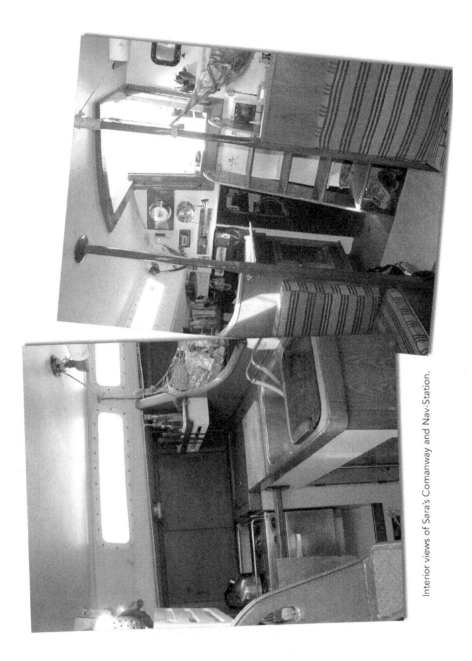

Interior views of Sara's Comanway and Nav-Station.

(Top) Ranen and Land Rover, "Boogie Mingi" in Kenya 1986
(Bottom) Shark eating Whale, mid Atlantic 1984

CHAPTER 10

Out of Africa

IT'S A LONG way from Mombasa to Phuket Island off Thailand, something like 3,200 nautical miles. Mombasa is at 4° South Latitude and Phuket is at 6° 42" North Latitude, which puts most of the voyage in Equatorial waters. The equatorial seas, also called by mariners, The Doldrums, are a world of very light winds and long periods of dead calm with strong squalls, the result of evaporation from the baking equatorial Sun. On the other hand, that means generally gentle seas. It is great hanging out on the equator if you have a comfortable boat, plenty of fuel, lots of great provisions, and no hurry. Those waters host some of the world's best blue-water fishing. In other latitudes you can sail for days, even weeks, without seeing anything but the occasional jellyfish, but the warm equatorial water seems to be alive with tiny sea life that attracts right up the food chain.

Despite the prospect of an easy voyage, I was nervous about leaving. Well, really, I'm always nervous about leaving after a long break from voyaging. This time I was extra nervous. Already out there both culturally and geographically and now heading further out, I have to admit that I was somewhat insecure about the next unknown playing field... Asia. Nervous about my *un-plan* and my ability to get it organized out of thin air, and then do it, I was trying to get my head around the responsibility of blithely sailing into the unknown with an inexperienced Arianna.

I was having a major "reality crisis," but keeping it to myself. In some ways having to be cool because of Arianna kept it all going on. My years of experience had taught me it simply will not do to have your crew thinking anything but the captain is omniscient. However, I have never considered myself a great sailor. In fact to this day I say with all honesty, "All of my friends are better than I am at everything I do." The only thing is, is that I do it… and in the end I have sailed more miles and more places then all of them.

As a child I was a reader, always fiction, always bold characters. I had fantasies about being brave and adventurous, bold and coura- geous. What other options for an imaginative little boy with no broth- ers, or even an interested father? I needed to know how to become the person I imagined I wanted to be, but didn't have a clue. Not even a clue of how to get strong, how not to be intimidated by my fears, how to dive into unknown waters. Somehow from that need to see and do the things that I dreamed, I came up with a formula: Convince myself I could do something, get in the middle of it, then do it or die, or fail, or whatever. Trick my frightened self into leaping into the mael- strom, then swim... or sink.

It was just after daybreak, the engine was running, the mainsail was raised, and I was pulling up the anchor chain hand over hand. Now the restraints were off. The exhilaration of leaving the land was giving me an adrenaline rush. "Fuck Kenya, Fuck President Daniel Arap Moi, WE ARE OUT OF HERE!" I shouted so loud that the cliffs rang.

Now we were on our way. All the anticipatory fears were left behind as Arianna and I settled into the daily routine…Sleep, eat, steer and make love.

The winds were light or non-existent, and to be honest, I didn't care if our course was off. Looking at the chart on the third morn- ing Arianna and I were laughing at our meandering course during the night. We looked each other in the eye and clinked our mugs of tea. "We've got loads of great food, plenty of water, so here's to the lon- gest, most fun, Indian Ocean crossing ever."

Still, when the breeze came up we did our best to keep *Sara* on a decent heading. *Sara* had a Magnavox navigation system that was being replaced by the newer GPS system, which in those days, was very expensive. Magnavox hadn't shut down our old system, they were just letting the satellites degrade and coverage was getting pretty unreliable. Sometimes the position fixes were way off and at that point we would go days without a good position. I had been crossing oceans ten years before having any electronic navigation, so just having occasional position fixes was still a luxury. We kept a log, updated every hour and plotted a position on our chart every four hours at the end of each watch or when we changed course. The sat nav was just one of our tools. I had been navigating by the sun for many years and had all the publications needed to do the calculations, but never having really enjoyed the necessary math theory, celestial navigation was a necessary evil. However, we had a beautiful sextant and a handy Texas Instruments calculator that made printouts to make celestial navigation less painful. When people asked me which stars I used for navigation, I would always answer, "The big one that comes out in the daytime. THE SUN."

Every few days in the calms, I started the engine and we would motor for a couple of hours to make some headway and charge the batteries. Otherwise when the wind quit, which was often, we would drop the sails and go for a swim or just hang out listening to music on our sound system. That sound system was amazing, Alpine cassette and CD player, Bose outdoor speakers, and a Bazooka sub-woofer in the starboard overhead cabinet. I had a huge music collection, spanning four decades of various genres.

Some mornings as the sun was coming up, we would collect the flying fish that had hit the sail and flopped about on deck. They were delicious grilled with salt, just like the classic British kippers and eggs breakfast. Life was good. We knew it, and appreciated every moment.

CHAPTER 11

King Neptune

AT THE END of the second week as we approached the equator, I started thinking about what to do for Arianna's first crossing the line ceremony. Sailors had been performing this hazing ceremony since the days of wooden ships and iron men as an initiation into the "Kingdom of Neptune." Studying the chart at the beginning of my late night watch, I figured that we would be crossing the equator right at the time to wake Arianna. So I got busy organizing the ceremony. The first task was to create an official "King Neptune Crossing Certificate." I was all set up for this one. The "Captain Ranen certificate kit" had plenty of official looking blank filigreed parchment for creating documents when I needed to change the name of the boat. Some fancy script and some artful stains and it was done.

Next, I had to turn myself into King Neptune, starting by cutting up an old baseball cap and gluing colored cardboard points to it for "King Neptune's crown." I let Arianna sleep quite late to get ready. To make Neptune's robe, I spent a couple of hours collecting sargasso weed out of the sea rushing by. For the trident I used my snorkeling spear with a cardboard three-prong tip. The next half hour was spent painting my face green and draping myself with my seaweed robe.

When I was satisfied that I *was* King Neptune, I dumped the genoa, put on my "crown," grabbed my "trident", and called to Arianna in my deepest loudest King Neptune voice, "WHERE IS THE POLYWOG CALLED ARIANNA?"

Arianna popped out of the aft cabin hatch blinking in the bright sunlight to see King Neptune sitting on the bow pulpit. "YOU HAVE

CROSSED THE EQUATOR INTO MY KINGDOM, POLYWOG. NOW YOU MUST BE INITIATED INTO THE RANKS OF TRUE SAILORS." The shocked look on her face was precious. She never saw this one coming.

The King ordered her to crawl on her hands and knees to the foredeck, and explained that this was a serious matter of life or death. Neptune controlled the seas, and all who sailed those seas were at his mercy. He ordered her to pick up a dried out disgusting plankton off the deck with her mouth and bring it to him. Next he reached deep into one of the sail bags lashed on deck and came up with a bottle of rum and two jelly glasses. First, Arianna was ordered to pour a libation overboard. Neptune then tapped his trident on each shoulder and proclaimed Arianna a "Shellback." They each had a couple of shots and he presented her the certificate.

By now King Neptune had become seriously aroused by Arianna who was wearing her usual sleeping attire, panties and a cut off sleeveless tee-shirt. The King was thinking that his solid was so hard it would cut coral. Arianna, who was still kneeling on the deck noticed and parted the curtain of Neptune's seaweed robe then took him into her mouth. Ranen was immediately back and we rolled onto the deck with my hands holding her firm butt and my face so buried in her sex that I couldn't breathe. This had to be the ultimate form of suffocation, death by passion. We drank deeply of each other while making love on our bed of seaweed. The scent and taste drove us to want more. Arianna slipped me in. She brought me in so deep that I felt every thrust reach the end of her. We were relentlessly locked together, mouths, chests, and hips, refusing to lose contact until finally we were spent. So far from civilization, both mentally and physically, our lovemaking had no boundaries.

When we came back to reality, giddy, spent, and slippery we looked up and around us at a perfectly flat sea. There were thousands of dolphins leaping out of the water in every direction as far as the eye could see. I climbed the mast to the spreaders with a pair of binoculars and it was the same, dolphins leaping for miles in every direction. That was the first and last time I have ever seen that phenomenon… the dolphin celebration! Eventually the wind came up, the dolphins moved on, and *Sara* continued moving slowly, east by north.

CHAPTER 12

Monsters From the Deep

WE WERE HEADED toward the Maldives but with this wind it could be a long sail… maybe weeks. One bright tropical day we were becalmed on a perfectly flat sea. The water was so clear that we could see the sparkling blue water turn darker blue then purple the further down we looked. Without a thought I dove straight down into the blue, and kept swimming straight down into the purple. I stopped and looked up. The surface looked like a shining hole in the water far above me. *Shit!* I thought. *I hope I have enough oxygen to get back up.* A minute or two later I burst to the surface gasping for air and completely energized. Arianna commented, "You looked so small down there."

I answered, "Throw the long cockpit cushions over. Lets relax in this big pool."

The cockpit cushions were canvas covered closed cell foam that made perfect floats. We kissed and wrestled in the water then spent some time lying on our floats watching the clouds far above us. After a while I got out of the water to make lunch.

Down in the galley, I could hear Arianna climb aboard. She called out, "Ranen, what are these large fish?" I came up on deck with a soft drink in hand. There were five or six big great white sharks milling around the boat, six meters down! I felt a little queasy thinking about us splashing around in the water just minutes ago. "I wonder if they're hungry?" I said, as I threw the can out into the water. Then, out of the purple depths, a monster shark came straight up like a missile launched from a submarine. It broke the surface with its maw wide open. It seemed as if it happened slowly, because we could see its huge open mouth with all of its rows of teeth visible, and the can disappearing into that cavern, but it continued to rise right out of the sea until the full size of the creature crashed back into its home environment.

In that profound moment when we could both see what might have been lost, I became acutely conscious of how much Arianna meant to me. Profound love? That would be a whole new concept for this self-centered thirty-five year old captain. As usual, neither of us felt comfortable talking about any of this. British reserve made even more difficult, talking about feelings in general, much less how we felt about each other. Of course, as a guy, I never wanted to talk about anything emotional.

However, we often talked for hours, philosophizing on every sub-ject, from human behavior to business and culture and the relationship of these things. In some ways I think I was mentoring her for what life would be like when we were no longer on our "honeymoon." She was fascinated by the "Kung Fu" sailing lifestyle. Arianna was already an experienced alternative traveler who had been on her own from an early age. So, as we got to know each other better, I was more and more sure she was perfectly cast for the role of a smuggler.

She talked about her life, growing up as a British Colonial in East Africa, with a beautiful "fast lane" hippy mother. As a teenager, Arianna's ex-model mother was living with the famous Playboy pho-tographer Peter Beard. So, how Arianna looked was very important to her competitive mother. Never mind that Arianna was a world-class beauty along the lines of Marilyn Monroe, except with long perfect legs. She was never skinny enough for Mom who regularly put her on diets and was constantly comparing her to her friend's children. They were always slimmer, had better style, and wore trendier clothes.

Although her dysfunctional childhood in East Africa was the cause of her insecurities, somehow it also gave her the toughness, the abili-ties, and the stubborn confidence needed to face the stress of smug-gling and the hardships long distance nonstop sailing.

CHAPTER 13

Sojourn in the Maldives

A FEW DAYS after the shark incident, we were suddenly sailing in bright turquoise water. Even though we knew we were about to enter the Maldives archipelago, it still was a startling event, after weeks of deep blue water sailing to cross a clear line right into bright turquoise. The ledge below must have been dramatic, a vertical coral wall a thousand meters deep. We slowly sailed for miles, threading our way through dozens of tiny islands, some of which were only half a football field in size, and only a couple of feet above sea level. Most of them were deserted.

> *From Arianna's journal: Maldives*
>
> *About 200 miles before we were due to arrive in the Maldives, Ranen became very anxious, impatient and angry. I wasn't sure what I was doing right or wrong. I felt that he was not interested in me any longer, had enough and that I was not good enough. I was young and had my problems and with Ranen being distant and freaking out, I was ready to leave.*
>
> *Ranen then mentioned that we would leave the boat in the Maldives and would be going to Europe for a couple weeks to sort out a few issues.*
>
> *What I did not realize was that he was risking the last of his funds to put into one last mission. That was it! But I had no concept of such responsibility. I didn't need a house, or nine-to-five job. My life was free. I had no responsibilities. All that mattered to me was that Ranen and I were on a mission*

*together, and I needed to know that he loved me, even though
I was not very good at giving love back.*

All the native inhabitants lived on Malé, one of the larger islands, a few miles from the airport. It was a filthy, poverty stricken place. We only remained in that crude sewage filled harbor for the hours it took to clear customs and fill the diesel tanks. We never even set foot on that island.

However, we did meet Satya and his wife Nishela who were an unusual couple living on a sailing boat in the harbor of that horrible capital town. Nishela was a pregnant buxom blonde, blonde, blonde, a political refugee from Czechoslovakia who had become a citizen of the Netherlands. Satya, a tall, thin, kind of goofy Dutchman, was a carpenter and the captain of this rundown Dutch registered boat. What was amazing was that Nishela was about to have their child right there in that filthy town in the midst of a cholera epidemic. In a way the epidemic was a good thing, because there was a large team of doctors from Médecins Sans Frontières there. Satya was a natural sailor and a hippy world traveler…We immediately bonded. Arianna remarked, "I hope we run into Satya again, he really is an interesting chap."

We arrived in the Maldives, and found a heavenly place to anchor the boat just off a small atoll with a German run hotel. Ranen then announced that he would travel alone and leave me to look after Sara. I was not prepared, and although I was honoured to be left with this responsibility, I was scared. Before Ranen left he made sure he secured Sara with two anchors and wrapped the chain around a few coral heads so she was not going to break free. He also left me with a few instructions in case there was a storm. So I took note and was ready for a couple weeks of beautiful weather, lots of snorkeling and pol- ishing the boat.

Arianna and I anchored *Sara* over a white sandy bottom amongst some impressive coral heads. A few hundred meters away was a tiny island just big enough to contain a hotel filled with German and Italian tourists. The Maldive archipelago all around us consisted of tiny low islands, each of which had a hotel, filled with tourists who had no contact with the reality of this tiny nation. They cleared customs and immigration right at the airport island, and took water taxis a few miles right to their hotels, isolated and scattered among the archipelago.

The only reason we stopped in the Maldives was that I knew I could get a cheap charter flight to Europe. I needed to fly to Switzerland to clean out the dwindling funds from an investment there. I also wanted go to London to buy some marine charts for Thailand, the Red Sea, and the Mediterranean, as well as some injector tips for the engine and some rigging bits. At this point I had not been in the first world for two years and was in need of a little R & R at the Portobello Hotel in London.

There was no way I was going to leave *Sara* in the Maldives without someone onboard to keep watch. Although we were within one degree of the equator, where there were no cyclones and the reefs afforded good protection, still there was a possibility of a storm. Arianna and I may have been lovers, but she was first mate and staying with the boat came with the territory. The boat always comes first, something that has caused problems with my crews and relationships over the years. So I left Arianna and took the water taxi to the airport to catch a direct flight to Zurich.

We had only been in the Maldvies about two days when Ranen flew off to London. I was left with this beautiful 46 foot yacht all to myself. There was only one other boat in the bay, owned by a Swedish couple who were also on board. Later in the afternoon the weather started to build up. I checked the anchors and all seemed fine, then the storm came in with a bang.

The waves were bursting over the decks and Sara was jerking the anchor chains. I was terrified. I could only think about the anchor breaking away and Sara drifting out over the atolls and out to sea. I then decided to start the engine and just keep it idling in gear to take some strain off the anchor chain. I was so worried that I couldn't sleep the whole night. I had no one to call but I could see the other boat was still there.

The next morning, the sea was calm and I decided to go to the hotel on the island. A few of the people working there asked if I was okay. They said they had tried to drive out to see if I was okay during the storm but they couldn't get through waves that were pounding onto the island. There were small boats that had been thrown onto the middle of the island. I then realized that this was more than just a normal squall.

I had been getting high whilst cleaning and sorting out the boat. I met a few people on the island and invited three young lot out to the boat, a couple of blond girls and a blond guy. I was so crazy, I had a Quaalude and some joints. I was dancing in the galley, took my top off and carried on dancing and cooking bare breasted. We were all a bit crazy. I'm not sure if I ever saw them again... I think I may have scared them.

I met up with a couple of German guys who were working at the hotel. I was always high and taking Quaaludes. One evening they asked if I would join in with the Karaoke, and I actually went on as Tina Turner and sang one of her songs. I then invited them back to the boat, we partied and one of them stayed the night. The next day he invited me to one of the other islands for lunch. It was beautiful and we stayed until evening. I was happy to get back home to the boat, and wanted to be left alone. But this guy kept coming back to visit, day after day, and I was starting to get annoyed. Finally, one day he came out and asked if he could make dinner and bring it to the boat, but when he turned up, I asked him to leave and said

I wanted to be on my own. He insisted, so I pulled out a gun and told him if he didn't leave I would shoot him. He left pretty fast!! A couple days later Ranen came home.

Author's note: Even after thirty years and even if I did request her journal piece about this period, it still hurt. I knew that she was going through something at the time, but didn't want to know about it then, because somehow I also knew that was not the moment to find out. However, It might be important to point out that the hypnotic sedative drug methaqualone (brand name Quaalude or Mandrax) was responsible for some uncharacteristic wild behavior, bizarre thought processes, and blackouts during the 1980's, which is why it is now no longer manufactured anywhere. KR

I grabbed the train from the airport to the Zurich Bahnhof, and then a taxi to see my old friend Hans. Hans and I had met many years before in the Caribbean. I had invested in a business of his and when it was successful, I asked that he hold my share for a future opportunity. Well, he had returned to start a family in Switzerland, and in my view, a Swiss friend is the next best thing to a Swiss bank. I asked him for ten thousand dollars. He made a call and less than an hour later some guy in a suit arrived to hand him an envelope.

Hans handed me the envelope and said, "I want to thank you for encouraging me to buy the sailboat. My family has spent many wonderful hours on Lake Zurich sailing our boat. I know you have a plane reservation, but allow me to take you for a wonderful Swiss meal first."

I caught the first flight to London that afternoon. I walked down the mirrored hallway, backpack slung over my shoulder and a uniformed British customs officer came out of a doorway. He said, "Excuse me sir, please come with me." He politely escorted me to a small interrogation room. I was dressed in clean jeans, a button down collar shirt and a dark blue ultra suede sport coat. I was wearing red Converse All-Star sneakers and my thick curly hair was below my shoulders.

There were two customs officers present, one of whom asked me to take off my clothes. While the other went through my pack, I took off my coat, shoes, pants, and shirt. One of them found the ten grand in a pocket in my pack.

He asked in a nasty tone, "Where did you get this?"

I answered in a calm business like voice, "At my bank in Switzerland."

"What are you going to do with this money?"

"Look guys, I live on a sailing boat in the Indian Ocean and I'm here to buy parts, some foul weather gear, charts and other supplies."

He said, "Lift up your genitals."

I was losing my temper but not raising my voice. "Now you listen, I've just come from the bank in Switzerland and intend to spend money in your country. I could have easily gone to France or Holland to spend this money. You can see by my ticket that I haven't visited any country that exports hard drugs. Whatever is under my balls isn't going to put a dent in your drug problem. There was a flight coming in from Pakistan right behind mine. They're all passing in the hall now. Go search them. Forget it, I'm putting my clothes back on. I'll just return to Zurich."

One of them shrugged and the other said in disgust, "Get the fuck out of here rich boy."

When I finally got out into the airport, I called the Portobello Hotel and asked for Fiona, the manager. She wasn't in. I said, "This is Captain Ranen. I want a room for tonight and another three days, a cabin if you have one."

The receptionist replied, "I'm not sure we have a room."

I said, "Look, I don't know you and you obviously have never heard of me, but I stay there all the time. Call Fiona and check it out but do not give away my cabin or you will have a problem. I am at Heathrow and will be there shortly."

The Portobello was a discrete, small private hotel on a quiet street between the Portobello Market and Notting Hill Gate. It catered to musicians, artists, and filmmakers. You couldn't get a room there unless the management knew you or at least somehow knew of you, or if you turned up and were obviously their type of guest. It was one of the only hotels in London that had an all night bar and restaurant. The rooms were all decorated in different styles from super plush to a few "cabins" which were like boat cabins where I felt right at home. This place was steeped in rock-n-roll history. All the bands stayed there, except the superstars and even some of them. The whole cast of the movie Little House of Horrors stayed there for weeks. It was perfect for artists who were recording because of the homey atmosphere, the all night restaurant and bar, and because there were no uncool tourists staying there. Captain Ranen fit right in.

I had been going there for years, whenever I made some money and needed to go somewhere where I could cut loose and not have to worry about letting something slip about what I did for a living. Maybe tell stories and even brag a bit. I have attended some amazing middle of the night impromptu parties there.

The next couple of days were spent running around London picking up parts and charts. Andy, a Portobello regular who was a studio drummer from New York was staying, while he worked with Bryan Ferry. I loved listening to all the rock music gossip over drinks in the bar at three in the morning.

Fiona, who over the years had become a good friend, invited me for dinner to the apartment she shared with her boyfriend David. The three of us had a laughter and alcohol filled evening. We all realized that one night was not enough and decided that they would come stay on the boat for a couple of weeks in Thailand sometime during the coming London winter. The next day I caught a flight back to the Maldives.

The launch from the airport island dropped me at *Sara*. Arianna cheerfully helped me get my bags and all the gear onboard and put away. After dinner we exchanged stories about the week we had been apart. She nervously told me that some German guy swam out to the boat quite a few times and that he was hitting on her pretty hard. Then one night when she couldn't get him to leave, she pulled the .38 caliber Smith and Wesson revolver on him. Problem solved. There was a reason that there was a deadly weapon within reach almost anywhere on *Sara*. You might need one.

The next day Arianna handed me the in-flight magazine she found that I had used for padding in a box of electronic parts, "Read this article. This is something I am dealing with."

It was an article about bulimia, something I had never heard of. However it made perfect sense, considering her mother's need to force Arianna into her concept of a perfect daughter. I told her that the next time she was inclined to vomit up her food we should have sex instead. I suppose I was a bit naïve, but she laughed and agreed. In the end, training her to be a long distance sailor and giving her the responsibilities that go with being a smuggler, gave her the self confidence to get past all those issues. I like to think so anyway.

That evening at dusk a boat anchored far enough away so that we could make out the outline of the boat but not see the details with our naked eyes. The thing was, it looked just like *Sara*, like identical. I grabbed the binoculars and glassed the new boat. Although the profile was the same, this was a larger vessel and was a ketch not a yawl. I recognized the design. It was an Ocean 60.

We jumped into the dinghy and zipped over to our new neighbor. We were welcomed aboard and introduced to the American crew of four. It was an unusual encounter. We shared a couple of drinks and talked about how our *Sara* was just a smaller version of their boat. It was pretty well established that Ocean Yachts had patterned their Ocean series after the Bowman Corsair, which is what *Sara* was. The Bowman had finer lines, less freeboard. The Ocean was built for sleeping a lot of people where *Sara* was built for racing with a small crew.

For some reason, we just dispensed with all the LPLs and started exchanging notes about smuggling in this part of the world. They had sailed here from somewhere far away to pick up a load of who-knows-what and were delayed for some unspoken reason. The captain was nervous about hanging around his pick up point and came here to wait. We didn't ask, and he wasn't volunteering any details, but he wanted any insider gossip about this part of the Indian Ocean. I gave him what info I had picked up, mostly from Steve in Djibouti, and our observations of shipping that we had seen, mainly empty ocean and no military type vessels. The Ocean was a better smuggling boat, but their profile was a lot more suspicious. That boat was a lot bigger than *Sara*, and could carry a lot more of whatever and with those four guys, could sail anywhere nonstop. I could see why these guys were nervous about hanging around. They were a big boat and a crew of hardened sailors, unlike *Sara* with her attractive young couple. They were a lot more visible. They needed to keep moving.

We all spent an enjoyable couple of evenings with our colleagues. Then one morning they were gone.

When those boys on the Ocean left, we pulled the anchors and headed east toward Thailand.

CHAPTER 14

Medical Emergency at Sea

A LIGHT BUT steady breeze was pushing us east away from the Maldives toward Sri Lanka. Arianna and I were hiding from the blazing equatorial sun under the scrap of canvas that served as an awning while underway. It was Arianna's watch and I was absently staring at the fishing lines that we always trailed behind the boat.

"Whoa! We just hooked something." All in one fluid dance, I leaped out of the cockpit, grabbing and jerking the thick monofilament line, and a big Wahoo cleared the water fifty feet behind the boat. "Fresh fish is on the menu tonight." I grabbed the gaff lashed to the rail, "Head up into the wind to stall us while I get this guy onboard." While I was stripping one-meter fillets off of the carcass, I looked over at Arianna. She seemed kind of distant. "You okay?"

"Just feeling a bit off. I'll get some sleep as soon as my watch is over."

"Go now, the wind is steady and she's keeping the course, and I've got to get this fish marinated. Go!"

The next morning Arianna woke up with a sore throat. By her evening watch her throat was really raw and she felt feverish. "I never get ill, just get me some more of those vitamin C tablets and two Ibuprofen and I'll be better in the morning," she croaked. I swung down below to catch a nap.

An hour later, I got up and lurched down the cabin toward the closed up head where *Sara's* pharmacy was. I opened the EMT box and grabbed a thermometer and a tongue depressor. Arianna was making a log entry at the nav station. "You look flushed," I said, and swept back two pounds of hair, put my hand on her forehead and the thermometer in her mouth. "You definitely have a fever, over 101," I said, shaking down the mercury in the thermometer as if it were a wand. "Open your mouth, stick out your tongue and say AHHHH." I pushed down her tongue and shined the flashlight down her throat. *Not good*, I thought. Her throat was inflamed and there were a couple of white pustules near her tonsils.

I had been a blue water smuggling captain for years, so a medical problem, weeks away from medical help was not something new. Still, it *was* one of the big worries. A look at one of my medical journals confirmed what I suspected. Arianna very likely had a bacterial infection, possibly Strep.

"Listen, take these four Ampicillin, then two every four hours and go to your bunk and we'll see if we can knock this out. Now go!" I always carried a good stock of antibiotics in the ship's medicine chest, and I had started her on the Ampicillin, hoping this infection wasn't a resistant strain. Fortunately the NW Trades were blowing a steady fifteen knots generating a long easy swell and *Sara* was pretty much sailing herself with a breeze blowing fresh air through the boat. We were out of the shipping lanes so single handling *Sara* was no biggie. No way was Arianna going to be on watch for the next few days.

At daylight her temp was down to 100° but her throat was still raw. That evening her temp had climbed to 102.5 and she was starting to exhibit a nasty cough. While Arianna slept I got on the HF/Ham radio and called in to the Maritime Emergency Medical Net. Two hours later I was in radio contact with an Aussie MD who provided medical advice for isolated ranchers in the Australian outback over HF radio.

"Right mate, what have we got? Over."

"I've got a pretty sick but otherwise healthy 22 year-old woman on board. Over," I answered. Then I ran down the symptoms and what I had done so far.

"What kind of medical supplies do you have on board?" he asked.

"I probably have most of what you have at your surgery except the machines."

"Good on ya mate. I want ya to get your stethoscope and listen to her breathing, Tap on her chest and listen. Then get back to me, I'll stand by and listen on the hour and the half hour."

The medical cabinet was in the head, which I kept shut off at sea because marine toilets are one of the most common causes of serious leaks and even sinking of yachts at sea. Really! Imagine using the toilet in any kind of seas. Picture what happens when the boat takes a good roll. Since we weren't using the head, all the ventilation was shut off, so, when I opened the door, I was greeted with a blast of humid hot air. I dug around the EMT kit and quickly found the stethoscope.

In the aft cabin Arianna whispered, "That feels so cool" when the stethoscope touched her fevered chest. There was a crackling sound in her breathing. Her temp was up a few tenths. My mind started running down the options a mile a minute…*I hope to hell this isn't pneumonia and if it's going there, can I deal with it onboard? Sri Lanka is the closest port and not a good place to be in the hospital. Fuck! We're in the middle of nowhere. Well, I might as well call the doctor.*

The doctor listened, was silent for a bit, then asked, "What other antibiotics have you got? Over."

"She's taking Ampicillin and I've got, Erythromycin, and Keflex. And, I've got to tell you Doc that we are nowhere near a safe medical facility. The closest first world hospital is a month away or three weeks with luck. So tell me what I've got to deal with here."

"No point in guessing. Let's just try to kill it. Keep her on the Ampicillin tonight but start the Erythromycin immediately then stop the Ampicillin in the morning. I'll be listening on this frequency at 1700 and 2200 GMT tomorrow."

Once again by the next morning Arianna's fever was down, but by the time I called in to the doctor it was back up to 103.5°. "Right mate, let's get out the big gun. Start her on the Keflex immediately."

The following morning her temp was down to 101° and I was thinking we might be okay. By evening it was up half a degree. *Shit!* I thought. *I hope this isn't a resistant strain, cuz we're out of options.* Worry was sneaking up on me, but I knocked on the teak bulkhead and thought *too soon to worry.* In the eighties Keflex was the answer to resistant bacteria, yet I must have been worried because I started looking for ships and thinking about the possibility of putting her on board a container ship bound for Singapore or Hong Kong

The next morning Arianna's temp was down to 99° and I looked at the thermometer and said, "Well, that was somewhat scary."

Sara continued heading east by north 120 miles a day.

PART 4 — Thailand, 1987

CHAPTER 15

A Smuggler's Guide to Good Manners

As *SARA* APPROACHED the Bay of Bengal we started listening in on the SE Asian Ham Cruising Net on *Sara's* HF radio. Steve had given us the times and frequencies for when all the cruising sailors in Thailand tuned in. I had fabricated a call sign from Panama, which would work unless some uptight ham operator took it upon himself to look it up and find it was non-existent. The South East Asia Cruising Net was set up for the cruising boats in this part of the world to keep contact with each other. You could listen in to find out where your friends were, if Susan had her baby, or whether the Indonesian government would bust you for anchoring off a great surfing break in Java.

This net was pretty loose, so after tuning in and listening for a few days, I started talking. It turned out that Steve had passed on a message to his friends in Thailand to look out for me. We got a warm welcome to the net and I got the feeling that we would fit right in with this crowd. It looked like all the sailing boats in Phuket were anchored in a bay called Ao Chalong. I had a talk with some guy, Terry, who would end up becoming a friend. So, long before we got there we knew all the gossip in Phuket, but no names of people or boats. I was not the only one with a Panama license.

Twelve days later we were sailing our way through tiny islands along the coast of Malaysia approaching Thailand. I sat at the chart desk looking at the chart of the Andaman Sea with the details of Phuket and surrounding seas. "I think we should drop the hook at this island across from Ao Chalong. We can clean *Sara* up a bit and get in radio contact with these guys from the Ham Net to see where to anchor."

Two days later, having rested, cleaned up *Sara*, and inflated our sport-boat, we sailed over to the anchorage that was to become our home for quite a few months. We made our "grand entrance" threading through the anchorage under sail looking for a good place to drop the hook. At my signal, Arianna at the helm headed down wind and I dropped the anchor in 12 feet of water, fed out 36 feet of chain and cleated it. The forward motion laid out the chain perfectly and when the anchor set itself, the boat abruptly stopped and swung into the wind. We anchored perfectly without starting the engine, and for sure anyone awake in the anchorage heard the anchor and chain clanking and was watching us anchor under sail. *Sara* had left her calling card.

Arianna and I took our time furling and bagging the sails, and getting the dinghy and the outboard organized. We took a tea break on deck and glassed the anchorage with the binoculars. Ao Chalong was a large crescent shaped bay with a sandy beach along the edge. It was open on one side to the south but protected from the waves of the Andaman Sea by the big island next to which we had anchored for the last two nights. The water was not really clear but kind of cloudy light green. Occasionally a sea snake head would pop to the surface. Although sea snake bites are deadly, they were not something to worry about because their heads are too small to bite anything as big as a human.

We could see that this was a bustling village. There were a few funky restaurants in palm-roofed makeshift open buildings built right on the beach. The sailing boats anchored in the bay were all unique, very seaworthy boats. There was only one production built boat out of the ten or so sailing boats anchored, all the rest were custom built boats. Judging by the flags, the boats were an even mix of three continents. Three of the boats were American. Obviously this place was way off the beaten track, just our kind of place, probably not a Cruising Magazine within five hundred miles.

There were also three or so big Thai fishing trawlers anchored in this protected bay. Frequently, one of the trawlers would display a whole lot of flashing lights, immediately another big trawler would go alongside for a short time. I later learned that they were signaling for a collection boat to pick up their fish. In those days, Phuket Island, and Thailand had no yachting scene. This corner of the world had too many pirates and not enough marinas for the "sailing around the world crowd" to feel comfortable, which was a big attraction for us.

"There are some dinghies pulled up on that beach. Let's go to Thailand for some lunch. We've got to clear in with immigration. I'll get the passports and boat papers." We jumped into the dinghy and raced into the beach. There were four dinghies pulled up out of the water in front of a mostly open sided beach bar with a palm-frond roof and a sand floor. There were a few tables outside and more inside. We walked in to find a couple of foreigners having beers at one of the tables. One of them looked up and said in an Australian accent, "She's a beauty mate, your yawl that is. You're Steve's friend from Africa, right? Heard you on the net last week."

I noticed he didn't really introduce himself, but to me that just meant I was in one of those places where everyone was cautious. From the look of the boats in the anchorage I was guessing that this was a safe harbor for outlaws and probably some of the owners of those boats didn't have passports or at least not valid ones. I had been in harbors like this before. You just don't ask personal questions and folks don't volunteer personal information, at least not until they've checked you out.

"Right. Steve told me to stop in here. We hung out for a few weeks in Djibouti. I'm Ranen and this is Arianna." I shook his hand, "Where do we clear in?"

"Well mate, you're gonna love this place. Here in Thailand you just need a visa. The Thai government isn't really interested in clearing in your sailing boat; they figure all that rigmarole isn't worth it for a yacht. You can take a tuk-tuk to the government building in town to get your passport stamped and they don't even look too closely at that. You might as well have a beer and some food first. Those offices don't open 'til two o'clock. That's Champi, Pan's pet. He won't bite you. Pan owns this place and Pan is a good cook."

It was then that I noticed the large monkey, like a gibbon or something. Then a small good looking twenty-something local guy came out of the kitchen holding a machete in one hand and a green coconut in the other and asked if we wanted something to drink. So we asked for two coco waters and for whatever smelled so good on the stove. Our first meal in Thailand was a gourmet tam yam soup made with chunks of fish and crabs flavored with hot chilies and redolent of lemongrass, served up right there on the beach. We shared a huge bowl of the soup that was so beautiful to look at that it was almost a shame to eat. The people in Thailand were very conscious of beauty and design. Once again *Sara* had ended up in one of those special scenes that fit me like a glove, just what we needed.

After lunch we caught a tuk-tuk (a motor scooter taxi that has two back seats with a little roof over them) to town, where we officially entered Thailand. As we were told, the clerk never asked a question. We asked for a visa and he gave us a stamp with a six month visa. Actually, I'm sure he didn't speak or read English. Phuket wasn't an official port of entry so that office probably saw few foreigners.

I was looking around and blinking in the bright sunlight after filling out forms in the dark government building. "We need local currency. Where was that market we passed on the way here?"

Arianna pointed, "Down that street. We need fresh food as well. Let's get some fruit and veg for salad as well. I wonder if they sell bahngi in the market here? It could be legal here."

"That would make it easy," I laughed.

We soon found the market housed in a big open building with spotless concrete floors and bright white pillars. Honestly, it was so clean you could eat off the floor. The experience was a riot of scents and color. I don't know that I have ever seen such an impressive array of food as was displayed in that building. There was an amazing amount of different types of fruit, a hundred types of bananas alone. Okay we had been at sea for a while, but still it was impressive. Then there was the endless display of perfect vegetables. I'm sure that you wouldn't find a more complete selection of fresh fish outside of Japan. It was all there and all of the food was appetizingly presented, even the giant cockroaches! Well maybe not the cockroaches. I never saw anyone eating those insects but maybe they were reserved for sneaking into rude tourist's meals. It turned out that weed was not sold in the market because it was illegal in Thailand. However we did find a place to change dollars for bhat.

After changing money with a street vendor at the market and picking up some fresh fruit to go with our breakfast cereal, we caught a bus back to Ao Chalong.

It was late afternoon, and the tables at Pan's were full. There were three other *falong* (foreign) couples and six or so guys, all from the anchorage. One couple made room for us at their table and introduced themselves as Muriel and Terry from the catamaran. Pan's was kind of a semi-private beach club for expat sailors.

I was glad we made the effort to "make an entrance" because they had all seen and appreciated us anchoring under sail. Real sailors love *Sara* not just because of her clean no-nonsense lines but because she was such an obviously seaworthy sailing vessel. We spent some time answering questions about how she sailed. Then the conversation flowed on about boats and sailing.

All of these people were long-time, full-time, live-aboard sailors, and were obviously members of that small worldwide community of what my friend Hugo used to call "Kung Fu Yachtsmen." During the evening some non-sailor expats stopped in for beer and food. I'm pretty sure that years ago one of them, an American, many years before, had walked away from the Viet Nam war into Thailand. He was a full-time resident, married to a Thai woman. I got the feeling that some of Pan's patrons were on the run, from the law or worse. There were also a group of wealthy treasure hunters living here, who had found, and got away with loot from two major shipwrecks. All in all, it was a fascinating mixed bag of real adventurers. For a change we were not even in the running for the most interesting boat and crew in the anchorage, which was a good thing!

We spent a pleasant evening drinking beer, smoking weed, and talking about sailing and life, without having to be too careful about everything we said. No one asked any of the normal impolite questions that "straight" cruising sailors ask, like: How can you afford that nice boat? Or what do you do for money? Or how come you never go home? It was always a relief not to need an *LPL*.

We slid right into anchorage life here. We became quite close with Muriel and Terry. One day I said in Swahili to Arianna." I think Muriel is the heavy in this couple." Terry said in perfectly accented Swahili, "*Indio Bwana.*" It turned out that his father was Idi Amin's personal pilot until his death. So Terry must have lived in East Africa at some point in his life. He was a thin, very fair complected, very laid back Australian who hadn't grown up in Australia. He spoke English with a mixed accent I couldn't place. Come to think of it I'm not even sure what kind of passport he had. Once again, wouldn't ask, and never did.

Muriel was a powerful, smart, very fair, beautiful lanky Australian woman in her twenties. She sported a look that was total disarray with flyaway curly blonde hair. Like a lot of Aussie women she was a hard, no-nonsense woman with a thick Aussie accent.

CHAPTER 16

Touristic Reconnaissance

WE JUST FELL into the expat lifestyle. Ao Chalong was not a tourist town. The hotels and tourist spots were on the other side of the island. The sailors in the anchorage were the only *falongs*, but we had our own bar and restaurant and there was great bus service to the markets and communication points in Phuket town, for making phone calls, sending telexes or receiving mail. Cell phones were in their infancy in the eighties and didn't exist there yet, and email and internet were still a rumor.

I for one was quite okay with being out of contact. Out of sight, out of mind was a good thing in our world and Ao Chalong was definitely out of sight to Western law enforcement. An informer wouldn't last long in Ao Chalong, these folks were way too street wise. Although the possibility of people watching always exists, it just seemed a remote chance that any government would spend money to put someone here. Bangkok for sure, but Phuket was just too far from the action.

At this point Arianna and I had become more than lovers. We were partners having shared adventures, and more importantly our relationship existed on all kinds of levels. Our conversations were in English with a lot of Swahili thrown in and sometimes I would realize that a whole lot of a conversation was only half spoken. We just knew what each other were thinking and we never got it wrong. It makes sense when you consider that not only were we lovers, but we had been living within a meter of each other for a couple of years.

Life was easy in Phuket and we spent our time hanging out with the expats, as well as sailing and exploring the west coast of Thailand and Malaysia. The mix of Muslim and Buddhist culture with British Colonial and Chinese influence thrown in, made for some fascinating travel in this part of the world. On one of our little cruises we stopped at a tiny island, just a big rock really, that had a shrine to phalluses. The local Buddhist fishermen would come and leave offerings and penises, some of which were ornate carvings and others were just driftwood that were naturally occurring penises. Arianna insisted that I leave an improved driftwood penis. Sailors are a superstitious lot!

We sailed to Langkowie, an island resort in Malaysia. We left *Sara* on a good mooring there and took a really modern catamaran ferry for a weekend in Penang. Penang, Malaysia was one of the most important cities in the Eastern British Empire until WWII brought an end to the rubber industry.

We stayed in the historical, if somewhat frayed, Eastern and Oriental Hotel. We imagined ourselves on our "grand honeymoon world tour" in 1890, while having an English Sunday curry with a gin and bitters. We wandered through this dilapidated British colonial town, which was now an unimportant city in the Muslim nation of Malaysia. The food however, was a vacation of its own. Malaysian soups or *laskas* are an adventure in exotic flavors. I can still remember a tamarind flavored *laska* with fish and noodles. The British rubber plantations brought Indians here, and with them came Indian food which seemed to be everywhere in the streets. We were only there for a two-day food safari because we didn't feel comfortable leaving the boat unattended any longer than that. Too bad really, but then we were headed back to Thailand whose cuisine is world famous and where smoking weed is not a crime punishable by death.

When we arrived back to Phuket there was a message waiting at the Pearl Hotel where we received our messages. The woman at the desk handed me a copy of a telex (faxes didn't exist yet) and I turned to Arianna, "My friend Fiona from the Portobello Hotel is coming with her boyfriend David next week. This is amazing. I never expected them to get this far from London. Showing these two around is gonna be a lot of fun."

We met them at the Phuket airport and loaded them into a tuk-tuk. The look on David's face was too funny. This was going to be great for a lot of reasons but one was that neither of them had ever visited an Asian culture before. We had a meal at Pan's before going out to the boat. They had been in London eight or so hours before and now they were sipping coconut water from a straw in a green coconut while Champi, Pan's gibbon looked on. Lunch at Pan's was a perfect opener for David and Fiona's two-week vacation, the first in years for both of them. Muriel and Terry and one of the treasure hunters were there at the beach bar. And of course sailors were coming and going, since this was the dinghy beach. No time for culture shock, Fiona and David were immediately members of our little community of pirates. Pan had a big kettle of his fabulous tam yam soup going. The whole thing must have been overwhelming and I'm sure wherever they are now, they still have a clear memory of that first day. I'm surprised they made it through the soup before heading out to the boat.

Close to noon the next day, Fiona pulled aside the canvas and peeked out from their cabin, blinking in the bright sunlight. She managed to get her wide shoulders and long legs through that little hatch and down the main companionway ladder to the galley where I was making a pot of tea. I passed her a cup, "Arianna's putting up sails and getting the anchor up. We'll be well on our way to some outlying island or empty anchorage by the time David wakes up."

David wanted to go scuba diving. Unfortunately in those days I didn't have any scuba onboard, but I did have lots of masks, fins, and snorkels. So, we headed to a pristine reef anchorage at Pi Pi Island where he could snorkel over untouched coral in four meters of clear water. We dropped the hook in five meters of water over a white sandy bottom. I threw a mask, snorkel and fins to David and asked him to go down and make sure the anchor was buried deep in the sand. Once David got a look at that reef, he wasn't going to be back anytime soon. So I got out more gear and gave Fiona a quick review of safe diving tips and over we went. I had my spear with me and managed to kill a few lobsters and a snapper for dinner that night.

We spent days anchored off PiPi Island, diving and beachcombing for seashells. Fiona actually found a chambered nautilus. This was 1987 and there were no hotels on PiPi Dom. Some fishermen had built a restaurant on the edge of the bay, mostly of bamboo with a palm roof. Sometimes we had lunch at the little restaurant.

Both Fiona and David were tense and pretty stressed when they arrived. She was the manager of a trendy London hotel, on the best hotels in the world list. He was a manager at a well known London restaurant, Julie's, in Holland Park. Both the hotel and restaurant were frequented by the rich and famous and had clients who expected a lot. They were both tired and rundown. Fiona had Psoriasis, which covered a lot of her legs and arms at the time. Originally, they were going to stay for a week. I had told them that they were going to stay for at least two weeks and made them change the reservation right at the airport. "Listen, you may think that you cannot afford to stay longer. However, looking at you two right now I can tell you with complete confidence that you are not going to even relax until next week. Then you're not going to be able to make yourselves leave for another week after that. This holiday isn't going to cost you anything except air fare and if you change now they won't charge you extra. They always have empty seats on these charter flights. Give it up! You guys are going to return home feeling completely renewed."

We stayed anchored around Pi Pi for four days. By then Fiona's Psoriasis had nearly disappeared. The cure for Psoriasis is obviously sunshine, seawater, and no stress. David had lost his pallor and his ironic sense of humor was in full bloom. We were having lunch at the little beach restaurant one day when eight young German tourists showed up on a local boat from Phuket. They sauntered up dressed in very brief swimsuits and even smaller bikinis, basically naked. The place was run by Thai fisherman, who are all Muslim and were all dressed. David just said to the Germans as we walked out, "I hope you don't mind if they spit in your food." One of the German woman's face turned really nasty and said "You English are so restricted and uptight. You think you can control everything." They had no thought to how offended the local Muslims were about their nudity. I'm sure they had no idea that there were even Muslims in Thailand. The women cooking weren't wearing traditional Muslim clothing, but their shoulders and legs were covered. The Germans were the new ugly Americans.

We sailed back to Phuket for a couple of days to visit the market, look around the island, and hang out with Champi at Pan's "beach resort." The whole pirate scene fascinated both David and Fiona. Everybody liked David's dry sense of humor and Fiona's tales of rock stars misbehaving. In the end, good manners in the world of the rich and famous were very close to good manners in a nest of pirates.

My plan was to make sure they left Thailand relaxed, body and mind, so we left again to explore the myriad of islands along the coast. David loved the island with the shrine devoted to penises and the next week passed too quickly. A clear skin, suntanned and fit Fiona laughing with her buff, suntanned David disappeared through the gate on their way to another world.

It was during this period that Muriel and Terry asked us to help with a charter that they had lined up. Terry had a Dutch friend who owned a bar and "coffee shop" in the Netherlands. This guy's business must have been pretty successful because he spent his winters in Phuket. I knew from my many trips to Europe that a "coffee shop" is the name the Dutch give to establishments that sell and serve hashish and marijuana as well as drinks. Every year Terry's friend Jack took a group of good customers and employees with their girlfriends and wives to Thailand. Obviously Jack was a dealer with plenty of cash to spend.

Jack wanted Terry to take his friends for three days and three nights on a cruise around the adjacent islands. However, the group was too big for their 40 foot catamaran to handle. Plenty of room for sleeping with some people crashing on deck, but not a big enough galley to support the food for this crowd. Our plan was to sail to day anchor-ages and raft the boats together in the evening, giving a lot more party space both above and below deck. By then we were pretty close friends with Muriel and Terry. The money was good and it sounded like fun. I also had an idea in the back of my mind that it might be a good idea to find a marketing contact in the Netherlands, where weed was legal.

We all decided to do the cooking on *Sara*, which had a bigger galley. Terry's catamaran had lots of deck space and two cabins, so most of the partying would be happening on the cat. *Sara's* head was crammed with cases of beer and ice-filled coolers. We bought chick-ens and vegetables for stir fry and salads. There were dozens of eggs and loaves of bread for breakfasts. This was going to be a floating party for a group of beer drinking, weed smoking Dutch guys.

It was a pretty rowdy bunch, six single guys and a couple. This gang was definitely *not* into deep intellectual conversations about Russian literature. Both boats stank of cigarettes and alcohol flavored sweat within hours of these Dutchmen coming onboard.

Jack's bar was in a small town near a big chemical factory, where I'm pretty sure these guys worked. The couple was Jack's bar man-ager and his wife, here for a week on a holiday, paid for by the boss. Aloysius was a quiet kind of Walter Mitty. His wife was a mousey, scrawny woman with teased up hair who saw herself as glamorous in leopard skin patterned tights and spike heels. She fit right in with the rest of that crew.

The second evening of the party/charter we were anchored off Pi Pi Dom. Most of our guests went for dinner at the little beach restau-rant. Jack, the bar owner, was sitting in *Sara's* cockpit drinking a beer and smoking a joint. He was a tall, well built kind of rough looking guy who was both smart and manipulative. He was paying us for this party and without being rude, always behaved as the boss. I have to say that he was respectful of my experience and intelligence, never conde-scending toward me in any way. However, he *was* condescending to

Terry, Muriel and Arianna in varying degrees. He was a good example of something I have always believed, that it takes some kind of intelligence to become rich. Stupid people do become wealthy but they can't hold onto it. Jack didn't come from money. Raised by a single mother, who worked in the local chemical factory, Jack was under educated and underneath a good guy mask, somewhat ruthless. However, he was intelligent and had developed street smarts. My thought was that since he was sharp enough to start and maintain a very successful business from scratch, he was good enough to feel out for a plan I had in mind.

I told him that I was thinking of sailing to Holland with some weed and asked if he was interested in selling it. I also said that I was thinking that he might want to go up north to Laos to pick out what he wanted to sell. I would pay for the cargo; I always liked to own my cargoes. He was more than interested; Jack was keen to do this. All dealers want to be smugglers. This would be something he could brag about in Holland.

Honestly, I wanted someone else to do some of the organizing. I made this decision even though I didn't really like this guy. I didn't exactly have a bad feeling about him, but heavy drinking bar people weren't my preferred colleagues, and Jack had more than a bit of a biker mentality. I suppose I was rationalizing being lazy by telling myself that I was cutting down the risk by not personally showing my face in the Golden Triangle, as well as having a dealer that actually had a stake in the game. In the end it turned out to be a mistake.

Time passed and the SW monsoon started to blow hard right into Ao Chalong. So all the yachts moved out of the wind to an anchorage off Nai Harn Beach on the opposite side of Phuket Island. Nai Harn had a beautiful, somewhat sloping, white sandy beach. Unlike Ao Chalong, Nai Harn Bay was very touristy with big hotels and none of the local flavor of Ao Chalong. On the other hand it was exciting. Just going ashore could be an adventure. Sometimes the waves wrapping around the headland created six-foot breakers that we had to surf to the beach in our orange speedboat. Getting back to the boat without flipping the dinghy in the surf was even more tricky. We had to get the boat out in the water inside the surf line, pointed out, with the motor running. Then at the exact right time just after the last wave broke, but before the next, we had to jump in the boat and gun it to climb up and over the wave just before it broke. It turned out that we were practicing, because months later we would be making those same moves on a much larger scale with *Sara* out in the Indian Ocean off the Horn of Africa.

The bars and restaurants in Nai Harn were filled with tourists from all over the world. There were coffee bars serving espresso, rock bars blaring, lots of restaurants open to the street and some large, stylish western hotels. We stole our Christmas tree from the Club Med garden, which had the only evergreen trees in Phuket.

We met Steve Hatchee in Nai Harn. Steve was an artist who had a tee-shirt business. I gave him my crude drawing of a biker-shirt revision. "Smoke Em Till the Keels Fall Off," a "Harley Davidson Marine" concept. A sailing boat with a wake of skulls, and a man in the clouds giving the finger. He took the idea and created a front and a back design on acetate that I could get printed at some point.

It's a damn good thing I commissioned Steve for that artwork. I would need his bold, striking design later in this story. I had learned the hard way, sometimes things don't go as planned, and if I ever get stuck needing to sell my own cargo, it's important to have marketing ready to print. Fortunately, people who smoke tons of weed together love wild, off-the-wall images, and Steve made it so badass, people *still* ask me about the tee-shirt when I wear it today, some thirty years later. It's a conversation starter.

At Nai Harn I got sick of getting my pants wet wading out to the dinghy, and came up with a design for some three quarter length sailor pants. I made some sketches of what I wanted, and found a tailor in Phuket who would produce them in high quality for an amazing price in quantity. He made me a prototype. They were in heavyweight cotton with tabs to adjust the waist, reinforced patches across the butt and at the knees for sitting and kneeling on rough decks, a webbing loop across the back pocket, and tabs and rings to shorten the legs for wading. I ordered forty pairs in navy blue with red stitching, and another forty in white with navy blue stitching. They were beautiful, and wonderfully practical.

CHAPTER 17

Getting It Together

ONCE AGAIN THERE were many things to organize beyond a cargo, which in itself looked like a long process. Terry and Jack took on the job of finding someone who could sell us 150 pounds of good weed. They had been buying their smoking stash from a local Chinese guy, so it seemed that we had to start with him. I left them to it, but closely followed their progress.

Meanwhile there were boat issues to deal with. It is the little subconscious things that the mind of a policeman sees, which ring his alarm bells. We were about to make a long voyage to Europe with a load of contraband and *Sara* needed to arrive in our first Mediterranean port looking as if she had arrived from a day trip, not like she had just blown in from a nonstop voyage from SE Asia. Saltwater is not just corrosive, but also abrasive. The last time I had painted the decks was in the States, so by the time we arrived in Europe, the paint would be looking shabby. Same with the interior varnish, especially the cabin floors, which would also take a beating.

Sara definitely needed to come out of the water to have the antifouling renewed, do the maintenance on the propeller and shaft seals, and replace a few through hull fittings. Phuket had a shipyard that mainly serviced fishing trawlers. This was a proper shipyard that had a marine railway with a limited number of tracks. We would need to work day and night to get our task list finished, because commercial vessels needed our spot. Oh, there was one other thing, no one in this shipyard spoke anything but Thai.

The day came to haul out. As we motored into the harbor, a big Thai fishing trawler was just coming down the ways festooned with garishly colorful garlands and strings of loud firecrackers. Arianna and I were blown away... a going back in the water celebration! Who does that? What a great concept. All that experience I had racked up in yards around the world wasn't going to have anything to do with this boatyard on Saturn.

A guy from the yard waved us in as soon as the trawler cleared the railway. We motored into the cradle the trawler had vacated. The same guy dove under the boat to adjust the cradle supports. *Sara* seemed secure so we jumped into the dinghy and tied up to the dock alongside the railway. There was a woman with three children, ages five through ten, who greeted us with a respectful *wai*, a slight bow with her palms pressed together in a prayer-like fashion. She was attractive, in her early thirties, with hair bobbed just below her ears but shorter in the back, dressed like all the workers, in a tee-shirt and classic baggy Thai fisherman pants with a huge waist tied in a knot to fit. I got it that she was somehow involved because she was gesturing to the guy in the water who was setting up the cradle.

As the boat rose out of the bay, the man and woman seemed to be giving orders to each other, the children, and including us with gestures. By the time the boat reached its final spot I realized that this family was going to be our crew for the refit! And then Grandma arrived with both long and short handled brushes and she and the kids got started scrubbing the bottom.

Grandma fed us a meal each day. The whole concept of a business relationship in Buddhist Asia is way different from the western one. Karma and face (as in saving face) are higher priorities than profit.

I am sure that we weren't this family's first foreign boat, because the mother, Dao, who seemed to be our liaison, was quite good at hand communication. From the very beginning she was constantly forcing us to learn to speak, or at least to communicate in Thai, because even

Dao didn't speak a word of English. Within an hour, Dao and I had composed by hand signs and pointing, a comprehensive list, in order by priority, of the tasks we wanted done during this haul out. She would point at something and slowly say the word, repeat it then make me say it three times. Dao was the boss, the organizer, and the parts purchaser.

Dao's husband, Kiet, did the heavy work and the mechanical jobs. Like many of the Thais we came to know, Kiet was a gifted mechanic. We needed a non-metric propeller shaft. Kiet found a non-magnetic metric shaft that he had machined to fit our very expensive variable pitch Max Prop. He also machined and installed a hardwood cutlass bearing to replace the expensive Duramax bronze and rubber one that was worn out. I even understood Kiet's explanation, in Thai, of why the wooden replacement would outlast the old one and that the shaft would last longer with the low tech bearing.

While Dad was replacing bearings and through hull fittings and their valves, Grandma and the kids were painting the antifouling below the waterline, waxing the white hull, tuning up the varnish, and sanding and oiling the cockpit teak. Dao kept the paint, brushes, sandpaper, mechanical parts, spares, and the language classes flowing.

Sara wasn't the only sailboat in the yard. There was a wild Aussie, a reckless adrenalin junkie who had a nice sailing boat out of the water. I think Muriel came to Phuket on his boat. Lance was a thin, natural athlete and a super strong windsurfer, who had a hang glider that he used to fly over the anchorage. He was one of those long haired blonde surfer types who are always sporting awful herpes lip sores triggered by sunburned lips. Lance didn't bother to protect himself from the brutal tropical sun, no hat, no shirt, no sunscreen.

When we got to the boatyard, I noticed he was repairing a hole in the keel of his boat. I tried not to look but I couldn't help commenting to Arianna, "Lance is glassing in some kind of secret compartment in his keel. It's small, must be opium or heroin. Jesus! I hope I'm the only one who notices."

A few months later, I heard that he was shot and killed during his arrest in Malaysia. The story I heard, was when they tried to take him he dove into the water and they shot him. They say he was killed but his body was never found. Lance was an expert free diver, and I like to think he got away. I don't think anyone in the boatyard said anything and the local police seemed completely uninterested in what foreigners might be up to. It is more likely that he drew the heat when he bought the drugs, but as I said, Lance was reckless. We all knew that we were players in a small, very connected league where the penalty for losing could be prison, torture, or even death. For a lot of reasons I felt that I was one who would always win. I was careful, never did the same trip twice, judiciously maintained a believable profile, and I always could always smell danger. Maybe the ability to sense danger was an inherited genetic trait passed down from my Jewish ancestors who escaped the genocides throughout history.

The day came to go back into the water. At first light we jumped on the motorcycle we'd rented for the haul out, and stopped at a roadside stand for an early sticky rice and tea breakfast. No eggs for breakfast on this coast because they taste like the fish parts they feed the chickens. When we arrived back at the yard, *Sara* was gleaming. Every piece of chrome and stainless was polished and the entire boat was hung with colorful crepe paper, Thai Buddhist decorations, and strings of firecrackers to frighten off the evil spirits. Everyone in the boatyard was there to watch *Sara* slide down the ways to the water. Grandma lit the fuse, and the fireworks were deafening. I was watching Dao who was wearing a wistful smile. I saw her lips whisper *soay*, beautiful. In twenty-eight years of boatyard experiences, the Phuket haul out was one of the best.

Meanwhile Jack, Terry, and Muriel had gone up to Laos with their Chinese Thai contact. It seemed that what we all called "Thai Sticks" was weed grown in Laos or somewhere in the "Golden Triangle." The expat legend has it that Thai Sticks was a marketing project created by a frustrated Peace Corps worker to generate a real cash crop for a village somewhere in the Golden Triangle, during the Vietnam War. He was obviously successful, although I am sure he got the boot from the Peace Corps. I hope he made a fortune on it, and is an old man living happily somewhere, like Bali.

Jack had seen and picked out some excellent weed, and committed to paying for seventy kilos delivered in Phuket. Unfortunately, the growers packaged the weed in paper bags, which was good to somewhat cure it during the weeks it took to get it to the coast, but not good enough to survive a long ocean voyage. Packaging is pretty damn important. After all, marijuana is a vegetable that can get moldy. Years before, I did a run from Columbia, and after two months at sea, and another month buried in a sand dune, I opened up a bale to find that I had a ton of moldy weed to sell. So yeah, packaging is important. I couldn't think of a solution to this major obstacle. Terry came up with a brilliant solution, beeswax. We decided that if the weed arrived sufficiently dry, that we would wrap it in Thai newspaper, then dip the packages in melted beeswax.

Now we had to wait... major problem that I had not seen coming. Summer was almost here and with it the southwest monsoon. Everyone in Asia understands what the southwest monsoon means. Bad weather! If we could leave before the southwest monsoon hit, we would have gentle winds in our favor. If we left after, we would be fighting to sail against strong winds and potentially deadly waves off the Horn of Africa. The Chinese Thai guy who we were buying the weed from knew that we needed to leave before the southwest monsoon, but kept putting us off. Ling was a clever guy and had to know that if this trip went well, it could be done once a year with larger quantities. He knew we were committed, that this product wouldn't keep, and that we had to leave once we had it loaded.

So now I was getting a lesson on doing business in a culture I didn't really understand. I had read the James Clavell's Asian saga, which is all about Asian business mentality, and here I was experiencing that very phenomenon. In Asian business deals, profit motive is not necessarily at the top of the agenda. I am sure that Ling was gaining face by making the deal happen on his terms. He was gaining face by putting us off until the bad monsoon came, and showing us we couldn't dictate the terms, even if it meant that there would be no repeat business. I was imagining Ling, who I had never met, laughing in a tea shop with his friends as he told them how some stupid American was paying him while getting screwed. I hadn't been clever enough to make the timetable an actual part of the deal.

For me this whole deal was kind of a proof of concept thing. However, putting us off until the wind changed wasn't worrying me as much as it should have. I was so fucking arrogant that I was actually looking forward to beating into the southwest monsoon, just to see if I could!

It was April when Arianna, Murial, and I caught a tuk-tuk from Pan's to Wat Chalong, the fabulous Buddhist temple in Phuket, to try to buy beeswax for our packaging. We arrived at the perfectly maintained two hundred year old multi-tiered multi-colored building, and managed to corner a yellow-robed monk to ask about buying candle wax. I had done my homework and learned quite a few words from Pan that I thought would be helpful. I'm not sure that it didn't make things more difficult, but somehow we got the general idea across. He led us around the temple to one of the smaller buildings. We took off our shoes and walked into a little shop, infused with the smell of honey, where the monks made candles for the temple. For twenty dollars in bhat we bought seven kilos of yellow beeswax blocks, all they had at the time. The blocks were flat chunks obviously taken right from their hives, complete with the odd embedded dead bee.

I went out and bought a small gas cooker and a large kettle to melt the wax. I also found some large baking pans to cool the packages on. All the provisions for the voyage were listed and stowed onboard except for the final fresh food: dozens of eggs (not from fish fed chickens) packed in straw filled baskets, cabbages, citrus, garlic, onions, green mangoes, and lots more. We arranged for Pan to pick everything up for us just before it was time to pull the trigger on this voyage. All that was left was to nervously endure the days of good winds blowing away as we waited for our cargo.

I never did meet Ling. Didn't want to. I figured the less he knew, the less he could tell...if it came to that. Terry was our go-between and one morning he came by the boat in his dinghy to say that it was on for that night. Pan brought a boat load of fresh food in the early afternoon, while I was stowing and lashing down everything for a long hard voyage.

Terry and Muriel were anchored not far from Ao Chalong near a tiny beach in the middle of some mangroves. The beach was hidden from a little-used dirt road. Terry had set up the meeting for one o'clock the next morning. After dark, we pulled up *Sara's* anchor, motored out of the harbor and an hour later tied up alongside their catamaran. Around midnight we got our little packing plant set up on Terry's boat, and I got ready to go ashore to pay for, and pick up the weed. We were all on *Sara's* deck as we changed clothes to go ashore. Arianna and I were wearing our dark blue sailor pants, black shirts, and All Star sneakers.

Terry was visibly nervous and Muriel finally snapped, "God Terry! Fucking cool it mate."

When I checked that my little .38 cal revolver was loaded, Terry started to come unglued. "I, I don't like you carrying that gun, man. NO. No guns, we don't need guns."

"No is right. No way I'm going to meet a total stranger on a hidden beach in the middle of the night, with a lot of cash... without a gun. Listen Terry, this is a Smith and Wesson Airweight. It has no hammer and only carries five bullets so it can be completely hidden, which means that no one will know I have this, unless I need to use it. Calm down. You don't have to come with me, I'll take Muriel."

It was time to go. I always made sure I arrive well before the appointed meeting time. I didn't have a reason or even a feeling there would be trouble, but why not be in control of the environment? Our

Dinghy was packed up and lashed on deck and the outboard was stowed securely below under the forward bunk. We had got our fresh food earlier in the day, and we were ready to leave for a long, long voyage. Muriel and I jumped into Terry's dinghy and quietly motored to the beach. I just pulled the boat up on the sand, without an anchor or tying to a tree, so we could leave quickly. We walked around to check things out then sat on the dinghy to wait. After forty minutes a car arrived. Two middle aged Chinese Thai guys got out. I walked over as they opened the trunk. I looked in to see the compartment stuffed with burlap sacks full of prime buds. I started counting money into one of the guy's hands. Muriel and the other man were putting the bags into the dinghy. Less than five minutes later we pushed the boat into the water and quietly motored back to the boats.

Arianna grabbed the dinghy line and pulled us along side. Muriel and I handed up the sacks to Arianna and Terry. Terry was so nervous he tripped and almost dropped one of the sacks overboard. Muriel snapped at him, "Why don't you go below to get things ready. We'll take care of this."

The three of us set up a chain and quickly got the big sacks below decks into the galley. Terry had the cooker going and the wax was starting to melt in the big kettle. The weed was in one-kilo paper sacks in the burlap bags, and Arianna and Muriel began to carefully empty each paper sack. I had the English Thai newspaper laid out on the baking pans. The girls laid the weed onto the paper and I gently wrapped each bundle in the newspaper, and put a large rubber band at each end. Terry and Arianna each took a package and started dipping them into the melted wax. It looked like we were going to be dipping for most of the night. There were sixty packages and each had to be dipped repeatedly because we were going to have to make the coating pretty thick, and you could only coat half a package at a time.

It was hot down there where the wax was melting, but Terry was really sweating. He kept getting up to look around outside, then he would come down below to tell us to hurry. Muriel was getting more and more annoyed by his chickenshit behavior. Arianna and I just continued to dip the packages. Finally Muriel told Terry to go on deck and keep watch so we could work. As dangerous situations go this was as relaxed as it gets. I had never seen a police boat in Phuket, so the police wouldn't happen onto this. The only way we could get caught was if they knew, and if so they would have busted us hours before. Terry just wasn't strong enough for this business, but Muriel definitely was.

I have always held to one of the Ten Commandments of Smuggling that says "thou shalt finish all loading and unloading before dawn." And dawn came just as we finished putting the weed into *Sara's* very high tech, hidden cargo hold. The fragrance of honey blew into my face as I closed the hermetically sealed compartment behind the aft cabin bulkhead. I grabbed the main hatch and vaulted into the cockpit. Arianna already had the mainsail up and the engine started. We said our goodbyes as Arianna tossed Terry's lines back to the catamaran.

PART 5 – The Race West...
Against the Wind, 1988

CHAPTER 18

Kung Fu Yachting

THE MOMENT TONY caught the lines, our attention shifted. The catamaran was gone. The contraband cargo was stowed in the hidden compartment and might not have existed -- Arianna and I forgot it was there. Up at *Sara's* bow, I pulled heavy chain hand over hand until the anchor crashed into its slot and I bolted it solid. Arianna cranked up the mainsail, metal zinged. *Sara's* genoa went up, canvas snapping and Arianna sheeted it home. *Sara* gathered speed as I steered her into the Andaman Sea. Arianna adjusted the steering vane to keep the boat on a course just north of the entrance to the Sumatra Straits. I had been studying the route for weeks and had worked out the course and positions of waypoints days before.

The ocean beats out different rhythms. Running with the wind behind you, the water rolls the boat side to side in an undulating beat. Your hatches are open, the breeze is behind you, and your sailboat is swift. If the wind comes at you across the beam, you're reaching, and the boat rolls to a reggae beat. With the wind from the stern quarter, the boat is Bob Marley playing "Kinky Reggae". But the closer to the wind you point, the more insistent that beat becomes. A close reach is Jimi doing "Foxy Lady". The boat is no longer dancing to the Reggae beat but starting to hit the oncoming waves at a rock tempo, and the water is starting to come aboard by the bucketful.

But when you attempt to sail upwind into the teeth of the wind, you are beating. It's a brutal ride as you drive into the hard face of the waves every few minutes, always nailed to one side, slamming into water walls and the waves crashing the bow like a million decibels of

Rage Against the Machine. And you having to crank in the sails until they are as hard as sheet metal for that precious forty-degree angle that will curve the sail like an airplane wing, and make a vacuum so that you are pulled forward, though it feels like you are being pushed and you tack back and forth, fighting the wind that wants to blow you backwards from where you came.

For now, the wind was easterly and *Sara* flew south on her best and most comfortable point of sail, a beam reach. The wind across the starboard side blew the water away from the cockpit and gave the boat that steady Wailers beat as it passed the wave crests, but most importantly it allowed the hatch boards to be out and the breeze to blow through the boat.

Arianna sat at the top of the companionway stairs on her watch while I plotted a course through the Straits of Sumatra. I called her down to have a look. "Listen, This is a tricky bit, we don't want to get too close to the tip of Sumatra because it's a serious pirate lair. And there's a Russian submarine base somewhere on the Nicobar Islands. It's a secret base so I don't know where it is, but I'm thinking it's this first island. I know for a fact that people who have stopped there have left without their boat--I've seen them in Asia after their boat and all their possessions were impounded. They say people caught with contraband are never seen again."

"Sounds okay as long as we stay near the middle of the channel," Arianna said.

"The problem here is that as soon as we turn into the Straits, the wind is going to be right in our face. We're going to be beating against the wind and the pilot chart shows a serious current."

Arianna asked, "How strong is the current?"

"It shows one and a half knots. Let's try to keep the tacks short because the closer we get to land, the shorter our life expectancy," I replied. "Keep the boat moving well and we'll get the fuck out of here. Now try to get some sleep. It's my watch. I'll turn the boat into wind. Better rig the safety net on your bunk because I'm going to harden up the course."

Note written by Ranen on navigation worksheet: P.S. this is one of those places where when you see another vessel you turn out the nav lights and get out the shotguns

We sailed right up to Sumatra that night then tacked toward the dangerous Nicobars, when the watch changed an hour before dawn. *Sara,* true to her racing yacht heritage, was sailing fast, and charging through every wave ahead of her. The motion below decks was violent, but it was still possible to cook or sleep, provided you were wedged in tight. If you weren't holding onto something, you'd be flung down. The boat rose and crashed over and over.

By the next morning with the wind still fighting us, the Nicobar chain could be seen as a series of black bumps to port. I was eating a fried spam, cheese, and onion sandwich under the spray dodger when I heard the mainsail rip. The sail spat a wad of thread right over my head as an entire seam let go with a sound like a cosmic zipper. It was the sound of a serious disaster in the making. "Fuck!" I shouted.

Arianna yelled from below. "What was that?" I shouted my reply, "That was the sound of us approaching a Soviet naval base with absolutely no navigational control. Hope your Russian is good." Up on deck, she needed no explanation. The top and bottom halves of the mainsail were flapping like bed sheets on a clothesline.

"We need to fix the mainsail and we need to do it fast! Without it we have no power to move past these islands. We have to pull it down and put up the storm main. The trysail won't do much good, but at least it will keep us steady until we get the main back up."

"How can we get that huge sail off in this wind?" Arianna asked. The mainsail was too big and heavy--fifty feet high and 120 pounds--for me to lift by myself, even if it was nicely folded on land, but flapping around in the twenty-five knot wind the heavy, stiff canvas could sweep us both off deck and into the sea.

"I don't know but we've got to. We can't repair the sail without taking it off the mast and boom. We have to get this thing laid out on deck." I said sliding the metal slugs out of the track that held the sail to the mast. As I released each slide from the track more canvas was blown out into the wind. Arianna had to throw herself on it just to hold it down. Both of our hands were bleeding from getting the big sail under control. "I just can't figure out how we can pull this off with this wind" I shouted. "We need to get the ripped seam laid flat on deck so we can use sticky backed tape to hold it together while we patch and sew it. It has to be perfectly flat with no puckers or the sail won't draw correctly."

I had always had a good working relationship with King Neptune. After all, *he is* my astrological patron saint. Must be, because out of nowhere the wind stopped blowing altogether. An hour later the boat was moving slowly upwind under the storm main, we were making a lot of leeway but at least the motion was steady. Three more hours we had that seam laid out, and put together with a continuous strip of six-inch wide six-ounce Dacron sticky-back cloth and ready to sew. We folded the sail with the seam on top and carefully stowed it in the cockpit. I immediately went below for food and the ditty bag. It was Arianna's watch and as she scanned the sea she noted that the Nicobars were no longer bumps on the horizon, but clearly distant land. She came below to update the log and take the first position since the sail had ripped. "Listen, "she said, 'We're thirty miles from the first island."

"Thirty miles from real trouble," I said quietly, passing her on my way up to the cockpit with the sewing bag, and a cold fish salad sandwich.

By the time Arianna got back to the cockpit I was already sewing. I was pushing the big triangular sail needle through the thick layers of hard sailcloth, using my roping palm. I had bought the hard leather palm from a retiring New England sailmaker, who had got it from his sail maker father. It fit my thumb and palm perfectly, and the built-in bronze thimble was in the exact spot to safely push the needle as hard as necessary. I looked up and tossed Arianna another palm with a needle stuck through it.

Just then the monsoon returned and it was blowing just as strong as before. We looked at each other in amazement. Both of us

immediately knocked on wood as a big wave dumped enough water over us to fill the cockpit. We were back in the real world of strong winds, violent motion and, life on a slant.

The seam had to be perfect. We slaved over the canvas until our knuckles bled, but we had to sew and sew fast. Without the power of the big mainsail, *Sara* couldn't overcome the drift toward the Nicobar Islands and a bad end to the voyage. Every hour took us half a mile closer, and the islands just got bigger.

Arianna and I sewed for sixty hours or so, both of us, unless one ran down to grab something to eat or drink, and run back up. Without much sleep or rest, nervous energy kept us going. Our backs ached and our hands cramped, but we had to keep working, heads down and focused, to avoid stabbing the big triangular needle through our hand. Still, we loved each other, and when one of us went below to make some food, we shared it in the cockpit over sewing and small talk. I loved and never tired of hearing tales of Arianna's childhood in Kenya.

CHAPTER 19

Across the Bay of Bengal

From the Ship's Log:

4/18/88   God damn this place, hard on people/equipment!!! 6 knots to the wind.

4/19/88   main sail up again, but blown out (worse for wear). Three reefs. Lots of squalls. Sailing like crazy but not able to move further east.

ARIANNA AND I did a perfect job. "Keep the stitches small mind you." Fifteen feet of seam with stitches no more than one-quarter inch apart. The seam was secured with three lines of stitches, 2160 stitches total. It was late afternoon some two plus days later that we manhandled the big high tech mainsail up, now even stronger than before but a little stretched. We could see people on the beach pointing at us as we cranked in the main sheet and blasted through the first waves coming out of the Bay of Bengal.

Our departure from those islands was small relief. As the boat picked up speed, the motion was more violent and life was no easier. My note in the ship's log: *"Guess this is what we'll have for the next month to the Gulf of Aden."*

Now, we could have turned the *Sara* around, and sailed back to a deserted island anchorage in Thailand to do the repair. But I knew damn well that the voyage we faced could not be completed without a certain mentality of sailing. The kind of sailing that Moitessier, Hayden and other sailors like Captain Joshua Slocum taught me, that you don't wait for anything. If you want to get anywhere, you have to go, just go and keep going. You don't break the voyage. We had thousands of miles to go and we couldn't get there by going backwards. Not many yachtsmen sail like I did. It was Kung Fu Yachting, martial arts sailing. Arianna and I were now mentally there. Our heads were right where they needed to be to make this voyage.

What we had to do now was maintain course through strong trade winds going against us. Elemental forces were relentlessly pushing us back to the South China Sea, but elemental forces or not, we were seven hundred miles as the crow flies from Sri Lanka, the next land mass we'd see, but we weren't crows, and we sure as hell weren't going in a straight line. The two of us fell into a constant rhythm of four hours on watch, four hours off. Cooking, sleeping and steering were what we did. We joked above the noise of the hull pounding into the waves and we were mostly busy hoisting smaller sails when the monsoon pushed harder or larger sails when the monsoon eased. When the force of the wind stayed constant, we got more rest.

Note by Arianna on Nav worksheet: Ouch! Ouch! Our feet are raw Painful to walk on deck

A half dozen times a day, the wind would strengthen or ease, and immediately we had to take reefs[7] or change genoas, moving as fast as possible, for every minute the sails were down *Sara* would drift sideways, and the wind would push her back from where we had just struggled to come. She would travel four to six knots to leeward, and an hour of progress could be lost in minutes of drift. The trick was to the make the sail change in the five minutes before the boat lost its forward motion. We grew skilled and swift at the maneuvers.

Life was reduced to four-hour periods. For four hours, one of us was responsible for keeping the boat moving in the right direction, and maintaining navigation. Whomever was on watch was Captain.

The task was simple; you concentrated on keeping the boat moving well on course, this was done by tweaking the self-steering vane

---

7 Reefing is the means of reducing the area of a sail, by folding one edge of the canvas in on itself. The converse operation, removing the reef, is called "shaking it out." Reefing improves the performance of sailing vessels in strong winds, and is the primary safety precaution in rough weather.

(the mechanical autopilot) to keep the boat hard on the wind, but not so close she stalled. Everything was about keeping the course.

Sailing against the wind is an art. The physics of sailing, dictate that when beating against the wind, the faster you go, the closer to the wind you can sail. Too close, the boat stalls and you lose time and ground getting back to the right speed and course. So we would stay hard on the wind even when reefing or changing sails, a tactic usually reserved for racing boats.

It was day and night, twenty-four hours a day. At night, charging into the darkness, you cannot see anything other than flicks of white wave tops speeding from the bow. You never allow your mind to start wondering what might be floating around out there. Giant hardwood logs, half sunken vessels, a lost barge, sailing boats have been known to sink in seconds after hitting some barely submerged flotsam.

And then there's navigation. Once an hour you had to figure out where you were and log the current conditions. At the end of every watch or every time you tack, you have to plot the position on the chart taped down on the nav desk. Keeping the navigation current was more than just not getting lost, it was a constant feedback about our upwind performance.

We had to eat and we had to cook and we had to bathe, no easy task on a pitching deck. I shaved every day. Personal hygiene is part of the essential discipline. Sleep helped.

But it was not all hell. When the sea was not too rough, I would sit at the top of the companionway stairs and read, mostly dry, behind the canvas spray dodger with plastic windows that kept the forward part of the cockpit shielded from the weather. Plunging into a novel was a good escape. Every ten minutes or so, I'd pop my head out for a look around for ships or problems. Sometimes on a sunny day the boat would break through a wave, and the spray at the bow would send a rainbow over *Sara's* deck.

On rough days the prime watch position and the driest spot on deck was safely wedged between two rigging wire stays on the aft deck. From there you could see the compass, the set of the sails, and could easily adjust the wind vane steering without moving from your perch. My perch was really good because the boat is always on an angle and being firmly wrapped in the mizzen mast rigging is a big plus. You cannot walk on the deck without holding onto something or at least ready to grab a hold, but in my perch, I could relax and pay attention to sailing without worrying about being thrown. Beating into the wind, the rail is in the water and a sudden lurch could send you into the sea... then, treading water, you would be watching the boat sail away, your shipmate sleeping below.

After passing the Sumatra Straits, the strain of it all kicked our asses. We were exhausted. Every activity was on a slanted, moving platform. We never got real rest, so we didn't wake each other up for help, unless it was necessary.

Those first few days of beating with a sea running were, as always, difficult, but then our bodies adjusted to the strict regimen of the watches, and our circadian rhythm changed. After that the discipline of keeping up with the constant physical demand, combined with the revitalizing effects of being immersed in the living, breathing seascape, bestowed upon us a Zen-like focus.

Our appetites got better and so did our cooking. I got more serious about fishing and fresh fish was on the menu again. Life was still difficult, but no longer miserable. How could I complain while eating fresh tuna salad on fresh baked bread?

CHAPTER 20

Around Dondura Head

From the Ship's Log:

    4/20/88   2308 hrs   110 up back in biz again

    4/24/88   motoring. can see the glow of Sri Lanka at 224°.

    4/25/88   try to go around the south end of Sri Lanka, around noon. come out from under the lee of the island and run into gale winds, wild seas and run for Sri Lanka. "Boat's been battered, our minds are shattered, ours plans scattered, the sails tattered." Ranen.

    4/26/88   Well, let's try again to run the dondra head gauntlet. heavy seas, winds now 30 to 35 knots. (like 45 mph) Monstrous steep seas.

THE SHIP'S CLOCK rang six bells and Arianna looked up from the galley as I slammed open the hatch and jumped below, gallons of sea water pouring off my red foul weather jacket and bib overalls. I reached up over my head with both hands and slammed the hatch. "It's fucking dark and wet out there. My feet look like prunes. Is it possible we're getting used to this miserable beating into the weather?" I asked.

The relatively shallow Bay of Bengal fostered short, steep seas. I had to back the course off the wind to gain any speed. The waves were just too close together. So we tacked and tacked, back and forth making poor progress east.

"What kind of course are we getting?" Arianna handed me a cup of strong black tea with lots of sugar.

"We're sailing hard and going nowhere. Can't get any speed up in this chop. The seas should be getting smaller as we come under the lee of Sri Lanka. Then we'll be able to make some real headway toward the Indian Ocean." I took a sip of the sweet tea and asked, "How come you're not sleeping? Not that I mind the company, we haven't seen much of each other since we got the main back up."

"I woke up when you put in the reef. It's too fucking hot and humid down here to sleep anyway. Did you get a log reading? Take a break, there's some pudding. I'll put in the position."

Arianna took down the log and sharpened the pencil held by Pencil Teddy, who was a small stuffed bear that was strapped into the bookshelf above the chart table. She entered our position in the log and added, *"4/20/88 1642 hrs. Another horrible night."*

The promise of the island of Sri Lanka lay ahead. We really looked forward to the comfort of sailing in the flat water under the lee of that huge island.

Two days later there we were, sailing on a comfortable beam reach down the coast of Sri Lanka a mile or so offshore. Dondra Head, the reef on the southern tip of the island, was in view a few miles ahead. Arianna and I were mentally preparing for another round of tough seas. We had already left a lot of rough weather in our wake. I confidently figured we could handle the rest of the trip against the monsoon. Arianna put in a second reef in the main in anticipation of coming out of the wind shadow of the land. The medium genoa was up and *Sara* was self-steering. Squinting in the harsh sun, I was naked except for a tee-shirt and my foul weather jacket. I stood with my feet on either side of the cockpit, and both hands on the dodger, watching the course as we arrived at Dondra Head. We knew the wind would come back. I just didn't know the wind would get any angrier. We rounded the head and returned to open water.

In a flash, *Sara* was out of control. The true force of the monsoon hit her like a battering ram.

"Get your harness on," I shouted, "Clip in and get another reef in that main!" I jumped to the steering wheel. Neptune had switched on a gale and it was blowing thirty-five knots. The waves were enormous; as steep as I had ever seen.

In the diamond bright light, the ultra white breakers and the royal blue sea were blinding. The full sunlight created color spectrums everywhere there was spray, and that was everywhere we looked. The roar of the waves was right in our ears as *Sara* surfed out of control. I steered away from the breakers over my shoulder.

It was a surfer's dream and a sailor's nightmare. In the maelstrom of plans and strategies flying through my consciousness, I realized I had become dangerously overconfident. We needed to get this boat under control and get back under the lee of Sri Lanka to regroup. My mouth went so dry my lip cracked. My feet were jammed into the corners of the cockpit seats. Both hands gripped the wheel at my waist. It took total concentration and all of my strength to turn the boat. An over correction would result in a broach. If she broached, *Sara* would turn, get caught by a breaker and be rolled over or worse the bow would go under and she would flip stern over bow. Even a kung-fu sailor had to surrender to the wind sometimes.

Solid green water was coming over the bow as *Sara* surfed in and out of the breaking waves. My concentration was over my shoulder where the waves were coming from, but I could also see that Arianna was about to get the mainsail down to put in the reef. I would gain a lot of control once the main was smaller. Another ten minutes of running this insane maze and she would have it done. In this world of adrenaline, noise, and speed, time was fluid. Arianna cranked in the outhaul as I ran right under a breaker. Then she was cranking the halyard winch with a demonic look on her face and the main was back up. Suddenly she was there in the cockpit.

Even next to each other, we had to shout to be heard, "We're still way over powered. We need to get that genoa down and the storm jib up to slow her down and get control. Then we're gonna duck back under the lee of Sri Lanka to get our shit together. I can't let go of this wheel even for a second until we get this boat under control. You have to do it."

"Okay," was all she said.

"Clip your harness on. Go up forward and get it all organized in your head first. Then get it all sorted on deck before you start. You're going to be floating up there when that bow goes under. Make sure you stay on deck. Don't let yourself float off the boat when the big ones sweep the foredeck. I've been able to avoid the really big ones, but we're still catching some of them."

I was plenty uncomfortable sending Arianna to change sails up at the bow in these conditions. This really was a captain's job, but steering this boat in these conditions was something she couldn't do. I knew Arianna was strong enough to change the sail, and I hadn't ever known anyone more determined. The very idea of giving up just didn't exist in her mind. I also hated it because I wouldn't be able to see her on the fore deck from where I was steering. I would have no way of seeing how she was doing.

"Do it now," I said.

Arianna clipped the ten-foot line from her harness to a cable that ran from the cockpit to the bow. On her way forward she stopped to un-lash the storm jib from the base of the mast. Dragging the small sail bag down the deck meant she only had one hand to hold onto the windward lifeline. She was thinking how she used to curse Ranen for using such rough sand when he painted the deck, and how it would tear pants and skin. Now that she was staring almost straight down the deck to the sea, she realized the only thing between her and a bad fall was her hand on the lifelines and her feet gripping that deck.

Alone in this wild and threatening environment, Arianna was reciting the litany of the sail change in her head to stay focused. *Get this bag secured and the sail hanked on, get the big sail bag unzipped and open, to get that big genoa in. I can do this. Those waves are only water and I'm tied in. Keep moving Arianna!*

She was clipping the working jib hanks on the stay when a big breaker hit her with a wall of solid water. She was jerked off the deck and only the fierce grip she had on the sail stopped her from being flung overboard. She was floating above the deck and for a moment wondered if, when the boat rose out of the wave, would she be hanging on the other side of the lifeline? *Sara* rose out of the wave, shedding water like a surfacing sea monster, and Arianna kept on hanking.

Now I know why Ranen loves this kind of sailing. It is fucking wild! She thought. *I've got the rhythm now. Work like a maniac until a big one hits, then hang on for your life!*

Arianna was totally focused and flying on adrenaline. Nothing existed but the task in front of her in this wild place. Time was elastic, in a moment of consciousness she realized she was already at the mast gripping a small diameter line between her teeth, getting ready to bring the big genoa down. Then back into the vortex as she let go the halyard that held the sail up. Using the cabin as a diving board, she dove onto the sail, clawing at the yards of sailcloth to wrestle the wind whipped demon to the deck. No rodeo cowboy ever tied up a bucking calf as fast as Arianna got the line around that out-of-control sail.

Now, back to real time, she surveyed the situation while she unclipped the triced up genoa. *I just need to get this bastard zipped into the bag and the bag lashed down good and tight.* With the big sail down the motion was a lot easier. The smaller storm jib was all ready to go up.

I had heard the ship's chronometer sound seven bells, three o'clock, when Arianna went forward to get the genoa down, and then the next set of big waves came up. Surfing in and out of the breakers was all that could occupy my mind. *That one was fucking close Ranen, get it turned before they hit, and stop oversteering or you're gonna knock Arianna overboard!* I must have heard but didn't register that the clock sounded one bell, 4:30. When the clock sounded two bells the thought that she had left the cockpit two hours ago broke my concentration. I stood up as high as I could, to try to see over the spray dodger, but couldn't see anything but waves and that the big genoa was still up.

My mind was racing. *Over two hours is a long time. Well, she's doing everything with one hand and holding on with the other. Still, two hours? It's got to be pandemonium at the bow, give her more time before you really start to worry. Jesus, why did I send her up there? What the hell were you thinking?*

Another big set came and I was back into surfing and time became fluid. Again the clock sounded. This time two bells, 5:00. At this point I began to feel sick with worry.

What if she's gone? What the hell am I going to tell her mother? How am I going to live with this? I was gripped by fear, frustration, and guilt. Tears were running down my face.

Knees bent and flexible, my grip on the wheel kept me in control of the boat, kept me from being flung overboard, and kept me from totally losing it. Three bells or was it four? The motion changed, and the genoa started slowly coming down. A huge rush of love swept through my body. *She fucking well did it!* I thought. *Supergirl.* The clock chimed another thirty minutes and the smaller jib started crawling up the stay. We were back in business.

Hours later, Arianna and I were in an entirely different reality. *Sara* barely moved at anchor under the lee of Sri Lanka. We were sharing endless deep kisses in the motionless double aft cabin bunk. My love for her had taken itself to a new level. I was swept away by the intensity of this new love. I made love to her face, to her legs, to every millimeter of her body. I just couldn't get close enough or deep enough.

At first I could feel that Arianna was shocked by my passion. Then her natural reserve, and all of her protective barriers dissolved and she opened like a spring flower in the morning sun. We seemed to melt into one being. Then, as if being picked up by a waterspout, we transported to a different world.

After sleeping like the dead for twelve hours, we awoke with a new sense of determination. I was in the galley making a high calorie one-pot meal. I fried chunks of canned meat, then poured in a can of baked beans with brown sugar and topped it off by poaching four eggs on top.

From the galley I could see Arianna on deck lashing equipment down and getting the light weather sails put away. God, she was beautiful, just looking at her made me a little dizzy.

Obviously, she felt more confident having survived the day before, and was determined not to get caught unprepared again. The smell of food was tweaking her appetite. She was starving, and anxious to eat and get moving again. Arianna was a great believer in getting right back on the horse.

CHAPTER 21

Across the Indian Ocean

THIS TIME WE were prepared. It was the same scenario but we had storm sails up, and we had a different game plan. I knew that the steep seas off the southern tip of Sri Lanka were caused by the big long monsoon swells piling up as they hit the shallow water. The plan was to head straight out to deep water, getting out of the steep seas as quickly as possible. Being mentally prepared definitely made it more doable, and having the storm sails already set certainly made it easier. But, as we headed again past the tip of Sri Lanka, *Sara* started taking solid green water over the bow and continued to do so for the next twelve hours as we fought our way through the walls of water and against the force seven winds trying to drive us onto the reefs of Dondra Head.

There was no point trying to stay below for anything except making tea or looking at the chart, just too wild down in the cabin. Arianna was at the wheel and I was at my favorite spot, wedged into the backstays on the aft deck. Out of nowhere a big fancy motor yacht, some 150 feet long, appeared from behind one of the huge waves. It was beating its way around Dondra Head, probably heading toward one of the ports on the other side of Sri Lanka. I felt much better about our situation as I watched that monster try to punch through those waves. It came out of a big one with the bow literally bent. The captain would have been better off doing what we were doing. These conditions were harder on his big motor yacht than ours. Most of his vessel was exposed to the elements, as most of *Sara* was below the water. *Sara* was built low and lean for just what we were doing. But we were on different courses, and soon they were gone, and we were alone on a wild empty sea, with thousands of miles and many more days of wild seas to go before the Suez Canal.

We were now in deep water, but the winds were still just as strong, and the waves were just as big but not as steep. These weather conditions, and worse, were what we could expect the whole way to the Red Sea, except when we were near the equator. The winds were pretty much westerly, and we were going northwest. My plan was to head for the southern Maldives, and do as much motoring west in the calmer conditions on the equator as possible, at least as much as we could afford with the fuel we had. The farther west we were, the better the point of sail toward the Horn of Africa, and the route to the Red Sea.

Years ago, when I first bought *Sara*, we thought we would just refit the old original Mercedes diesel engine. Hugo removed the injector pump to have it rebuilt, but the diesel shop wanted a thousand dollars to rebuild it. Hugo suspected the whole engine was worn, so he decided to pull it to work on it. We were all helping as he winched the engine out and swung it over toward the dock. Hugo stopped as it hung suspended over the water. "Listen you guys. When I finish rebuilding this, it will still be an old engine."

Rick said, "Let's float test it."

I nodded, and Hugo let it plunge into the canal, and dryly commented, "Doesn't float"

I answered, "Buy a new Perkins."

We bought a 4 cylinder Perkins diesel engine which was strong enough to motor *Sara* at four knots in moderate seas. It had plenty of power for maneuvering in port or as additional power while under sail. It was also good for charging batteries when there was no wind. In the light wind conditions near the equator, with the 100 gallons of fuel in the main tanks, and the additional 50 gallons in the collapsible fuel cells stored in the bilge, we could motor five hundred miles due west, and still have sufficient fuel for getting into the next harbor and emergencies like getting out of the way of a ship. *Sara* also had a very powerful wind generator fixed to the mizzenmast, so normally under sail there was no reason to waste fuel running the engine. Anyway, we hated running the engine because it was noisy and heated up the cabins.

From the Ship's Log:
   21/7/88   0133 hrs   crew z-zik Boat sails on by herself. (There is a little sketch of two stick heads with little bubbles all around and x's over the eyes. My head says, "No One Home." Arianna's says, "Out to Lunch.")
   21/7/88   0818 hrs   Crew takes over again.

Four days away from Sri Lanka I was trying to make sense of our position, because the log had no entries for a day and a half, or at least entries that made any sense. I knew that we both had been feeling ill the last night after eating tuna fish salad that I had made with some old mayonnaise. But was it last night? I called Arianna down from her watch to ask about it. She and I remembered having some very weird dreams, which probably were memories of us doing things while we were so ill they didn't seem real. I couldn't remember any of my watches. The satellite positions didn't make sense at all, but at this point the system was giving us a lot of bogus positions, sometime for a few continuous days. I was beginning to realize I didn't even know for sure what day it was, not good when you are in the middle of the ocean and you need to navigate. For at least four watches there were no log entries at all. I finally tuned in to the time signature on the HF radio and started taking some positions with the sextant. We never did figure out what happened to us. At least we were off the shipping lanes in one of the least visited places on the planet, while *Sara* sailed along on her own merry way for thirty-six hours.

We held the boat as close to the wind as we could without losing ground to the wind and the waves. We were pushing *Sara* hard and ourselves harder. Arianna and I were getting stronger every day from the strenuous, demanding work of keeping the boat at its best performance.

It was already well into July, and the monsoon was at its strongest in August and September. The pilot charts showed red concentric circles at the Horn of Africa during those months. Those red lines were yelling at me not to be there, not during that period. The red circles meant that the wave heights would average fifteen feet or higher, and that was just the average. There would be a strong possibility of waves over twice that, and even higher, as we turned the corner out of the Indian Ocean. July looked nearly as bad, and there was no way to avoid Ras Asir, the headland of the Horn of Africa at the tip of Somalia and the entrance to the Gulf of Aden.

The sooner we got past the Horn of Africa the safer we were going to be, and we were still 3000 miles away, but in reality we were much further away. Since sailing boats cannot sail directly into the wind, we were going to have to tack back and forth for an extra two thousand miles, until we could get far enough west to maintain a direct course a little more off the wind.

We knew when we left, that we were a month late, but my arrogance allowed me to rationalize that it was no big thing, and, oddly, it was going to be okay, because we were rising to the occasion. Our first long tacks to the southwest were something like 1000 miles to the One and Half Degree Channel through the Maldives.

Every day South gave us lighter winds. We arrived at the Kolhumadulu Atoll in the Maldives after seven days of sailing. This was the unpopulated part of the Maldives. We dropped the anchor in four meters of crystal clear water over white sand. *Sara* left Thailand, but *Saga* was going to Europe. I always kept the green paint and the stencils I used to paint the name on the transom of the boat. In twenty-five minutes US registered sailing auxiliary *Sara* became British registered sailing auxiliary *Saga*. The papers had been prepared months before. Arianna took down the American flag and raised the British ensign as I raised the anchor. It didn't even occur to us to take the night off. We were late for an appointment with the Horn of Africa and the worst was yet to come.

From the Ship's Log:
7/23/88   1°54'07 S. 77°49'76 E.   A Belle is awarded Best Tuna Salad gold medal at 1988 Galley Olympics. Pencil Teddy protests white African participation in Olympics. Medal is revoked. Tough luck A Belle.

We sailed away from the Maldives on a light breeze, and hooked a fifteen-pound tuna as soon as we hit deep water. Sashimi for hors d'oeuvres and tuna sautéed in lemon, ginger, and soy sauce was on the menu. We still had plenty of cabbage and tomatoes for a salad the next day. The rest of the fillets I soaked in soy sauce, and put in the oven at a low temperature for hours until it was jerky. Fish jerky is a great snack on a bad night watch.

For the next week we motored, sometimes when there was a light breeze we kept the sails up, keeping the boat from rolling. Even though there was little or no wind, big monsoon swells were rolling up from the southwest, which made life pretty miserable when there was no wind to steady the boat from rolling.

At the end of that week we were ready to head north. We were still punching into the ever increasing strong winds, but with a better course. However, we still couldn't sail directly to Somalia. Crashing into waves means that salt water is dousing anyone working on deck, and we were constantly on deck, changing sails and reefing or shaking out reefs in the mainsail, as the winds got stronger or lighter. Now it was even more important than ever to keep *Saga* moving, even when changing sails.

It was summer and it was hot, but we were living and sweating in our foul weather gear. The alternative was to be cooler in shorts and cut off shirts, but wet all the time and constantly covered in salt and saltwater sores. Being hit by wave after wave is not like swimming in the ocean. Each wave adds another layer of salt, without washing off the previous. Our Foul weather gear was stiff with the salt build-up. Arianna and I would put on our jackets even to go out to pee, because the chances were only fifty-fifty that you could make it to the aft deck without getting hit by a wave, it wasn't worth a saltwater drenching to take the chance. We had no shower, nor enough fresh water to rinse off the salt whenever we wanted.

We only had two forty-gallon water tanks and another twenty gallons in two plastic containers lashed to the aft deck. Water was important onboard always, but on a voyage this long, fresh water was an issue, a big issue. The galley had two water faucets, one freshwater and one saltwater, both operated with foot pumps.

We washed with salt water and rinsed with fresh water, same with bathing. We bathed on the aft deck by filling a bucket with salt water and using Prim, a very detergent shampoo that would lather in seawater. Hanging on with one hand, and using a washcloth with the other, we managed to scrub down, then re-fill the bucket and rinse off the soap. We had a safari canvas freshwater shower bag hanging from the mizzenmast, which we judiciously used to rinse.

In these conditions something as simple as a shower became another strenuous task that had to be accomplished one handed, while holding yourself in place with the other hand. We bathed every few days, and I shaved every time I bathed. Maintaining hygiene was part of the focus process. It is a high priority not to become lazy about maintaining an organized life when chaos is just outside the main hatch.

We wiped down with fresh water before getting into our bunk. We were hot bunking. In these seas the only bunk you could sleep in without being thrown out, when the boat slammed into a wave, was the lee (down side) bunk leaning against the hull. There was comfort in getting into a bunk still warm with the scent of the woman I loved.

Day after day we beat into the brutal southwest monsoon. When we left equatorial waters it seemed that we could sail toward our waypoint off Ras Asir. However, the Wind Gods had other ideas. We were still tacking and beating into at least force 6 winds of twenty-five knots, which at times would strengthen to force 7 winds of over thirty knots. Wave heights were never less than fifteen feet, and the waves heights were increasing the further north we got. As predicted, the wind became stronger with every passing week.

I had just finished changing from the small working jib to the staysail[8] and reset the self-steering. It was time for Arianna's watch. I quickly slid open the main hatch and jumped straight below, closing the hatch at the same time, trying not to drench Arianna, who was sitting at the nav station staring blankly at the water stained chart.

"Look at this crack on my finger. I think you can see the bone! Shit, is this the bone?"

She looked at it, shook her head, and handed me the jar of Vaseline. Arianna and I didn't talk about how hard this was, in fact, I don't remember even thinking about it. Sleep, eat, and steer. There wasn't time or energy for small talk and reminiscences. It's funny how everything is relative. We thought we were at our max performance crossing the Bay of Bengal; then we passed Dondra Head into the Indian Ocean and, except for the brief respite passing through the Maldives, things got wilder. Now after a week of this, we were getting used to the new level of the game. *Saga's* forward deck was awash with every wave, and our hands were so cracked and raw that we wore gloves packed with Vaseline and vitamin e oil when we slept. Pulling the sheets and halyards was painful, but still, day or night, when the wind changed, we changed sails or reefed, or shook out reefs in the main. The only way to end this was to keep the boat moving out of the Indian Ocean toward the Mediterranean summer.

Arianna was becoming noticeably stronger. Her shoulders, her arms, and her legs were more defined, and even her face was leaner. She seemed to thrive on the adversity. She rarely woke me to help on deck. Still, we both would wake when the motion of the boat changed, put on a jacket to go on deck to check on each other. We were really

---

8 **Staysail** a small headsail that is set behind the Jib or forward sail, normally used when it is too windy for the working jib.

connected body, mind, and boat. Sometimes on night watches we would leave each other notes in the logbook or on the plotting chart.

"I'm sick of straining to stay on this shelf holding these pencils. I want to go to New York to be a ballet dancer."

Pencil Teddy

However wild the sea became, we cooked hot meals and baked bread. Beans and rice cooked in the pressure cooker, and stir-fry cabbage, onions, and carrots with eggs stirred in were often on the menu. Hot cereal made with canned milk and lots of honey was our high calorie breakfast, at all hours. We always woke each other up with a large mug of hot tea and a kiss.

Like climbing partners on a wilderness ascent, the hardship drove us closer, and made us more appreciative of each other. I took time to think of ways to take some of the stress from Arianna's watches, changing sails or reefing just at the end of my watch, to help her conserve her strength. It was touching to catch her doing the same for me. Nevertheless, We kept to the watch schedule. However tempting, we learned early on, that taking the other's watch just didn't do anyone any favors. Arianna and I were running flat out, and desperately needed whatever sleep we could get. There were times when one of us would have to call the other on deck to help, but only when not to do so would be too dangerous or would make us lose ground, or both.

Notes on the navigation worksheet, 9/8/88, 6°N 63°E:

Yesterday Arianna saw a ship and called them on the radio. Blah blah blah, the officer wondered what we were doing in the middle of the Indian Ocean sailing against the height of the SW monsoon. Looking at this fucking chart tonight, I also beg the question. Five thousand miles upwind? I answer money, but I know that isn't the answer. This voyage is going to cost most if not all the profit. Adventure hah? Really, more like misery. Arianna, look at this chart. Is this madness or adventure?

Stupidity perhaps? But then you can't call yourself a sailor if you don't go sailing.

At least now we are getting a course somewhere in the right direction toward the Horn of Africa where we know the worst weather awaits.

A Bell to Captain R,

Tonight was pure fucking madness. If I had any boxing gloves I would have thrashed the sails for not cooperating. But what can you expect when for an hour there was a curtain of rain clouds across the horizon sucking up all the wind. Two knots is probably what we're getting which is amazing considering we have 2 reefs in the main and the working jib.

CHAPTER 22

Around the Horn of Africa

WE WERE NOW into the second week of August, and the Pilot Chart for the month was spot on about the wind strengths and wave heights. Winds were consistently near gale force, around thirty knots,[9] and gusting to forty knots[10]. The waves marching up from South Africa were enormous, never less than twenty feet, and gaining height every day.

The noise on deck filled the air, and we had to shout to be heard above the roar of waves rushing past us. The boat would sail up the steep front of each wave, then, at the top, she would dig in, crashing through the breaking white water. For a moment *Saga* would hang in the air, before she slammed on her side to sail down the back of the wave. At the top of these three story waves, all that could be seen in any direction, as far as the horizon, were line after line of these huge waves, and their white breaking tops against a blue sky. Immediately, we would plunge back into the next canyon, where all of our world became just the next big wave ahead to climb, and the roar of the sea.

On August 8 we finally eased off the wind for a direct course to Ras Asir, on the Horn of Africa. Now the wind was just forward our left shoulder, a broad reach. This was *Saga's* best, most manageable course, going with the wind and waves, no longer fighting through them. For days we made good speed with our small working jib, and three reefs in the mainsail. Now, with the new course, we were flying.

---

9 30 knots = 35 mph
10 40 knots = 46 mph

Although the odd breaking wave sometimes swept across the boat, life on deck was drier and safer.

However, we still had nine hundred miles to go before we could turn "the corner" away from these seas and the waves were getting bigger each day. One of those big ones broke over the deck one day, and slammed into a sail tied to the lifelines, which are plastic-covered steel cables that need to be strong enough to hold the weight of a big person. The impact broke off a stainless steel stanchion[11] like a toothpick, I was impressed, because I always went bigger and stronger on equipment for my boats. A broken stanchion is no big thing, we had more than we needed, but it gives an idea what kind of forces we were dealing with.

Another week would see us at Ras Asir, "the corner". Sixty-four days out of Thailand, and thousands of miles against the wind and now we were approaching the end of this leg, and the conditions were getting worse. What the fuck? Over.

I was quietly worried about what would happen when our course crossed the continental shelf off Ras Asir. How would these long huge rollers marching up from the south behave when the bottom went from four thousand meters or twelve thousand feet, to five hundred meters. They might start looking like Waimia on a big day. What the hell, at least we didn't have to worry about pirates! They were out of season. No way they were coming out to board vessels in these conditions.

From the Ship's Log:
13/8/88   1952 hrs   Last 24 hrs, gale force winds, no mainsail, rigged mizzen stays'l and stays'l

The wind vane self-steering was mostly working, but one of us had to be at the wheel to make sure we didn't broach. It was too scary to risk

---

11 **Stanchions** are the upright stainless steel posts that hold up the lifelines

having the main boom jibe over if a big wave pushed the stern over and the boat broached. All kinds of bad things could happen if the boat broached in those seas, including rolling the boat or breaking the mast and the coast of Somalia is not the place to be shipwrecked, even if we did both speak Swahili. That is why we rigged a sail between the mizzenmast and a spot just at the base of the mainmast. With that mizzen staysail up we were not likely to break the mast if we broached unless the boat rolled, in which case all bets were off on that score. Anyway, we were still hauling ass with those the two stays'ls up, and the boat was easier to control.

With someone at the wheel at all times, sleep was a luxury we grabbed when we could. Fried canned corned beef and baked beans, or spam and eggs, were on the menu, with lots of hot tea with canned milk. Not much energy for gourmet cooking, protein with lots of calories was what we craved.

At 0725 hrs UTC, on August 14, I put up the storm jib and the storm trysail, reefed. The storm trysail is a bulletproof, free-footed sail set in place of a reefed mainsail. The storm jib was also bulletproof, and really small and high off the deck, so as not to catch a wave, and cause us to broach. I would have put up Arianna's bikini instead of these sails, but it just was not strong enough to stand up to this gale.

I was a strong believer in Bernard Moitessier's theory of storm management: as we flew down the steep faces of those giant waves, the safest strategy was to keep as much sail up as you could, and still maintain control of the boat. It was vital to be able to maneuver on the faces of those waves, and if we lost our forward thrust we lost our ability to steer. Although we were moving crazy-fast we had to move faster than the waves, or the rudder wouldn't function, and we would be a leaf in the current.

We were down to our smallest working sails, and still the boat was almost overpowered. For the last few days we had been sleeping on the cabin sole in the narrow passage between the aft and main cabins. The motion was too wild to stay in the bunks.

Two days later, on August 16, we sailed across the continental shelf. The comment in the log: *"Course 325°, Full Gale, Wind 45-55."*

The seas had become increasingly steep, just as we feared they would. We were steering full time, surfing down the faces of these huge waves, looking over our shoulders to veer away when the crests broke. The breaking crests reached as tall as our mizzen mast: thirty feet. When we were at the bottom of the trough the crest of the waves soared above the top of the mast: sixty-two feet. Over six stories.

We would have been terrified, but after more than sixty-five days of continually worsening weather, we'd become good at this! Arianna and I were just too busy and too focused on survival to worry. We had a lot of confidence in our boat, and we were exhilarated by the challenge. More importantly, I had become confident that Arianna could handle anything. She was that girl, the one who let nothing stop her.

Around midday I saw a medium-size cargo ship from the top of a wave, maybe a mile away, also headed toward the cape. I lost it for a while, then saw it again, this time closer. After four weeks of silence the radio shouted, "MAYDAY! MAYDAY! Deutsche Bulk carrier, twenty-five miles south of Ras Asir, taking water. MAYDAY! MAYDAY!"

Arianna took the wheel as I jumped below to answer, "This is the *Sailing Vessel Saga*, one mile east of your position. I will try to approach, but we have very little control in these seas."

"Sailing vessel, do not try to approach us. We see you. It is not possible for you. Save yourselves."

I saw the ship headed down a big one…and never saw her come up. She drove right to the bottom, and the sea swallowed her. I would like to say that we were shocked and horrified by what we had witnessed, but honestly, the whole tragedy just made real the danger of our own situation. We had to leave it in the wake of that adrenaline fueled nightmare.

We had our own problems.

By late afternoon we were within sight of the headland, around which was the safety of protected waters. I was at the wheel, literally surfing away from breaking waves, like the star of a big-wave surfing video, riding a sixteen-ton surfboard!

Arianna shouted over the roar, "What do you think it will be like tonight when we can't see the breakers coming?"

"I guess you'll be the first to know. You've got the first night watch." Arianna just looked at me and laughed. Really laughed.

At least we still had a sense of humor, always a good tool for maintaining some vestige of self-control. "Seriously, we only have to get through this fucking night. The minute we turn the corner all this'll be gone. I can't even remember what silence sounds like."

What I didn't voice to my first mate was the fact that we were in trouble because of my arrogance and bad judgment. We could have gone around Socotra Island and stayed in deep water until we were under the protection of Somalia, in the Gulf of Aden. I had made the decision to cut the corner into shallow water where the seas were at their worst, just to save a couple hundred miles of sailing, and to skirt a pirate stronghold I suspected was poised on the other side of Socotra.

If we make it through the night it will be worth it, I thought.

I stayed by Arianna for the first hour of her watch. The seas had moderated slightly, and she seemed to be doing okay. She could hear the breakers coming, and steer out from under them. I was exhausted, and went down below to get some rest.

Arianna stared at Ranen as he went below, *What? I'm going to have to sail through this alone? Ranen has been doing this for twenty years and he doesn't make mistakes. If he thinks I can do this then I can do it. He's right there on the other side of this bulkhead; I can see his face.*

Then, she looked over her shoulder, a wall of water loomed, and there was no more time to think. She mustered all her strength into wrestling the wheel to keep the power of the waves from taking control.

Sailing out from under the curl, she thought, *Okay, I'm afraid, but nothing is going to sink us as long as I stay focused on keeping this boat headed down these waves.*

Sleep was not a possibility. Lying in the walkthrough storm bunk afforded a view of Arianna through a port into the cockpit. I desperately needed rest, and was half asleep until I heard the roar of a breaker from astern.

The boat was catapulted off the wave, and landed on its side.

With a white-knuckled grip on the wheel and her legs wedged in the cockpit corners, Arianna was locked into position at the steering station.

I felt the breaker catch the canvas spray dodger, and *Saga* was held in the grip of the roiling water long enough for the rest of the fifty-foot wave to roll her down, until the mast went under.

I am not sure how far over we went, but suddenly I was lying on the overhead with bedding strewn everywhere. I could see Arianna gripping the wheel. Through the port she looked like an ice cube in a glass of freshly poured soda. She looked at me and mouthed, *"Is it going to come back up??"*

I shrugged. This was a new one for me.

The struggle between the eight tons of lead in *Saga's* keel, countered by the resistance of the mast and sails through the water, was putting a lot of stress on the rigging. I prayed to Neptune for the rigging to hold and the mast not to snap, and then… BOING! The mast popped out of the water, vibrating like a coiled spring, and *Saga* was sailing again.

I fought my way to the main hatch through all the tools, books, cushions, and other gear that had scattered everywhere. Just as I reached for the companionway ladder we were swept by another breaking wave. This time the mast didn't go under very far, but I was thrown across the cabin, crashing into the stove, and getting my forehead hammered by a flying pressure cooker.

The cabin was a mess, and a slick of oily bilge water covered the wreckage. I leapt to the ladder to help Arianna control this boat, which had become a wild, bucking bull.

From the Ship's Log:
   *16/8/88   1315 hrs   Swept by breaking waves, broach-
ing 4 times.*

I finally made it on deck, and looked around in sheer amazement. Everything was in its place. Nothing had come adrift. In fact, we found later that all we lost on deck were our flip-flops. I yelled above the din to a wet, bedraggled Arianna, "Don't bother going below, it's a wreck down there. I'll steer. Just watch for breakers and call out which way to steer."

"Go to port, Ranen! Fuck, that one was close. These waves are still quite large, Captain. So how close can we get to the light?"

"You mean when can we turn? Are you asking when we're going to get out of this? We just have to pass the light before we turn left, and it's thirty meters deep right up to the coast, but we still need to stay off a bit to avoid getting into more breakers.

"I can't even remember the last time I slept. I mean really slept."

She put her lips to my ear and teased, "Mmm, sleep."

"We're approaching the Ras Asir light now. Four more hours and we can turn. Jesus! As fast as we're going it may be less. And, by the way, you were brilliant up here when the shit hit the fan. Oh, what the hell, go down and see if you can get some rest."

It is fascinating how your body can do what it has to. Days of no sleep, amidst unrelenting physical labor, profound danger, plenty of stress, and then... Strange, I don't even remember turning past the Ras Asir light.

...This night just wouldn't end. I went down below, and was shocked to see the cabin had taken water through the tiniest

window beside the galley. I was exhausted, and fell asleep in my foul weather gear on the floor next to the engine compartment, as oily water ran past my face. There were no dry beds, and I wanted to be ready in case the waves picked up and Ranen needed me on deck.

This was the longest night of my life! The wind was still howling and the rigging still pumping. Then we entered the Gulf of Aden, and were suddenly protected from the wind. All was quiet. This was the most bizarre feeling: Just moments before Ranen and I could hardly hear ourselves talk, the next minute there was silence, and the boat rocked gently.

CHAPTER 23

The Gulf of Oman to Djibouti

AN OSPREY SPREAD its wings and launched from its nest high on the naked cliffs of Ras Asir. Hundreds of feet below, she spied something new in the clear, turquoise water. A scorching mid morning sun lit a white sailing boat with her sails dropped on deck. A woman in her red foul-weather suit slept on the pile of a sail with her head resting on a green canvas sail bag. In the cockpit a man lay sleeping with his leg wrapped around a winch.

I woke in the cockpit, having slept for ten hours, right where I was when we made it into safe waters and dropped the sails. No anchor, just drifting in the absolute calm, two miles off the rocky desert headland of the Horn of Africa. I couldn't focus, one eye was blinded by the light of the sun, the other was crusted shut with salt. For a moment, I didn't know where I was. Barely conscious, I opened the hatch, and went below to wash my face with fresh water. Both eyes now functioning, I needed a mug of tea to kickstart my brain. With the second cup of sweet milky tea in hand, lists started forming in my mind.

I reached over and turned on the bilge pump. It ran for fifteen minutes until it sucked only air. A lot of water, but not over the floor boards. I wandered back to the deck, now wearing my rose tinted shades, marveling that we were still afloat. Arianna was still dead asleep at the base of the mast. She looked comfortable in her nest of sails. There is a comment in the log that sums it up, *Becalmed. Hard to believe that yesterday happened!*

After a careful scan with the binoculars, and feeling satisfied we were alone (no pirates in sight), I jumped below to start sorting out the cabins. There was a lot to do today before we left this protected un-anchorage…get some food going, start drying out and cleaning up. In a few minutes I had a big pile of wet bedding ready to spread out on deck.

I looked up. A bleary-eyed Arianna peered down at me.

"Get out of those salty clothes and have a shower while I get you some tea. I filled the shower bag. Take my word for it, don't even try to think until your second cup."

"Cheers," she croaked.

A few minutes later, I heard her dive overboard.

Clearing up the cabins wasn't nearly as big a job as it looked the night before. There *were* a lot of wet clothes — not just wet, but wet and oily. When the boat rolled the oily water in the bilge soaked everything that had come adrift. We washed it all with salt water then hung it out in the rigging to dry. It was only a matter of hours to wash down the cabin, even at our glacial pace. We were right on the coast of Somalia, so thoroughly cleaning and oiling the guns was a high priority. The High Standard .12 gauge riot gun, the Colt 1911 .45 auto, the S&W .38 Airweight, and the Ruger Mini 14, all had suffered some degree of saltwater soaking.

Sometime in the early afternoon, the absolute quiet was shattered by the distinctive *Wop Wop* of a helicopter! Arianna and I looked at each other with *What the Hell?* clearly written on our faces. A few minutes later a U.S. Navy chopper flew by us at masthead height. I jumped below, to the VHF radio, to broadcast on the ship to ship hailing channel, 16, "This is British registered sailing vessel, *Saga*, calling U.S. Navy helicopter passing Ras Asir. Do you copy? Over."

There was no answer for five minutes. Then, "*Saga*, that chopper doesn't have a radio that can talk to you. Please switch, channel 12." On channel 12, "This is U.S. Navy survey vessel -------- *(I cannot remember the name of the ship and can't find the name in our log)*. Where did you come from and where are you bound? Over.'" He sounded genuinely astonished to find us here in this godforsaken place.

I answered, "We came from around the corner last night."

"Captain, are you aware that there was a ship lost with all hands yesterday in that vicinity? Over."

"Oh yeah. That was us talking to him. It was just impossible to get to them. We were barely able to make it ourselves. Over."

"*Saga*, please standby channel 12, our executive officer will want to talk to you. Over."

"*Saga* standing by 12."

Meanwhile, we started collecting all the clothes and sheets hanging from the booms and rigging, and straightening up the decks. I told Arianna to put on one of her briefest bikinis. We needed to look like a normal cruising couple.

"Wow! You look so beautiful! What happened to that girl who left with me from Southeast Asia?"

"You look pretty good yourself, Captain. Must be all the fresh air and relaxation we've had during our little sailing holiday."

"*Sailing Vessel Saga*, this is the X.O. of the U.S. Navy survey vessel. Congratulations on surviving the last few days. Where are you bound? Over."

"We are two months out of Langkawi, Malaysia, bound for Djibouti. Over."

"The captain would like to know if you are in need of assistance? Over."

"Since you ask, we are very low on fresh water, considering we have another four-hundred miles to the next safe harbor. Over."

"Are you sure that is all you need? Do you have enough fuel? Over."

"Well, actually, we barely have enough to motor into the anchorage in Djibouti, but this is a sailing boat, and we should be okay. The other thing is, we would love to have ice."

"We cannot come in to where you are. Can you come out to us? Over."

"Sure, we'll get a few things secured and sail out there. I'm guessing you are the ship with all the antennas a couple of miles north of us."

"That is us, Captain. Get any water containers and coolers you have ready for pick up. Over."

I always got on well with the Navy, not at all like the Coast Guard. The Navy was always good for a weather report, or a look at their charts, or even a sandwich, when we would visit one of their ships in some foreign port. The Coast Guard are really just ocean going police, and to be avoided. I would rather go to the bottom then ask help from those assholes. Just like their land-based cousins, they would find an excuse to arrest you before rendering assistance. Where the Coast Guard was concerned, I have to paraphrase Bob Dylan, "The Coast Guard don't need you, and man, they expect the same."

Good thing a very light breeze had come up because we had less than five gallons of diesel fuel left, so we put up the sails and slowly made our way out to rendezvous with the U.S. Navy. I looked at Arianna, "Now *this* is totally unreal."

"*Sailing Vessel Saga*, U.S. Navy, channel 12. Over."

"This is *Saga*. Navy, go ahead."

"The captain asks if you would sail around our ship so we can all have a look at your boat. He wants the crew to see the boat that survived those impossible seas off the Horn of Africa."

The captain was probably a U. S. Naval Academy sailor who could appreciate a very seaworthy and beautiful sailing boat and we were all of that. With Arianna efficiently trimming the genoa, looking dazzling in her bikini, no one on that ship twigged that we were smugglers headed for Europe with a small but valuable load of prime Laotian buds. This is why we spent all the time in Thailand painting and varnishing. The crew and officers on deck actually saluted us!

As we completed our circumnavigation of their ship a large hard bottom inflatable launch approached. The pretty young chief pulled alongside smartly, and a seaman held on while I passed over two coolers and our two water containers. She asked me to heave to while they returned to their ship to fill our containers.

Arianna asked, "Can this be happening?"

"Yeah, these last few days have been surreal. You know that ship is not doing any surveying. I've seen U.S. survey ships, and they aren't Navy. The National Oceanic and Atmospheric Administration, NOAA, is who does underwater surveys, and charting, and that is not one of their ships.

"All those antennas… definitely for collecting intelligence. Some of the people on deck aren't military personnel, not in uniform. They're probably civilian specialists and spooks. The deck officers and crew in uniform are definitely Navy. This is a hot part of the world. CIA, Defense Intelligence, NSA, they're all over the Indian Ocean Basin."

This kind of crazy shit was why I loved my lifestyle. It was all so exhilarating. It was always new, and often dangerous. I never was good at boring.

Just when we thought the day could never get more surreal, this inconceivable Navy scenario got better. The launch returned about an hour later with both water containers full, plus an extra full seven-gallon water container. The ice chests were full, and they gave us a bag of oranges and lemons. However, the best surprise was a fifty-five gallon drum of diesel fuel. They had the drum securely wrapped in a sturdy cargo net, which we clipped onto our main halyard, winched into place, and secured on the cabin top, just aft of the mast.

I called the ship and offered to pay for the fuel. The captain came on and said this was his favorite kind of thing the Navy did and they had no way to accept payment, "It's not like we have a cash register onboard." He wished us a safe voyage. We put out the fishing lines and set a course west for Djibouti.

As we moved offshore, out of the protection of the mountains, the wind came back, still not as strong, but strong enough for a reduced mainsail and the working jib. These waves were not the big rollers of the Indian Ocean that had thousands of miles of fetch to build upon. These waves were just waves.

The next afternoon we were making good speed on course to Djibouti when, out of nowhere, a propeller airplane flew really low past us, and the radio squawked, "Sailing vessel, this is French Legion aircraft. What is your name and flag?"

I answered, "This is Sailing Vessel *Saga*. What can I do for you?"

"We are searching for a French registered sailing boat, *Sloopy Blue,* two weeks overdue from Mauritius."

"French aircraft, we are not *Sloopy Blue,* we are British registered. We have not seen any sailing vessels since leaving the Bay of Bengal. Be informed that the conditions near Ras Asir have been very bad."

"Thank you and bon voyage. French Legion out."

"Those poor bastards. They didn't make it. They're lost at sea," I whispered to Arianna.

On that late afternoon watch change Arianna said, "Here's to being resupplied in Somalia by the United States Navy. Would you like an iced tea with fresh lemon, Captain?"

"That would be lovely. Tah," I replied in my best English accent.

At that moment the fishing line went tight with a loud SNAP as the cable set the hook. Behind the boat a shimmering, rainbow colored, four-foot long Dorado (Mahi) leaped high out of the water, trying to shake the hook out of its mouth. "Arianna! Pull in the other fishing line while I slow this boat down. I am suddenly starving for fresh protein, and now we have a better use for all those U.S. Navy lemons!"

The boat was just loafing along slowly with the mainsheet eased, so as not to rip the hook out of the Dorado's mouth. I put on my gloves, and hand over hand, gently started taking in the heavy monofilament line. When the fish started to run, or even resist, I gave it some line, but always keeping the line taut. The idea was to tire rather than to overpower the fish. After half an hour he stopped resisting, and I had him close to the boat. Arianna was right next to me at the rail, leaning over the lifelines with the big gaffe. One last careful pull, and she slipped the big gaffe hook under the Dorado's gill and out through its mouth. It took both of us to haul the powerful thrashing fish onto the deck. With my foot holding down his head, I reached into a cockpit locker and pulled out my homemade billy club. One blow killed this magnificent creature and I (as always) thanked the fish for giving its life to feed us. It was a sad moment, and as it died, all of its shimmering colors faded to a dull grey-green.

The next hour was spent skinning, filleting, and cutting the fillets into appropriate pieces for sautéed Dorado, fried fish sandwiches, fish soup (we still had a few soft, but edible potatoes), and fish jerky.

Things were looking up. The sailing conditions were perfect: steady and moderate beam winds with a gentle swell. Good cooking conditions as well. No real worry about pirates with the Navy around. Anyway, they knew the boat, and avoided us, because in our previous encounter, Beach Rat and I had greeted them with gunfire. Pirates prefer softer targets.

During the run from Thailand we were forced to put our love affair on hold in order to survive the long voyage. Now, we were alone in this empty gentle ocean, sailing along a deserted coast where we might see a band of nomads riding camels along an empty beach. We joked around, laughed together, and enjoyed plain sailing, having just survived an ocean holocaust.

Our changing night-watch routine was way different during this part of our odyssey. The winds were so steady that most nights I would get into Arianna's warm vanilla-scented bunk, and she would welcome me with sleepy vanilla kisses, her strong naked arms and legs wrapping around me as we made love in our private universe. Much better than the Indian Ocean's brief kiss, cup of tea, and fall into a dead sleep.

Ranen never stopped talking and had so much energy. I never wanted this life to end. The beauty and savage adventure of the voyages, the excitement of smuggling, and even that little

bit of fear in the farthest corner of your mind, that we would be discovered, made life so powerful.

And I was always learning so much about myself. I spent a lot of time thinking about my anger. I think I wasted some of those valuable days thinking negatively. But we had days when we just laughed about everything and if I was in an angry mood, Ranen would crack a joke and I would burst out laughing again.

The days to Djibouti were fine sailing. We had a lot of time to enjoy sailing, fishing, and getting to know each other on a deeper level. I always knew that Arianna had a dark side and some family issues. Now that we had shared and survived so much together it was easier for her to talk to me about the anger she harbored over the years her mother had led a promiscuous lifestyle. Her childhood was filled with adults she didn't trust, who were always stoned on one thing or another. Stoners are typically self-centered, and Arianna was largely neglected by her mother and her friends. In fact, they left her to raise her much younger brother.

Another issue Arianna began to unravel was the nagging anger remaining from the death of her father. Her life with him had been a wonderful contrast to life with her mother. He had been a scientist, an oceanographer and hydrologist. Life with her father was always interesting. His house was often filled with colleagues, who were mutually high-minded intellectuals. I remember her telling me about a big Kenyan ranch he lived at where they made their own cheese and experimented with ways to have what now is called a "sustainable lifestyle." She started realizing how much it pissed her off that she had never been allowed to mourn the death of her father after he had passed when she was sixteen.

We were having one of those long ramblings on one of those perfect days as the boat was sailing itself, the self-steering doing all the work. I was leaning against the mast, listening to Arianna talk about her life in Africa, when the boat lurched so violently that we both fell to the deck. I looked around–saw no land–and jumped below in a panic to look at the chart. No shoals in the neighborhood. Again, there was a lurch, as if we were bumping against something big. Up on deck, Arianna, mouth open in shock, was pointing at a large whale lazily swimming away.

The log said: *"Whale scratches back on boat."*

Our odyssey was formidable, not unlike competing in an around the world race. The difference was that we had no corporate sponsors, no world-wide support teams, and calling for help in an emergency was out of the question… and that was the biggest difference.

I knew that we would need to stop and refresh with food and fuel. Knowing where to stop is an essential skill for a smuggler. From the beginning it was in my mind to stop in Djibouti, a free port where cargo can pass through undeclared and untaxed. A free port also means, especially in Africa, that there is practically no hassle with authorities. We just needed to leave some info at the Port Captain's office and we would be in. Djibouti is a French protectorate set up after WWII, a small country, about the size of Los Angeles, at the bottom of the Red Sea, separating Somalia, Ethiopia, and Eretria. The French maintain a small naval base there and a huge Foreign Legion base as well–all of that French military prevents continuous open warfare in the region. Because it is still a free port, it remains a mecca for smuggling and sales of illicit goods to the outside world. All the spoils of war in that area, and a larger part of Africa, find their way to the open market in Djibouti.

There is a lovely little "yacht club" where you could get French food for breakfast, like fresh real croissants, and drinks on ice. Make no mistake, Djibouti is a filthy poverty-stricken port in one of the poorest areas of the world. It is a city-state positioned in the middle of three war-torn countries, and is overcrowded by displaced peoples.

The wharves were piled high with foreign aid food spoiling in the desert sun. Aid organizations had sent cooking oil, corn, rice, and dry milk to places like Somalia, Eretria, Ethiopia, and Sudan, but this was the closest port big enough to accommodate the ships carrying these cargoes. All of this food was sent by organizations like Geldorf's Band Aid and U.S. Aid, who campaigned for the money to pay themselves, and for the notoriety. Sadly, they couldn't be bothered with the organizational work to handle the actual logistics of getting the food to the remote places that desperately needed it. Even the local refugees weren't allowed to get their hands and stomachs on these precious commodities.

There is even a hospital in Djibouti, but no doctors, nurses, or medicine supplied by whichever organization built the hospital. Just a new building littered with medical equipment, and nothing else.

On August 23 we passed the breakwater into Djibouti harbor. It was in my mind to take the advice I'd given to other sailors about how to get up the Red Sea, namely to stop only briefly in Djibouti to provision, have a few good meals, then keep moving toward the Suez. With that in mind, I headed to the commercial wharves to find a mooring alongside the big stone wharf, so I didn't have to inflate the dinghy. There was a very new oilfield supply boat flying the British ensign alongside the quay. The name on the high bow was *Red Sea Trader*, she was well over one hundred feet long with a low aft deck. I thought, *This is a perfect place to tie up. Much better than that nasty, very high stone wharf with corroded metal ladders and easy access for thieves.* There was a thirty-something year-old man on the bridge of the *Trader* watching us entering the harbor, so I swung around alongside and shouted up to him, "Ahoy, can we tie up alongside?"

"Sure. Hold off while I get some fenders fixed," he answered in a London accent. At his call, a woman appeared with three huge fenders, which they hung alongside the low aft deck where we could more easily climb onboard. After getting securely moored alongside, we climbed over the rail and introduced ourselves. They were Bruce, the captain, and his British wife, Kate, who was obviously crew. Since they were stuck in Djibouti while some of his crew were in England on vacation, Bruce was happy to have new people to talk to and was fascinated with our story. He caught up with us as we crossed his deck, on our way to the Port Authority, and invited us for dinner.

Dinner with the rest of the crew, who were all English, was a lively affair. These guys were merchant sailors from Northern climates who had just discovered diving and were really into eating "bugs" (lobsters). I promised to take them out to the reefs in our inflatable. After hearing the story of our voyage, Bruce offered to let us make use of their shop to do some much needed repairs and maintenance.

Bruce had started a shipping company using a charted Maersk platform supply vessel to collect and deliver containers to harbors in the region that were too small and/or shallow to allow normal container ships. It was a novel plan, and all very exciting work for a commercial ship, because the *Red Sea Trader's* ports were pretty rough towns in Somalia, Eritrea, Yemen, and Sudan-—all countries that were in the midst of war, civil or otherwise, and had ineffective or non existent governments. These guys were also going inland to find and reclaim unreturned containers for which they were paid a good bonus. Bruce and company were high energy, creative, ocean-going cowboys, and all of us slipped into an instant friendship. We shared meals, sundowners, and piled into our dinghy for diving trips on the reef off the coast.

Arianna and I were having fun whilst licking our wounds. We weren't avoiding getting back on that horse, we were just enjoying the lifestyle with our new friends. Believing your LPL is what protects you from getting caught, but really, we just didn't think about our cargo. Our mindset was all about the voyage, and this leg of the voyage had become all about enjoying the company of these wild and well-mannered English cowboys.

We were making use of our neighbor's washing machine and watermaker, while replacing broken fittings that we had parts for. Those knockdowns we took on the last night in the Indian Ocean put an immense amount of stress on the rigging. Imagine eight tons of lead in the upturned keel, and the tremendous gravitational force that exists as the keel seeks its natural position under the boat.

All of that force did some serious damage to the stainless-steel cables supporting the mast as it dragged the whole rig, including the sails, to the surface. Thank Neptune that we didn't see the extent of the damage until the refit, long after the end of this story, because otherwise we might have never left that port. So we replaced the obvious stress-cracked wire terminals. Fortunately, I had rigged the boat with Staylock terminals that don't require a big press to replace.

I climbed to the masthead to check the terminals, and the forestay seemed to have sustained the worst damage. I shivered, thinking about our two weeks of sailing with that big foresail pulling a sixteen ton boat on that cracked cable terminal. If the forestay had let go under sail in a strong wind the mast would have surely snapped. But then, I am a Pisces son of Neptune, and he kept us safe. It was no accident that I had an entire forestay, complete with fittings, stowed in a dry spot in the tools locker, so Arianna and I spent a day putting it up.

Altogether, we spent a week working on the rig, no small job. Every terminal we cut off shortened the wire, so we used safety wired shackles to make up for the lost length. After all of that, we had to tune the rigging to equalize the wire tension to keep the mast in column. Not too tight and not too loose. It was a blessing to have use of the shop vice on the *Red Sea Trader*.

One evening, after dinner, Bruce asked if we were interested in being crew on the *Trader*. It was a tempting offer. A similarly adventurous lifestyle, but completely legal--very appealing. In that moment, I became tempted to come clean with Bruce and tell him the truth. However, you aren't doing your friends a favor by burdening them with illegal secrets. If you get busted because they let it slip, whose fault is it? So, as always, I kept my thoughts to myself. For better or worse, Arianna and I were committed to this voyage, so I politely turned him down.

Summer was getting on and we needed to get going. We still had another major gauntlet to run, right in front of us. Twelve hundred miles, against a daily forty-knot wind, up the Red Sea to the Suez Canal. After sixteen days in Djibouti, we set sail for the Suez, into the Mediterranean. We were rested and mentally prepared for the next trial.

CHAPTER 24

Red Sea

IT IS WORTH mentioning again: the voyage up the Red Sea is over twelve hundred nautical miles, against a fiercely hot strong wind. The desert nations along both shores were not at all hospitable. Yemen, Eritrea, and Sudan, were not exactly stable governments that welcomed visitors. Private vessels were forbidden to enter Saudi Arabian waters, and Egypt was off the menu because there was a death penalty for smuggling marijuana. Since these coasts didn't have pirates and we were not into stopping, the sailing conditions were the only problems and there were lots of those. Problematic sailing conditions, that is.

Although the direct route is twelve hundred miles, we really were going to sail more than double that, because the wind always blows from the north, which means tacking back and forth. The Red Sea is narrow, mostly less than a hundred miles wide of safe waters, with dangerous reefs and hidden rocky shallows extending out from both shores.

Then, throw in the hassle of big ship traffic. Almost all of the big ship traffic from the Indian Ocean, and Asia, heading to Europe, and Eastern and Western North Atlantic, goes up the Red Sea and through the Suez Canal. So, essentially, we had to sail back and forth across a freeway of ships. Big ships travel at upwards of forty-five knots, or fifty miles per hour. Even if they see you, and are inclined to give way to a sailing boat crossing their path, it is just not that easy. Many fully-laden crude oil tankers can take five or more miles to stop, and possibly as much to turn. You can call ships on the VHF radio, but often the crews don't answer because they don't speak English, they are off having a coffee or maybe they don't want to take responsibility for an accident.

I had a lot of experience navigating in a similar choke point, the Florida Straits. The Florida Straits is only a one hundred mile danger zone and the Red Sea was ten times as long with a lot more traffic. Yet we didn't even waste a moment thinking about possibilities, jumping off the edge was what we were all about.

Soon after leaving Djibouti, we passed the Straits of Bab Al Mandeb into the Red Sea, with moderate southeast winds behind us. Staying out of the shipping lanes by skirting through the Hamish Islands off Yemen, we made good mileage up to the Saudi Arabian Coast.

Six days later, we sailed through the line where the strong, dry hot north wind off the Nubian desert of Sudan blows. From this point, I knew that we would have an increasingly stronger wind against us until we reached the Mediterranean.

The temperature went from 90° to over 110° and the seas became short and steep. We closed all the hatches and put up a little canvas shade over the cockpit. It was like a sauna in the cabin below. To stay out of the shipping lanes we were short tacking up one coast or the other, carefully navigating to avoid rocks, reefs, and ships. This wasn't like any of the tacking against the wind out in the Indian Ocean, where there was nothing to hit, and weeks would go by without seeing a ship. Good thing we rested up in Djibouti, because tacking and navigating here required constant attention and was stressful.

The ship's log was page after empty page. In eight days, the only comment was, *"Close call with tanker."* There was no time or energy to make comments. Just jump below, put in the time, mileage, and position, then back up on deck to push the boat, dodge reefs, watch for traffic…and hide from the sun and the relentless hot wind.

Midday on September 15, we were sailing off the coast of Saudi Arabia when the sky to the east turned black. No doubt in our minds, *Saga* was about to be run down by a freight train of a rain squall. We were well out of the shipping lanes, so I dropped the jib, and Arianna reduced the main to a third reef, so we wouldn't lose the mast if there was a tornado lurking in those black clouds.

"All Right!" I shouted. "This looks like our fresh-water shower!"

I joined Arianna, who was already stripping off her sweaty, salty tee-shirt and shorts. We pulled up buckets of sea water and soaped up from head to toe.

"Let's wash some clothes while we're at it," She said, and dumped some of our favorite salty clothes into the sudsy bucket of salt water. We washed, rinsed, and wrung out the clothes, then hung them out to rinse in the downpour that was nearly upon us.

Then came the deluge.

Only it wasn't rain.

it was MUD.

Sandy, gritty mud.

For half an hour we stood in shock as our white sails, shining ice green decks, and our lovely dark green canvas all turned Arabian Desert brown. I turned to look at Arianna and laughed.

"Look at you! You've gone native!" We were caked in mud. We dropped the mainsail and immediately dove into the sea to get most of the mud off. My hair was still pretty short, so the mixture of soap and mud was pretty easily washed out. Arianna's thick hair was a whole different matter. She ended up with some seriously muddy dreadlocks, and I spent my off-watch time for the next few days, untangling and brushing out the muddy tangles from her thick hair—any excuse to touch Arianna was a better job than re-reading tattered Louis Lamour cowboy novels.

For the next several hours Arianna and I scrubbed the sails, decks, and sail bags. We sure as hell weren't about to enter the Med looking like we just sailed nearly nonstop from Thailand. Image is the key to success, or at least the key to staying out of prison.

From the Ship's Log

21/9/88   24°38.85 N. 35°10.16 E. Anchor for 24 hrs-transfer fuel water-cook-small repairs-night sleep. Open up boat for airing. Dry wet clothes bodies

We were fighting our way north against the Red Sea, hour by hour playing the slight wind shifts to get past those short, steep waves, and staying out of the path of the ships. On the twenty-first we anchored in four meters over white sand behind a reef south of Ras Baghdadi for a much needed break.

We were only a couple of boat lengths from a pristine coral reef, so I grabbed a spear, mask and fins, and went down to kill dinner. By the time I got back with a medium grouper and two lobsters, Arianna had taken a shower, opened all the hatches and had the wind scoop blowing dry, hot air through the boat,. We were within a week of the Suez so we emptied all the remaining spare water into the water tanks and emptied whatever spare diesel was left in containers, into the main fuel tanks. I figured we were going to need the fuel to avoid ships in the Gulf of Suez.

That evening we shared an elegant meal: fresh seafood curry with coconut rice. All the fresh veg was gone, but we didn't miss it. This was pure romantic luxury.

Without a word, we were kissing, then climbing into the v-berth up forward, on top of all the sail bags, under the wind scoop. My naked body, sculpted by months of hard work and limited rations, rejoiced in her equally hard embrace. Arianna's legs and arms, made incredibly strong by the months of struggle with the force of the sea, were wrapped around me holding me motionless inside her. The motionless total contact, both inside and outside of her, was so intensely erotic that when I finally exploded I was gripped by dizzy laughter. Who could do that? Make you climax by motionless will power? Arianna gave me a mysterious smile. I couldn't imagine not loving her.

Any man who thinks he knows what his woman is feeling or thinking is letting his ego get the best of him. We knew each other very well by this point. After all, we had been living, working, and risking our lives, within a meter of each other for three years. Yet, as well as I knew Arianna, that mysterious smile would appear, and honestly I am not sure I understood it. I don't think she had an orgasm. I think that smile said, "I loved this intimacy but more than that I enjoyed sending you beyond the edge of passion." That smile said, "I can send you there when I want, my Captain."

As much as that smile made me somewhat uneasy, the complex emotion and passion behind that smile was exhilarating.

The next morning we had a quiet tea and breakfast. Lost in our own thoughts, we quietly went about all the tasks of getting back to sea.

Two days later we passed the Straits of Jubal into the Gulf of Suez. I had sailed this passage before, but we had been going south, with the wind allowing us to easily maneuver on almost any heading. However, this time we were tacking north. The Gulf of Suez is two hundred miles long, and twelve to twenty miles wide-—really though, it is more like three to five miles wide, because there are busy oilfields obstructing both sides of the entire passage.

Totally out of character, Arianna cursed from below: "What in the hell are all these danger and forbidden symbols all over this chart? Is this seriously saying we cannot navigate anywhere but this narrow area in the middle of this channel? What the FUCK? It looks like the M1 motorway into London out there in the middle of that channel! What is this going to look like tonight?"

"I'm not looking at the big picture. Let's just start tacking north and when we have to cross the shipping lanes we'll make decisions as we approach. For now, since it's light, let's sail into the oilfields and see how dangerous it really is, and see what the icons on this chart really mean."

I tacked east into an industrial nightmare. We were going fast because the wind was blowing a steady twenty knots. There were 100 foot oilfield supply boats, like the *Red Sea Trader*, headed for the huge oil rigs. These rigs, or drilling platforms, were like houses perched one hundred twenty feet above the water with cranes, towers, and landing platforms for helicopters. There were more than a couple helicopters in the air, but they didn't concern us other than to add to the noise. Those were the obvious obstructions, but there were also big pipes sticking up out of the sea and long curving lines of buoys as well. It was like sailing through a partially built city.

Thankfully, the captains of the supply boats were real professionals, aware and experienced. We watched one back under a platform, and hold the ship steady in a four meter sea with the winds trying to blow him sideways, while a crane from above picked up a man off the deck. These guys all spoke English and were listening to their radios, which meant we could call them to avoid collisions.

Our plan was to short tack between the edge of the ship channel and the oilfields. However, the ship traffic wasn't continuous, and when there were lulls in the ship traffic we were able to get longer, more efficient tacks by pushing into and even crossing the shipping lanes. During the daytime there was a lot of fun to be had sailing around in the less crowded oilfields. Sleep was low on the agenda during the Gulf of Suez cruise, but Arianna and I had become pretty damn good at sailing our vessel--so, oddly, we were excited by the challenge.

When it got dark the landscape looked like something out of *Blade Runner*, like flying an airplane at low altitude through Chicago at night. All of the obstructions were lighted. The rigs were lit up with bright yellow sodium floodlights. The lines of buoys had a blinking white light on every buoy. Basically, all the hazards had some kind of marker, but there was so much ambient light that we had no depth perception, so all the hazard markers ran together. At times it was impossible to see which lights were closer and which were further away. Having one of us keeping watch with binoculars helped.

This was really stressful navigation, but we were addicted to stress. We were sailors with an attitude. It was exhilarating, sailing really fast on a moonless night, tacking through a maze of brilliant and blinding lights. We would be boldly pushing deep into the oilfield, on what we were thinking was a clear course, when a huge blast of fire would erupt from some unnoticed pipe one hundred meters ahead, forcing us to make a fast tack for an instant change of course. Every time they burned off some gas, it was good for a shot of adrenalin. Every time. Sailing through Hell? It seemed that way.

When we would pick a line out of the insane inferno, toward the shipping lanes, we were reminded that the shipping lanes were a lot more dangerous. The oilfields were fixed. The shipping lanes were busy and moving fast. Although you can make judgments on a ship's course by the changing position of its navigation lights alone, it is still really difficult to judge speed and distance. So during the night we stayed away from the shipping lanes. When the sun came up, and we could actually see them, we started tacking through the ships.

From the Ship's Log:

23/9/88 - 24/9/88   Tacking across the busiest shipping lane on earth through oil field after oil field all night with half a gale of wind. <u>No</u> sleep for us.

"Southbound Nedlloyd container vessel at 28°25.64 north and 33°06.3 east this is the *Sailing Vessel Saga* headed 300° do you see us? Please respond and switch channel 10."

"Sailing vessel this is Nedlloyd container ship *Rotterdam* switching channel 10. Sailing vessel this is *Rotterdam*. Good Morning."

"Good morning *Rotterdam*. Do you have us on your radar? We are wondering if we are safe to pass your bow on our present course, or would you prefer us to change course to pass your stern?"

"Sailing vessel, we have a visual and a radar fix on you. If you keep your course and speed you are safe to pass across our bow. I will adjust our course a bit just to be sure. You are also clear of all north-bound traffic for twenty miles."

"Thank you *Rotterdam*. Have a safe voyage. *Sailing Vessel Saga* switching and standing by channel 16."

"Safe voyage *Saga*. Nedlloyd *Rotterdam* standing by channel 16."

Polite exchanges like this were rare. Mostly the ships didn't answer, so when we weren't in the oilfields we were playing dodgeball with monsters.

CHAPTER 25

Suez

ON THE TWENTY-SIXTH we anchored close off the Sinai Peninsula at an oil terminal anchorage, to clean up, and contact my agent Mohammed, before approaching the Suez.

I had worked with Mohammed when I passed through the Suez Canal years before. Unlike many cheapskate "yachties" who tried to do all the formalities themselves, I used agents. As far as I was concerned, the less personal contact with authorities the better. When we originally came south through the canal I was planning to head back to North America by way of Cape Town and the Cape of Good Hope. But, as usual, the plan had changed. Instead, we were now heading for Europe, and it made sense to head back through the Suez again. Contingency plans were a good thing to have in my back pocket, and I had talked to Mohammed four years before about the fastest way to pass through the canal. All that was necessary was to contact him on the high frequency single-sideband radio to make arrangements.

I wanted to pass through the Suez Canal just like the ships, picking up ships stores, fuel, and water without stopping. Mohammed used a fifty foot "tender" to drop crew and supplies for cargo vessels and tankers. Even though agents only provide those services to big ships, Mohammed did it for our little private sailing vessel. Like most shipping agents, he could and would do anything for a price.

We needed to re-supply without going on land because as long as we were in the canal we were in international waters. Officially entering Egypt was not something that we wanted to do for a number of reasons. Even though the sealed packages of weed were packed away in a very tight compartment, it would be stupid to tempt fate by volunteering to be searched. Furthermore, our plan was to slip into the Mediterranean cruising crowd, and those boats do not turn up in Egypt. We just did not want to leave footprints for some government agency to pick up on. Covering tracks was hard wired into my lifestyle. Oh yeah, and as I said before, Egypt has a death penalty for smuggling drugs.

So I tuned up the single-sideband and hailed Mohammed, who was always standing by. He was quite happy to bring one hundred gallons of fuel, one hundred gallons of drinking water, and to do our shopping for fresh food. I also made it clear I wanted to pick up the required pilot[12] and transit the canal without stopping in Egypt. He could smell an inflated fee and agreed to pick up our papers when he dropped the fuel and water. Mohammed was good at his job. The first boat came the next afternoon. He dropped the provisions that keep, like citrus and cabbage, with the fuel. Food with a limited shelf life, like bread, he'd bring with the pilot.

A few days later Mohammed delivered our fresh bread, our papers for the Suez passage, and an appointment to pick up our official pilot later that day. He arranged for us to follow right behind the evening ship convoy.

The Suez Canal was built by the French in the late 1860's to make it possible for shipping to navigate from Asia to Europe without the extra mileage and danger of going around the Cape of Good Hope. It's really just a single-lane ditch connecting the Mediterranean Sea and the Red Sea. All canal traffic transited the canal in single-lane convoys. It is impressive to witness a mile long procession of monster ships sailing through the desert. There is a lake in the middle where we dropped anchor that night to wait for the morning convoy headed north. It was a huge relief to anchor and be rid of the day's pilot who was constantly pushing us to go faster to keep up with the convoy, while taking every opportunity to touch Arianna. What a sleaze ball!

---

12 The Suez Canal has compulsory pilotage. All transiting vessels must take onboard an official Suez pilot who coordinates the passage within the convoy.

PART 6 – The Mediterranean

PART 6 – The Mediterranean

CHAPTER 26

Into the Med

On October 4, we passed Port Said into the Mediterranean Sea, dropped our pilot, and set sail for Valletta, the capital of Malta, a central Mediterranean island nation. Word was, there was a yachting community in Malta. Valletta was the perfect port for slipping into the Mediterranean yacht scene. Another reason for Malta was the American and British Embassies there. We needed to replace our soaked passports that had gone for a swim when we were knocked down off the Horn of Africa. More importantly, we needed clean passports because our pages of visa stamps would land us on the elite list of who's who in smuggling. Having those stamps following us around Europe was not a good idea.

We could not have picked a more impressive destination to enter Europe. We ghosted through the harbor entrance with just the big fore sail up and a light wind behind us. The wind died as we sailed behind the ancient fortifications, and as we drifted along I could imagine knights riding those same narrow streets down to the harbor. The sun was lighting up some of the oldest buildings in the world. After months of seeing nothing but open ocean and desert shores, the contrast was shocking. Arianna and I were staring, hypnotized, at the ancient city above us. We had made it to Europe!

Yes, we had made it to Europe, but we were still thousands of miles from the Netherlands. Captain Ranen woke up from his reverie, and said, "Let's look for a place to tie up and find some food we don't have to cook. I would kill for a Coke with lots of ice."

"Looks like a marina over there," Arianna pointed to a bunch of masts. Thirty minutes later *Saga* was happily secure alongside a floating dock at a modern marina where Sonny Spiteri, the English speaking agent, directed us to the immigration office.

There were some beautiful boats in the marina. Most flew Italian flags. Malta was a perfect place for wealthy Italians to keep their boats: a picturesque Mediterranean island, with great beaches, only a short flight from Italy, and no Italian luxury taxes. The weather was still warm, the glut of tourists was gone, and there were some very sophisticated and wealthy younger couples living aboard their sailing boats.

Saga was looking quite the gleaming ocean greyhound, and she was definitely the most serious boat in the marina. Now all the work in Thailand was paying off. We were all business as we coiled the lines, zipped the sails into their green canvas bags, tightened up all the mooring lines, and generally got *Saga* looking "Bristol." Arianna and I were looking up to our part as well. My normally dark hair was growing out bleached by the sun and I wore the stylish sailor pants I had made in Thailand with no shirt. I was lean and hard. We were both in the best physical condition of our lives, after months of endless ocean challenge.

I am sure we looked like we felt, and we felt like gods.

As we stepped ashore I studied the impression we were making. This was the first test of our image in Europe and, I repeat, *Image is always the key to staying out of the clutches of law enforcement.*

Arianna vaulted across the lifelines to the dock in one effortless motion, wearing a long, white silk blouse and a dark blue (very short) skirt, landing smartly on her feet, adorned by a pair of white Topsider moccasins. She sported an array of antique African jewelry: necklaces and bracelets of Ethiopian and Somali silver, and antique Italian glass beads. Her belt was a beaded museum piece with links made of tiny matching bones, gone yellow with the passage of centuries.

There were two couples holding glasses of wine on a Nautor Swan up the dock staring at Arianna in shock, utterly dumbfounded. I am sure they fancied themselves very cool sailors, until the real thing appeared on their radar. Just the impression we were going for.

I stopped by their lovely, well-kept sailing yacht. "Wow. Is this a Swan thirty-six? This is the first I've actually seen up close. She's a beauty."

"She is a thirty-six," answered a late-twenties, blonde Brit with a thick upper-class accent. "Why not come aboard for a glass of wine and have a look around? I'm Robert and this is Natalie, James, and Alison. "

"Pleased to meet you, Robert. I'm Ranen, this is Arianna."

Arianna stepped forward to shake Robert's hand and said in her best classy British colonial accent, "Good to meet you all. Actually, we are off to clear in, but let's get together a bit later." She was right in her element and they all knew it. The exotic and charming Arianna Bell, her wild looking American sailor boyfriend, and their classic racing yacht fit right into the Euro yachting scene.

We eventually found our way to the customs house. Despite our polished image and confident stride, when we walked through that door I found myself tense. If there was an Interpol notice out on us, now would be the moment for things to go south. However, the officer there officially welcomed us to Malta with only a cursory glance at our passports and ship's papers. No one came to look at the boat. We had officially arrived in Europe.

Another hurdle was behind us, but there was still an entire slalom course ahead that was never on our radar, about which we were still blissfully ignorant.

It was going to be late September before we got out of Malta. Then we had another twelve hundred nautical miles to Gibraltar and the Atlantic. Cracks began spreading in my wall of denial. In the back of my mind I was beginning to have doubts about our ability to make it past the Bay of Biscay before the winter storms set in. Although weed was quasi-legal in the Netherlands, it was a serious crime in France, so if things were to go wrong there would be no going into port. I was thinking that most of the mast rigging would need to be replaced before we got hit by the kind of storms that might intercept our path on the way to the North Sea.

We were busy. I had a plan and we needed to keep moving, all the while maintaining the face (or *farce*) of the fun loving cruising couple. So, in addition to having dinners and drinks with the Brits and Italian sailors, we had to get passport photos taken and submitted for new passports, as well as prepare to sail nonstop to Spain.

The American Embassy fixed me up with a shiny new passport, after a few nasty remarks about being irresponsible with their precious document. The twenty-something Yale graduate made it clear that the U.S. Department of State did not exist to support American tourists. I, in turn, made it clear that I would present no further problems for his royal yuppie self.

The British High Commission gave Arianna a hard time about her citizenship. Although she was born in Kenya, she was a British citizen with a British passport. There were a lot of left-wing bureaucrats in the British government who were resentful of the whole British Empire history, and this guy she was dealing with obviously resented her colonial status. In the end she did get a new passport, but he wasted weeks of our time.

Not that we weren't having fun. We were... having fun. We were enjoying the sunny Mediterranean weather and selling our sailor pants. One of the young Italian women asked about them so I sold her a white pair for $15. We were both wearing the pants (not at the same time, of course), and some other sailors were interested, so I upped the price to $25. By the time Arianna had her papers in order the price had rocketed to $75, and we were out of pants to sell.

As it turned out we would have been better off spending the last of my stash on filling the boat with custom-made Thai clothing, rather than premium Thai weed, because those pants made a killing, and they were entirely legal. You cut a lot of smuggling costs when you don't have to do any smuggling. But this was 1988, and the magical crystal ball was yet to be invented.

CHAPTER 27

On to Spain

ON NOVEMBER 3 we set sail for Spain. We were a thousand miles to Gibraltar, the gateway to the Med. A thousand miles to decide if I was willing to tempt fate by trying to force our way a couple thousand miles past Spain to Holland, in the North Sea during winter. Just to put it into perspective, the biggest wave ever surfed was up toward the Bay of Biscay, right on our course. Besides giant waves, there are rocks everywhere, vicious currents, and at this time of year, blinding fog for weeks on end. We were starting to see broken strands of wire and the telltale blush of rust that meant corrosion within the metal. I just didn't have the confidence that *Saga* could sustain another severe pounding. I was feeling less bulletproof.

Nevertheless, when things seemed to be in doubt I always found a way to keep moving. Some old rock song said it best:

Everyone is goin' nowhere, baby.
They're all in line to be last.
We may be goin' nowhere, baby.
At least we're goin' nowhere fast.

So we just kept heading West towards Spain.

This is the thing about smuggling, or, in fact, about any new adventure: big wall climbing, ski mountaineering, or company startups--you follow The Plan until it becomes irrelevant. We were at that point, and I knew it. I was getting ready to break the voyage. Playing it safe, by sailing directly to Holland where weed was legal, was no longer a safe plan. Somewhere south of Sicily I made up my mind to stop in Spain, and I had a port in mind.

I wasn't going to consult with Arianna. She trusted me to make these decisions. The less you dwell on danger the calmer you remain. Worry and panic raise red flags, it shows in your body language. I had to consider the dangers, but it wouldn't help to involve Arianna in the worry. Welcome to being captain.

I was living on two levels: There was the voyage to Spain, the daily reality of sailing in the winter. Then there was the nagging list of options running through my head of what to do when we got to Spain.

The log doesn't show much for this part of the voyage. We had become a well oiled machine. The weather was getting colder and we started wearing wetsuit booties on watch. It was going to be December by the time we got to Portugal. There was no doubt that we had missed our seasonal weather window to continue nonstop to Holland.

Thank the Gods I didn't have that crystal ball, because the shit was about to hit the fan.

CHAPTER 28

Latest Pack of Lies

NOVEMBER 12 WAS warm and sunny. We moored alongside the port office in Almerimar and cleared into Spain. The formalities were just that: fill out forms, show passports, get tourist visas. No search.

We moved to a floating dock near the bar. This place was a whole different scene than Malta--less sophisticated, no fancy yachts, no jet set sailors, and very Spanish. We had been at sea for over two weeks and were anxious to get to the bar for a cold beer and some of those delicious tapas I remembered from when we stopped here six years ago, on the way to the Indian Ocean.

As we tied up, two British sailing couples in their forties stopped and watched us from the dock. One of the women asked Arianna, "Where have you sailed in from?"

"From Malta," Arianna answered.

"But where did you come from last?"

"From Malta," Arianna repeated.

"What was your last port? Where did you spend last night?" she asked impatiently.

"We left Malta two weeks ago. We spent every night at sea since we left Valletta."

Once again, our fellow yachtsmen were running into the *real* version of who they had convinced themselves they were. This was a recurring problem throughout my life as a sailor. Most people with sailing boats adopt their self-image from sailing magazines, and become angry when they meet the real thing. These people are often uncomfortable at sea.

We would have to be careful not to be seen as arrogant here. Making enemies was not what we were after. It was crucial that we fit in and fade into the crowd. So we introduced ourselves to these couples and even invited them to join us at the bar for a beer and tapa. I don't remember their names, which gives some idea for how interesting this crowd was. Maybe I'm a bit of a snob, but the rich "yachties" in Valletta were more to my taste.

I had narrowed my options down to two: Sell the weed in Spain or figure out a plan to smuggle it north to Holland.

Stupidly, I never considered waiting until spring to sail north to Holland. Big mistake. I've gotta say, I'm having problems writing this part of the story, because, in retrospect, I could have made better decisions. It's ironic that all the best stories are stories about crisis. Who wants to hear about a K2 ascent when the weather and snow conditions were perfect? Well, I wasn't making smart choices and this story is about to get a lot more interesting.

Almerimar appeared to be a quiet backwater with very little action and very few boats. Still, this was just up the coast from Gibraltar, across the straits from Morocco. Huge traffic in illegal substances came out of there, and probably still does. Even though I knew the risk, our profile was polar opposite to the local smugglers, and I had no intention to get involved in their traffic.

Soon after we arrived Arianna and I were having one of those wonderful Spanish breakfasts in the bar: Café con leche, pan con tomate, and a slice of Spanish tortilla, that lovely, baked, potato omelet. As usual, the place was nearly empty, just ourselves and a marinero at the bar having a carajillo, an espresso with brandy.

A short guy with a pot belly, maybe fifty years old, came in with a tall, thin, fair woman, in her early forties, and sat at a table near us. After obviously checking us out, he came over to ask if they could join us.

Paul was a Russian immigrant who left the Soviet Union in the early eighties, and his wife, Annie, was Belgian. They had a sailing boat in the boatyard. Both spoke perfect English.

They were curious about where we came from. We were vaguely honest. I sure as hell didn't tell them we sailed from Thailand with only two stops. Our LPL included that we met and fell in love in Kenya, and cruised the Indian Ocean, with emphasis on Kenya.

Paul asked if we stopped in Thailand. He homed right in on it. They had apparently visited both Thailand and Africa. This was not a straight cruising couple. They were players, but in what game? I wasn't foolish enough to think we were the only ones hiding in plain sight. They didn't feel like cops, but we couldn't feed them total bullshit either. They were way too sophisticated.

I was an experienced player and Arianna hadn't just fallen off the farm truck. This wasn't Thailand, where everyone was an outlaw and played by the rules. We were in Europe, on a hot coast, where not everything was what it seemed, where no one could be trusted. Making friends could be very dangerous. On the other hand, we needed information, intelligence.

We had legal visas, and for the moment we were not under suspicion, at least I didn't think so. I had learned from years of smuggling that the key to survival is to stick to the LPL, stick to the Latest Pack of Lies. The riddle was how to get rid of our cargo, whilst maintaining our LPL. I needed to get this place wired without attracting attention.

It was almost Christmas, most of the boat owners weren't here full time, and very few people were in the marina. This was a good time for us to travel. Almerimar Marina is a small, very well protected harbor. Even a bad storm wouldn't pose any threat to the safety of the boats moored to the floating docks. The boat was in plain view of the officina and the staff would notice anyone jumping on board.

I wasn't at all concerned about someone stealing our cargo. First of all, no one knew about our cargo, and to find it someone would have to break in and literally tear the boat apart.

CHAPTER 29

The Dutch Connection

WE DECIDED TO go to the Netherlands to meet with Jack's lieutenant, Aloysius. So we caught a cheap flight to Hamburg, then a train to a small town in Holland, just past the German frontier, and walked to Jack's bar.

I remember getting off the train with Arianna and hiking into the old town center from the station, bags slung over our shoulders. We wandered down the narrow streets and cobblestone sidewalks, searching for the address, passing few buildings newer than one hundred years.

Eventually we found our address. After we walked through the door, it took us a few moments until we could see again, and found ourselves in a bar where working class men came to drink and smoke weed--a rough looking crowd. We sure as hell didn't fit in. Arianna was the only female present (and usually was, during our many visits afterwards). However, we didn't feel uncomfortable in any way, even though it was one of those bars where as soon as you walk in you have to decide whether to just turn around and walk out, or save face, have a drink, and *then* walk out.

The bartender, who we met in Thailand during the three-day party on *Sara*, recognized us immediately, gave us a beer, and called Aloysius at home, who told us that Jack was still in Thailand. He eventually showed up and drove us to his comfortable two-story house on the edge of town. It had been nearly a year since we last saw Aloysius and his wife, Ilse, who had stayed in the aft cabin on *Sara* together, and they were happy to see us.

Part of the smuggler's lifestyle included staying with the dealers. It was important (for all kinds of reasons) that I knew what my retailers were up to. Staying at their homes cut through the bullshit. I could see who they really were. Aloysius and Ilse were definitely not members of the cocaine snorting, gold-chain wearing crowd, but Ilse did have some pretensions for the fast lane. She favored tight, leopard-print dresses, spike heels, and starved herself skinny. On the other hand, Aloysius was quite the middle-class bar manager, a bit over weight from drinking beer and smoking hash. A sweet guy, actually. Turned out Ilse was expecting a child--they were definitely headed for the middle-class.

We had a lot to discuss. I had planned to sail *Sara* right up to their front door, where I could drop my cargo easy as a bale of hay, and that's what they expected too. Instead, I asked if they had any connections who could bring the weed up from Spain.

Aloysius said he sold hash to some British guys that smuggled it into England. "I wait them to pick up some Moroccan from the bar, maybe tomorrow. It is possible they have interest in doing this."

"Good, because I can make arrangements to sell this weed in Spain." I did, in fact, have a contact that I intended to call, even though I didn't really want to do business in Spain with someone I didn't know. Too risky. But no sense in letting Aloysius become too comfortable.

Aloysius and Ilse treated us as family members, sharing meals and walks with the dog. Really generous, considering Ilse was six months pregnant. They went out of their way to welcome us into their home and I think they genuinely enjoyed us staying.

The next day the English blokes showed up, just as Aloysius said they might. Charles and Ronald were a couple of tough, white villains in their early thirties from Cardiff, Wales. Smugglers from the United Kingdom were mostly thugs, as opposed to your basic hippy smugglers in the States. These two were actually proud of having done time in jail. I wasn't overly pleased with their attitude, but they were polite enough, smart, and interested in doing the transport from Spain. They had a camper van with hidden compartments and a young couple to drive it.

The catch was, they wanted a *lot* of money for the job. It was the kind of job that I could organize. I knew a lot about secret compartments for eluding searches, but I didn't have the infrastructure, the money, nor the time to organize and do the work.

I told Aloysius that as far as paying these guys goes, I knew how much money I wanted, and it was up to him to broker a deal that Jack could live with. If he couldn't afford them, then I would figure something else out. I was sure that Aloysius was worried Jack would be furious to lose the weed that he had personally picked out, the weed that would elevate his status to that of a smuggler.

The Welsh boys seemed our best prospect. They knew what they were doing, and had all the pieces ready to go. I figured, since I wasn't going to have to work with these "Jack the Lads," aside from passing the cargo over, their attitude wasn't going to be my problem.

What the hell was I thinking? If Aloysius and Jack decided to work with them, of course their attitude would become my problem. Not a problem for Aloysius or Jack--my problem.

In spite of my reservations about the Welsh lads, I didn't want the hassle of making new contacts in Spain, and the risks associated with opening that door. I was anxious to be done with the project. Every time we came around a corner we found another difficult roadblock. Over and over it was roadblocks. Every solution to a roadblock created more roadblocks. The voyage was harder than I had any idea it would ever be, and we were way off course from the original plan.

We left the Netherlands hoping Jack would pay Charles and Ronald to pick up the load.

CHAPTER 30

New Year's Eve in London

BEFORE WE LEFT Almeria, bound for the Netherlands, we had called Fiona at The Portobello, and she invited us to the hotel party they threw every year for their favoured guests. An exclusive holiday event, from Christmas to New Year's Day, tab on the house, including (Fiona ordered,) fancy dress for the New Year's Eve bash.

So we caught a train to Calais, a ferry to Dover, a train to London, and the Underground to Fiona and David's flat. In the span of two days we went from the Netherlands to a fancy room at The Portobello Hotel. We had traveled a long way to attend a famous party, and we were not about to miss it.

Christmas Eve afternoon found us shopping for presents in the renowned Portobello Market--a number of city blocks filled with small specialty stores--a little village in the middle of the city. One tiny store only sold cookbooks. Another was brimming over with clever toys. The streets were crowded with stalls. Stalls after stalls, selling every fruit, vegetable, and flower known to man. I ducked into a likely hole-in-the-wall boutique, and bought Arianna a wool minidress that would look great on her. Of course, Arianna would look fabulous in a plastic sack.

Christmas day in London was predictably cold and snowy, but Arianna and I were quite cozy in the hotel, which remained closed to all but Fiona, David, and their rock and roll guests. We all shared a bottle of Bollinger during a fruit and yogurt breakfast, and exchanged the delightful little gifts we had found in the Portobello Market the day before.

The Portobello kitchen and bar was open all the time, since most of the guests were artists and musicians who kept late hours. The entrées were all pre-prepared and served up by the bartender, or, if it was busy, you could get your own. Fiona had stocked the kitchen, and the cook prepared an assortment of the usual meals before the staff left for the holiday.

After all we had been through, living in a luxury London hotel was just magical. We spent our days going to films, doing a lot of window shopping, and having a lot of fun.

One day we took a train up to Mersea, in Essex, to meet Don Pye, the marine architect who designed our boat. We drank tea in his loft, and thanked him for our lives. He was eager to hear how *Sara* behaved in those monstrous seas. "You know," he said, "no one ever comes back to tell us these things. I always thought the Bowman Corsair was one of our best designs."

We also took advantage of being in London, one of the most well-stocked cities in the world, to buy the rigging and engine parts we needed. Going to the yacht supply stores in London was a real treat after needing to scrounge makeshift parts in Djibouti, and even in Malta.

As the New Year approached, guests started to show up for the New Year's Eve celebration, it was time to take down the Christmas tree and get busy decorating. The day of the party Fiona, Arianna, and I went to Portobello Road to buy armloads of flowers, and fresh-baked bread for the hors d'oeuvres. I was put in charge of the Champagne. The hotel only served Bollinger, so I put three crates into the walk-in and another crate on ice. Sebastian, a sailor friend from Kenya, came up from the coast to help prepare the festivities, and immediately fell in love with Fiona. No big deal, everybody falls for Fifi.

This was a costume ball, but in England they call it fancy dress, which I thought meant formal wear. So, when Arianna started putting together a costume I realized my mistake and thought, *SHIT!* Fortunately, I never go anywhere without my pocket face painting kit, and I ran back to the Portobello Road to find a little, funky, used-clothing shop where I purchased a purple silk vest and bowtie.

Arianna and I sipped Champagne and added the finishing touches to our costumes. I painted an ornate, psychedelic mask over my eyes that matched my bow tie. Arianna went as a devil. She wore a red suit that a young Dutch designer had made for her, red pants, and a matching red jacket with tails. She sported a pair of cheap, plastic, red horns, and I painted a thin, sexy, venetian-style mask to frame her dark, striking eyes. We rode the rickety elevator down to the bar and joined the party.

By now the hotel was full. A lot of music-industry people flew in for the gathering, mostly studio musicians. Lots of London musicians, artists, and friends of the hotel stopped by as well. The hotel staff--the maids who changed the sheets, and men who scrubbed the toilets--were all young artists and musicians, and they were also invited and came. The bartender who could often be found playing the sax behind the bar when the morning sun rose and the crowd thinned showed up with a stunning fashion model.

It was a rarified and uninhibited crowd. The music was eclectic and loud. The Champagne flowed. Arianna and I danced and kissed, and kissed and danced, far into the New Year. For the two of us, this all coalesced into a celebration of our entire voyage. As it turned out, however, it was premature to be celebrating.

Two days later we caught a cheap charter flight back to Almeria. When I called Aloysius from Gatwick he told me the boys from Wales would drive to Spain in a few weeks. Meanwhile, I was considering not using them. I wasn't sure I felt good about what I had set up: I wouldn't have any control once I turned over the cargo, and I was taking a *lot* on Aloysius's word. Arianna must have read my mind, because as we fastened our seat belts she said, "It will be good to be back on *Sara*, but the rest of it is going to be a bit dodgy."

From the airport in Almeria it took forever to get to the boat. Three buses, some hitchhiking, a lot of walking later, and we were back to the boat. I wondered how in hell the tourists got from the airport to the various crap resort towns barely surviving along the coast.

However comfortable it felt to get back home, we were back to living on a razor's edge. We had a load of weed onboard we needed to unload, and it had to be done carefully. Whatever danger lurked around the next corner stalked us from out of sight, like a leopard in the trees.

On top of it all, we faced a major, unexpected boat problem. Our first morning back I tried to start the engine, but the starter motor couldn't budge anything. I jumped below, opened the engine room, grabbed a wrench, and removed the keeper bolts on an injector. When I pulled the injector, oily salt water sprayed in my face. Bad luck that salt water had leaked into the engine when I shut it down before we left, because it had been corroding the engine for the whole two and a half weeks we were gone. Now the rings were rusted to the cylinder walls, and we needed to pull the engine out.

This was, however, a good excuse to move into the boatyard where it was safer to unload the cargo off the boat. I have always liked the plan of unloading in boatyards while hiding in plain sight. There's always a lot of stuff coming off and on boats in the yard: sails, equipment, cargo, even engines. Plus, you can pull a vehicle right up to the boat--handy for obvious reasons.

CHAPTER 31

Now Starts the Game

THE NEXT DAY we were having a Spanish breakfast with our new "friends," Paul and Annie, when they became very open about whom they really were. He had been in the KGB, the Russian security service. Normally I would have been skeptical of such a claim, but somehow it rang true. He spoke perfect English, Spanish, and his French seemed just as proficient. He was incredibly knowledgeable, on almost any subject, and was very well traveled. The wall was down, Gorbachev was in, and the Russians were just now getting out into the world, but Paul's knowledge was definitely first-hand from years of travel.

One little incident really convinced me that he had been some kind of intelligence agent. I was at the payphone near the bar, calling a contact, a German weed dealer in Garrucha, on the coast north of Almeria. When I dialed, the call didn't get through, and I muttered, "Shit! Now I have to look up the number again."

Paul came over from where he had been standing at the bar, and said, "950.732.4475."

It was frightening to realize he had watched me dial from the other end of the bar, *and* memorized the number! In that moment, I was convinced, in no uncertain terms, that he was just who he said he was... a well-trained, runaway spy.

Even though he didn't feel like police, it made me uneasy that I couldn't imagine what he stood to gain. For sure, he wanted *something*. I was concerned, but not worried--maybe he was the leopard in the trees, but I was not about to walk under his branch. Anyway, we weren't going to open any hidden compartments before we were ready to make a move. Until then, we were safe…ish.

I considered the strong possibility that Paul and Annie were also smugglers, and in a bind similar to ours. After all, it takes one to know one. Neither Arianna nor I were all that pleased to be working with Charles and Ronald, the boys from Wales. Even if Paul and Annie seemed iffy, at least they were sailors, and maybe they had contacts we could use. I considered opening up to them, but it's always a mistake to hope someone else will solve your problems for you. No. That's how you get caught.

We had a third option. It was time to take a sample of our weed to Garrucha.

We chose to travel by bus, because I didn't want this German dealer to know anything about the boat, or us, until I looked him in the eye and got a feel for him. After all we had overcome, I was determined not to screw this up. Every decision now could lead to fatal consequences. Even taking a little weed to Garrucha was dangerous. If the Guardia Civil were stopping busses, looking for narcotics on this coast, and if they somehow figured out we were on a boat… we would be seriously fucked.

By distancing ourselves from *Saga*, we could get the information we needed about the weed market in Spain and Europe, without risking our cargo. I even caught myself fantasizing, *Maybe this guy will buy it all and we'll be done… Come on, Ranen, await the unfolding of events.*

These were the kind of nagging issues running through my head for the many hours we sat on the bus to Garrucha, watching the desert pass by, where Sergio Leone filmed the spaghetti westerns a dozen years ago. Where was Clint Eastwood now that I needed him?

We were feeling the pressure of opening the show in Garrucha, and meeting some unknown Euro drug dealer, but long experiences at sea had trained us to stay calm under pressure. It was essential to our LPL that we projected the image of calm, fun-loving tourists.

The bus stopped at a café in Garrucha, where I dialed Kurt, and he showed up twenty minutes later in a high-profile, late-model BMW 7-series sedan. Kurt was a tall, dark, good looking guy in his early thirties, accompanied by Ulrica, a striking, leggy, young woman with long blonde hair. He was well dressed in loose-fitting, cotton trousers (probably custom made from India), a hand-woven, Guatemalan shirt, and Birkenstock sandals. She wore a dark blue sarong, white cotton blouse, and Birkenstocks. Both looked hip, wealthy, and not too flashy, except for the car. *Euro-dealer chic,* I thought.

We introduced ourselves without surnames (no last names in this business). "Our house is not far, in Mojácar," he said, placing our bags in the trunk, "We can have some lunch and get to know each other." He actually held the door for Arianna.

As I climbed in, I could swear I caught a glimpse of Paul and Annie driving by. But I dismissed the sighting as impossible.

After a short drive, we crossed a river into Mojácar, a whitewashed, mountainside village overlooking the blue Mediterranean Sea.

Kurt made a snap decision to pull over at a market for a loaf of fresh bread, and I saw them again: Paul and Annie drove past! This time I had no doubt, I saw them clearly.

Okay, now I was paranoid. There's a saying Joseph Heller coined in *Catch-22*, "Just because you're paranoid, doesn't mean they aren't after you."

I had said something to Paul and Annie about visiting some friends in Garrucha, and they had offered to drive us there, but we refused. So why in the hell would they follow us here?

I compartmentalized Paul and Annie. I put them in a box and pushed the box aside. It was another puzzle to put together, and I needed to be in the moment.

Kurt and Ulrica had a new, four-bedroom house with a seven-foot-high, whitewashed stone wall enclosing the yard. We talked a bit about the Swiss friends we had in common, who I met in Sri Lanka, and he knew from India. They told him I might look him up when I got to Spain. Identity verification out of the way, we all relaxed. I pulled the weed from my pack, and he loaded a large, sticky bud into a pipe from India, called a chillum. We all got sufficiently high, passing the pipe in silence, and afterwards we began to really talk.

Didn't take long to realize Kurt was a real narcissist. An intellectual bully. He lectured us about his way of life, informing us of his Buddhist ways, and kind of bragging about it. Who brags about being a Buddhist? Why did we need to know that Kurt insisted it was against their Buddhist practice for Ulrica to use tampons? He wasn't entirely obvious, he did talk about other things, but the real Kurt showed himself bit by bit, like his pride for maintaining total control over his girlfriend. I was there to make a judgment call, and he was looking arrogant and over confident--potentially dangerous attributes in a law breaker.

I was noticing red flags here, but we had come all this way and I needed more time to sort out my feelings. Kurt came with good references from experienced and reliable people, and I owed it to both myself and Kurt to think this through. Just because Kurt was a bit of arrogant dandy didn't mean he couldn't do the job. So Kurt and I continued to feel each other out.

We discussed where we could make the cargo transfer, and even took a drive back to Garrucha to study the harbor. It might have been an okay place to unload, but not near as good as Almerimar. The Garrucha marina was way more visible, overlooked by the whole town.

Another problem: the harbor was just a few minutes from Kurt's little village. Dealers know too many people. It's never a good idea to let the dealer get too close to the boat. Best they don't even know where the boat is.

The advantage of being a smuggler, is that the smuggler is at the top of the food chain. There are only two times a smuggler is in danger, during loading and unloading. Contact is usually with one person, or team, on each end of the voyage. Dealers, on the other hand, have to maintain contact with a broad network of people. Being too close to the dealer makes it easy for the authorities to connect the dots back to you.

When the smuggler drops his cargo it creates ripples in the pond of the local economy. By the time the law detects the ripples, and starts tracing them to the source, the smuggler better be long gone. I am the smuggler who is not only long gone, but I never come back. I never return. A ghost.

All smugglers, at some time or another, for one reason or another, end up having to sell their own cargo. Every smuggler has to have the ability to do the dealer's job, but, on the other hand, very few dealers posses the wild assortment of skills that smuggling requires. So, even though I wanted to be in the wind before the cargo hit ground, I wasn't about to admit that to Kurt. As long as he feared I might sell the weed myself, I held the upper hand. He wouldn't jerk me around, for fear I would disappear with my cargo.

The following day Arianna and I grabbed a bus back to Almeria, then another to Almerimar, and spent those hours discussing the Germans. We decided not to pursue that connection, we just didn't know enough about Kurt, and neither of us felt comfortable about them.

Option three was off the table.

CHAPTER 32

Pebble in the Pond

THE NEXT ITEM on the agenda was a serious talk with our "friends" Paul and Annie. This needed to be handled carefully. We didn't need enemies, especially smart enemies.

They stopped by the next morning, behaving as if nothing had occurred, so I remained friendly, but I cut to the chase, "So why are you following us around the country? I know you saw me see you in Garrucha. What do you guys want?"

"We just felt like going for a drive," Paul started, but a quick look in my eyes changed his tune. "When you said you had friends in Garrucha we decided to go up there. Look, we have some hash and we need to sell it. Our contact fell through. Here is some for you to smoke," and he slipped me a chunk that resembled a small, light-brown bar of soap.

Without saying it directly, he was declaring that he knew we were smuggling. But he just *thought* he knew. He didn't actually know anything. My inclination was to neither confirm nor deny, and see where he would go with it. For the time being, he let the conversation rest, and once he was out of sight I tossed that chunk of hash into the sea.

The boys from Wales were still our best option, so we passed on the message to Aloysius that we were ready to unload. It would still be a couple weeks before they started driving the camper our direction. Time for us to get organized.

Meanwhile, we met an older couple that lived on a wooden, fifty-foot, 1940's-vintage English motor vessel. Nigel was a retired British Navy engineer, who was sixty-eight, and Mary was probably a bit younger.

We both enjoyed their company, sitting in their enclosed cockpit, having a beer while he told stories about being a ship engineer during WWII. After hearing about our voyages, he offered to rebuild my engine if I would do the heavy lifting. He wasn't just being nice, he was an engineer, and he actually wanted to do it.

When I showed him the engine, he quickly saw the reason it flooded when we shut it down. The siphon break wasn't functioning properly because it was too close to the waterline.

"Let's get her towed over to boatyard quay and get Antonio to pull that Perkins out with the crane," he said. "I know those Perkins. The Royal Navy used an older model on their lifeboats. This'll be fun. You better start scouting around for parts and gaskets. We might as well put in new rings and bearings. We can get a local machine shop to resurface the head. Might need new valves, but we'll see when it's all apart. Better talk to Antonio and get it organized. I'll help ya' tow it over."

Nigel and Mary were such a pleasure to spend time with. No need for lies, or fishing for who they really were. These two had both feet planted firmly in reality, and were a refreshing change of company.

The next day we tied alongside the boatyard stone wharf. Paul and Annie were the only other people living aboard their boat in the yard, out of the water. We seemed to be stuck with them.

A few days after we moved into the neighborhood Paul showed me the hidden compartment where he kept his cargo of "chocolaté." I am sure he expected me to reciprocate, but I never showed anybody my secret compartments. I never considered it. Furthermore, I still wasn't ready to admit to him that we were smuggling. However, Paul and Annie worked hard to earn our trust, and we both came to enjoy their company. Even the ever-reticent Arianna warmed to them.

It's easy to look back and see my mistakes, but the fact is I began to trust Paul and Annie... just a little. I had my reasons. They were smugglers in a similar situation to ours. With careful management, I figured they could be useful. It's easy to see my mistake in hindsight, but at the time it wasn't easy to sort out and measure all the characters.

They had a car and gave us rides to markets in the next town. We went for day trips down to Malaga to shop, explore bars and wonderful, dark restaurants that hung cured hams from ancient, smoky rafters. The winter days were chilly, but those bars and restaurants were warm and snug.

Around a table littered with plates of cured *jamón*, little tapa dishes, and empty Jerez glasses, Paul opened up about when he was busted on an Interpol warrant. He got caught pulling an extracurricular con while working for the KGB in Africa. Using his diplomatic passport he convinced Indian businessmen he could get their currency out of Africa in a diplomatic bag, and into a Swiss bank. The "bank" was a telephone in a Zurich apartment where Paul's co-conspirator played bank official when the "clients" called to check on their accounts. For that scam he did some time in a Spanish prison. As I said, Paul and Annie were sleazy, and I was not surprised at their lack of morals--however, in a lifetime of smuggling, they weren't the worst people with whom I've done business.

Meanwhile, I called Aloysius daily from a pay booth at the phone company, on the main highway running through El Ejido. Paul and Annie were helpful: waiting patiently and politely asking no questions. I'd like to say they entertained Arianna, joking and laughing in the car while I made my call, but Paul's Russian sense of humor was dry and sarcastic, at best, and Annie had no sense of humor at all. I honestly don't know what Paul saw in that woman. She was like somebody's grandmother.

One day, after three weeks of phone calls, Aloysius finally said Charles would meet us, the next day, at the bar in the marina.

We met Charles for an early breakfast, long before Paul and Annie would get up. He told us a small camper van, driven by a young British couple with a baby, were ready to pick up the first half of our cargo. I pointed out where they should park and set a time for early the next day.

Now it was all happening. We were at the smuggler's danger point. The contraband was about to be exposed to the light and us with it.

Arianna and I were too wired to sleep, so we made love, which calmed us down enough to fall into a restless doze.

Before first light I carefully pried the trim from the aft cabin bulk-head, revealing and then removing a line of almost invisible screws. Next, I used a thin tool (I had made just for this task) to jimmy the teak wall away from the hidden storage bin. Shannon, my genius boat-builder friend, constructed this compartment to be impossible to see, and nearly impossible to open.

Using the tool on one edge, and applying upward pressure with my free hand, I wiggled the teak wall until it separated, bit by bit, from what appeared to be a solid bulkhead. After painstakingly shimmying the wall the rest of the way up, and just a little to the left, I could fully access the bulkhead. It looked and felt solid, but if you knew where to find the invisible joint, and knew where to push, the entire wall came loose.

When the epoxy-impregnated plywood compartment opened, the sweet, overpowering smell of honey wafted into the aft cabin. Shannon had built this, and other compartments, to be completely smell proof and waterproof. No policeman or policeman's dog was going to find this.

Gods bless you Shannon, I thought, removing seven bees-wax encapsulated packages. Half the cargo. Arianna stuffed them into three sail bags while I carefully re-assembled the compartment.

"Okay, we're ready."

Arianna said nothing, just nodded.

We shared coffee and toast in the cockpit, and started the chores you do when you're about to put your boat on land in a dirty boatyard--clear the deck, and pile the sail bags off the boat.

Around 8:00 a.m. an English camper van (a well-used but well-maintained Austin, or something similar) pulled up next to the sail bags. A neat-looking, working-class young man emerged from the driver's seat, opened the side-panel door, and climbed in.

An attractive, plain, but attractive young woman held her baby, and I chatted with her while the father opened a storage compartment under their bed, and Arianna emptied the sail bags into it. I always kept a small perfume bottle filled with wolf piss onboard, for just this situation, and Arianna neatly sprinkled a few drops into the carpet before she was done.

All the while, I continued chatting with the couple, relaxed, but constantly scoping out the yard. Arianna and I both waved goodbye when they drove off.

I hadn't seen anyone... until half an hour after the van left, when an older, retiree-looking guy walked by. The boat he was walking away from was a vintage wooden power boat I had seen around the yard, but had never seen the owner. His profile fit the type of boat. His presence seemed ordinary and harmless, but after a lifetime of smuggling, his presence still makes me wonder, what if he was the real reason everything went to shit...?

The next morning Paul and Annie took us to Roquetas De Mar, a nearby resort town, and I bought Arianna a charter-flight ticket to Hamburg, leaving that afternoon. One of us needed to be there, in Holland, to weigh the weed when it arrived. The four of us ate a huge seafood lunch with lots of Spanish white Rioja wine, and afterword Arianna caught the Almeria airport bus, just like any other tourist.

It was strange coming back to the boat without Arianna. There was more than enough work to keep me busy, but I couldn't stop thinking about Arianna, and whether or not the weed made it through French border inspections. French customs were some of the most relentless police in the world.

Charles dropped by the day after the load left, and somehow Paul had forced an introduction. He was persistent. They immediately bonded, a perfect match, a couple of shady, long lost brothers.

Charles told me, right in front of Paul, that the camper had been stopped by the French border patrol, a hundred miles past the border. *I guess I can't care anymore if Paul and Annie know what's going down. Charles just told him everything.* I had a rush of anger, but shrugged it off.

Charles went on to say that when the police dog got in the van, he immediately lifted his leg, peed right where Arianna had dropped the wolf piss, and then jumped right out. Any domestic dog that smells the presence of *canine superior* just wants to be somewhere else, anywhere else. Thanks to my wolf piss, our cargo was safely past the worst checkpoint. Score one for us!

I waited another day to call Arianna. She confirmed the weed had arrived, been weighed, and she had received the first payment. She was staying with Aloysius and Ilse. They were expecting the child in three months, and Arianna bought them a teddy bear.

The next morning would find her leaving for London, to stay with Fiona and David. We both said goodbye, and hung up.

The next evening found me in a Spanish jail!

PART 7 – Prison, 1989

CHAPTER 33

Winning the Battle with Fear

LET'S TALK ABOUT real stress.

I was under arrest in a country whose language I didn't speak.

A country with no civil rights.

No one I trusted knew that I was in prison.

Before first light of the next day filtered through the tiny, barred window in the cell door of the police station lock-up, my panic-fueled mind had worked over the whole unreal, nightmare scenario, time after time.

That's what I can say about stress. It is no substitute for sleep.

Not until sometime early that morning, after a guard brought in a café con leché, and fresh bread and butter, did my head clear, and my manic thinking slow. I was in a remote mountain village, locked in an old, stone jail that had only one large cell big enough to house seven men.

Soon after breakfast, a state appointed lawyer came to see me. The guard let him into the cell, and he actually sat on a bench to talk to me... and he spoke English.

He told me I would see a judge that day. The Guardia found 150 grams of weed, and 100 grams was the legal amount for a personal stash, so there was a good chance the judge would let me go. It was good news, but that small amount of weed was not what fueled my panic.

I didn't think they would seize my boat or send me to prison for that. Throw me out of the country with a stiff fine, maybe. What worried me most was that marijuana was not a common drug in this area.

Almeria was so close to the hashish capital of Morocco that virtually no one smoked weed.

I was seriously worried the Guardia would wonder, *How did this American happen to be in possession of an exotic drug?*

Or worse, maybe they already thought they knew. Some places in the world, when the law thinks they know what you've done, they don't even need proof to begin processing you. They can always do that later.

I sincerely hoped my LPL would explain away any suspicions. I needed to convince the powers that be they didn't have any reason to keep me and seize my boat, or go back to it at all.

Lunch arrived. Must have been from the local bar--two sandwiches of *manchego* goat cheese and fresh-sliced tomato on super-fresh, hard-crusted bread. I ate the last of it while being guided over to the courthouse, another ancient, stone building that reeked of fear. I wondered, stepping through the arches, if Inquisition victims were brought here for trial, long before Franco condemned republicans here in the Spanish Civil War.

When I was called up to the bench I saw the judge looking at my passport, clearly issued from Miami.

I knew at that moment I was truly fucked. *Miami Vice* was the most popular show in Spain at that time.

Immediately, he asked in broken English if I was from Miami.

"No. That's just where the passport was issued from," I replied to the woman who translated to the judge.

The judge sized me up, and told me "unusually strong" drugs were found on the boat.

This was a backwoods, mountain town. The judge was in his early fifties, and anything but sophisticated. The Guardia Civil knew exactly what they were doing when they brought me all the way up to the mountains. If they had brought me to the nearby city of Almeria my case would have probably been thrown out by a judge with more pressing problems than 150 grams of weed.

I slowly related my carefully-crafted story to the translator. I told her my girlfriend and I were sailing around the world, and that we had visited Barcelona, where I bought the marijuana from some person on the street. I had no idea how much was in the bag, nor any idea what the legal amount was.

As soon as I finished my statement, and listened to the end of her rapid translation, I clearly realized that this woman hadn't actually spoken any English back to me. Only Spanish from her to the judge, and then broken English from the judge to me. I didn't even know if she could really speak English.

The Judge struggled to find the right words to communicate that the Guardia Civil had confidential information he couldn't reveal. There was more to this than what they had found. I asked myself, *What the hell does that mean? Paul and Annie?*

He committed me to stand trial in Almeria at an undetermined date.

Shit! Not good!

I was walked back to the jail to await transportation to another jail. Exhausted and sick with worry, I remember thinking, *Well, half the evidence is already in Holland, and Arianna is safe in England, which has no extradition with Spain. Spain is where English crooks come to hide out.*

The jail truck drove south, through miles of hydroponic greenhouses, to deliver everyone from the jail in Berja to a big, new concrete prison sitting on a hill overlooking the sea. This was no jail, but a proper prison. My situation was getting worse.

Thank the Gods I had picked up a tiny bit of Spanish in my life. I knew the days of the week, the months, how to count, about twenty verbs (all in present tense), and probably another hundred assorted words. None of this helped much for understanding what anyone was saying, unless they happened to use those words I knew and were willing to speak slow enough for me to understand. One of the first phrases I learned to say was "ablas más despacio," speak more slowly.

I also knew enough to ask questions, and I knew how to ask, "How do you say in Spanish...?"

The guard who brought me to my cell somehow communicated that I would be in a private cell for two days until I was assigned to a regular part of the prison, "celda de la cárcel temporal." I was okay with a couple of days to get used to being here.

The private cell was unpainted concrete for all surfaces, with a polished floor. An industrial bed was bolted against the far wall, with a plastic-covered, hard mattress that felt like a cheap futon. Clean, rough sheets, a pillow, a clean pillow case, and two wool blankets were stacked on the bed. A modern toilet and roll of toilet paper were in the corner next to a sink, where a bar of soap sat and a short towel hung. A bucket and mop were stored under a concrete shelf. Besides the overhead light, there was a barred window to outside, and a small window in the steel door that closed from the outside.

All in all, it was surprisingly comfortable for a prison cell. I didn't leave that cell once for the next two days. All there was to do was read from a stack of *Holá* magazines, basically *People* magazine in Spanish.

When they transferred me to my new "home," the guard led me to a different wing of the prison while I carried my sheets, pillow, blankets, and towel.

We passed through a barred gate into a corridor about two hundred feet long with cell doors along both sides. About halfway down he stopped and knocked on a closed, steel door, then opened it and walked off.

There was a guy lying on one of the beds, reading a magazine. A tall, dark, twenty-something Arab-looking guy.

He got up, "I am Rafa."

"Olá, I am Ranen. You speak English?"

"I espeak a leettle Englis," he answered.

He spoke English! I felt a big rush of relief and my shoulders actually relaxed for the first time in days. When they arrested me I grabbed some money and my down vest, but no dictionary. Having a cellmate that spoke a "leettle Englis" was a big deal for all kinds of reasons.

For starters, he could teach me the rules, and who the players were in this place. Also, he could teach me Spanish.

"Why they put you here?" Rafa asked.

I told him I had a sailing boat and that the Guardia Civil found weed onboard. He immediately said, with great respect, "*Contrabandista!*" I didn't even know the Spanish word for smuggling, *contrabando,* which made me a *contrabandista.* That's when I got my first inkling of the class system in this prison.

Rafa said that it was 9:30 a.m. and time to go out on the yard, until lunch.

Blinking in the bright desert sunlight, we walked out onto a concrete courtyard the size of half a football field. One wall was an outside prison wall, one was a wall adjacent to another cell-block yard, the third was a wall of the administration building, and the last was our cell block wall with cell windows looking down on the yard.

There were maybe thirty or forty men in the yard, some bunched in groups just standing around talking, some purposefully walking laps, and some sitting against the wall facing the sun. The groups seemed to be segregated along ethnic lines. There were Catalans, Basques, Gitanos, Andalusians, and Moroccans.

Rafa joined some of his Moroccan friends and I took the opportunity to do some stretches and basic exercises, push-ups and sit-ups.

Soon after, everyone filed into the cafeteria for lunch.

Surprise! The food wasn't bad at all. There was a small loaf of crusty, fresh-baked bread, some kind of meat stew, a salad, and an apple. It turned out that everyone got a small bottle of beer at both lunch and dinner.

I was eating at a table with Rafa and the "Moros." I decided not to eat the meat or drink the beer in this place, for a number of reasons, so I gave my beer to a Basque at the next table. He gave me his orange.

After lunch Rafa showed me where I could buy things like toiletries, candy, soft drinks, chips, and magazines. I had seventy-five dollars in pesetas, plenty to buy a toothbrush, toothpaste, soap, and a razor. It wasn't a razor big enough to make a knife out of, and I guess they didn't give a shit if any prisoners decided to slit their own wrists.

The cells in our block were open in the late afternoon and some of Rafa's friends came by to smoke hash. They put together a bong made from a large plastic soda bottle, some foil from a cigarette pack, and a bucket of water.

So far, prison didn't seem too bad, except I couldn't leave. The food was actually pretty good (this was Spain after all), there was quite a bit of freedom within, and you could get whatever you wanted, if you could afford it.

I wasn't at all claustrophobic being locked up after months of endless, open ocean. Thing is, life on the boat was *more* confining. This place had a *lot* more space to walk around.

Obviously, despite the relative comforts, I was still incredibly stressed. In fact, over the first three days I spent incarcerated, the hair on my chest turned completely white. People tell me that's impossible, but I was there, and it happened. You want to talk about stress? That is stress!

From what I understood about Rafa's situation, who was also busted for a small amount of weed, it appeared that I couldn't be released until I came before a judge. Without a lawyer I wouldn't get a court appointment until the Guardia Civil arranged it, or dropped the charges, or they might just leave me here for their own reasons. The Berja judge indicated the Guardia Civil wanted to nail me, and even *he* didn't understand why. This was an inbetween time in Spain. It wasn't a dictatorship anymore and the new constitution was in the works, but the Guardia Civil still ran the Spanish criminal justice system.

During this first week I was constantly thinking, *What if? What if I couldn't get out?* What kept me in control was the suicide option.

Those first few nights after the arrest were much more stressful than any other nights in my life. I needed to get control of my thoughts because if I couldn't think clearly then I was "well and truly fucked." *So*, I thought, *this is bad but I can always kill myself if it gets any worse.*

The concept that there is always an ultimate way out gave me the ability to cope with the pressure of not having any control. Sure, I had been through situations more dangerous and even more stressful. Still, in those situations I had control, or at least had things I could do to get me out of trouble. This thing about being absolutely powerless was new to me. So, every time I started going down panic road I would think, *It's bad but is it bad enough? To kill myself? No?*

It all seemed hopeless because I was alone in a foreign prison, and the only people who knew I was inside were the very people who (I was pretty sure) put me here. How in the world was I going to find a lawyer? I needed to learn to speak Spanish... fast.

I became resolved to get on my game, to power up. I was trapped and I needed to deal with it.

First of all, I wanted a shower. I actually knew the word for it and walked up to the guard.

"Navigante, que pasa?" he asked. So I guess I had a new name, *Navigante*, Navigator. Not bad, kind of classy. I guess the whole prison already knew the details of my situation.

"Donde esta la ducha?" I asked for the showers.

He pointed.

I found a big deserted shower room, like the showers at my high school. The weather wasn't freezing, but it was February, and it was close to freezing. Of course there was no hot water. So I took a fast shower and felt a lot more human.

I came out on the yard afterward and my down vest was gone!

Something snapped in my brain. All the frustration--not just of being arrested--but all the frustration of the past months overpowered any self control I may have had.

I remember raving about thieves while rifling through everyone's jackets and possessions piled around the walls of the yard.

I found my vest in a pack and yanked it out in a rage.

Some guy grabbed me by the shoulder to turn me around, and I amped up the turn and used the energy to hit him square in the nose with my elbow.

The next thing I remember was that it took Rafa and two of this guy's friends to pull me off of him.

Rafa told me later that the first blow knocked him to the ground, I kicked him in the head over and over, and then tried to strangle him. Everyone thought it was a good thing that I was wearing sneakers or I would have surely killed him.

Poor guy, he paid for a lot of things that had nothing to do with him. I was so strong in those days. Maybe the guards thought he deserved it, because he went to the infirmary for two days but I never heard a thing from any *funcionarios* about it. Nothing. Like it never happened.

The next day the Basque terrorists gestured for me to join their table, and they, the *Vascos*, were at the top of the prisoner hierarchy. Maybe they liked me because I was not Spanish, like them, and I had proven to be someone who would not be pushed around. Maybe they liked that I gave them my beer at that first meal. Who knows why, but for the rest of my prison time the Basques were my allies.

Early in my residence, Marcel arrived on a transfer bus from the prison in Malaga. He was a stocky, thirty-year-old Dutch guy who was in for dealing cocaine down in Puerto Banús. Actually, he was a biker badass from Eindhoven, whose gang were the security and enforcers for some Dutch coke smugglers and dealers down on the South Coast. The Guardia busted the lot for twenty kilos of coke they found in their big villa. Marcel was looking at a lot of time as a guest of the Spanish government.

Like most Dutch, he spoke perfect English, French, and Spanish. Even better, he really knew the ins and outs of the crumbling Spanish legal system.

He asked me the question everyone in there asked, "What in the hell did *you* do to get put into *this* prison? Almeria is for serious criminals. This is where they put the fucking Basque terrorists!"

"That's a good question! I think they're pissed off they didn't find a big load when they searched my boat. Their dog wasn't even interested. I made them look like fools, and those fools have huge egos. I fucking hate cops. Now I'm in here, no court date, and no one knows I'm here."

"Yeah, well, the Green Hats aren't exactly my favorite either. I'm not on any court list, but I don't want to be. I'm hoping to get my case transferred to Holland before they convict me."

"So, do you have a lawyer? I know they don't have enough evidence to convict me of anything but a very small charge. But the thing is, I need the name of an attorney to call."

"Sorry man, but the guys I worked for are paying the lawyers, and those guys are all in jail down in Malaga. I've no idea why the Guardia transferred me up here, but I am hoping they have lost me in their fucked-up system.

"Things are disorganized in Spain now. When the new constitution goes into effect a lot of things are going to change, and they might let go of a lot of people whose rights have been violated."

Even if Marcel couldn't help me, it was good to have a person to talk to, and learn Spanish from. It must have been good for Marcel too, because one day we were walking out on the yard together and he tried to hold my hand.

I have never slapped a hand away so fast. I was not going to let these goons in the yard think he and I were lovers. I didn't care that Marcel was bisexual. He was part of the whole biker leather scene, as masculine as they come, not a guy you want to meet in a dark alley. I just didn't want anybody to get the wrong idea about me. Nevermind the fact that I'm heterosexual, I did not need that kind of attention, and in that situation everything needed to be crystal clear.

It was such a surreal moment that I almost didn't write it here. My whole life, from Haight-Ashbury to Salmon, Idaho, I've always had gay and bi friends, but I never get hit on by men. I asked a guy once, "What, am I not good enough looking for you?" He laughed at me, "You? Captain Ranen? The most ultra-heterosexual guy in the world?"

Every day that went by without hearing from the law meant they hadn't gone back to tear the boat apart, and, just maybe, they were starting to lose interest in my case.

The winter storms had moved in with strong, wind-driven rain. I had left my boat unlocked, and not-that-securely tied to the stone quay. It was a temporary mooring. *Saga* was supposed to come out of the water the day I was arrested.

I felt ill with worry when I thought about her, and I thought about her every time a gust of wind-driven rain hit the barred window of my cell. I kept reminding and reminding myself to stay in the moment, but I couldn't help myself, worry seemed to be my main mental exercise just now.

One stormy day a guard approached to tell me that I had a visitor.

When I finally found my way to the meeting room, I was caught off guard to find Annie waiting.

"It took us a long time to find out where they were holding you," she said. "I've brought you some clothes from your boat and an English/Spanish dictionary. We have found you a lawyer as well. He is going to look into your case and then he will come to see you. I called Arianna and told her that you were arrested. I also told her not to return here until you have talked to the lawyer."

"How did you know where to call her?"

"I got the number of the bar in Holland from Charles."

This was so strange. They were playing their game, pretending to be my friend. I needed them and they knew it, so we were pretending to trust each other. These con artists were clearly amoral, so who knows what their concept of friendship was? I think, friendship for amoral people is sharing common self-interests.

I sure as hell wasn't going to let them know I thought they had turned me in. "Listen Annie, thanks for your help here. What I am most worried about is the boat. Will you lock it up and hide the key under the water container on the deck, check the fenders and the mooring lines? Ask Paul to make sure the bilge pump is working? That would take a lot of worry off my mind."

I walked out of that visit feeling like a new person. The dictionary alone was golden. Now I could look up the words I needed, speeding up the process of learning Spanish. Annie hadn't said anything about the Guardia coming back to the boat. If that was the case, the lawyer would be able to get me out, based on what evidence they *actually* had.

I needed to get back on the boat now more than ever. The Guardia hadn't found the guns onboard. As much as I loved those weapons, they needed to go overboard. If the court knew about my arsenal, the judge would never believe that we were an innocent couple sailing around the world. Sawed-off shotgun, Ruger Mini-14 assault rifle, Colt .45 automatic pistol, and a S&W .38 Special… more weapons than people?

I was thinking that Paul and Annie hadn't ratted me out about the rest of my cargo, at least not yet. If they had, the Guardia would have returned to tear *Saga* apart. I was thinking my "friends" got what they needed by simply getting me out of the way so *they* could hook up with Charles to sell *their* cargo.

CHAPTER 34

El Banco del Fruita

MY NEW LIFE in Almeria prison carried on into the third week. Three twenty-year-olds arrived, real hippies, who begged me to translate the Pink Floyd album, *Wish You Were Here*, into Spanish. Getting it right was a challenge, especially these lines:

> You were caught on the crossfire of childhood and stardom,
> Blown on the steel breeze.
> Come on, you target for faraway laughter.
> Come on, you stranger, you legend, you martyr, and shine!

It was good for me to tackle a translation job that pushed me right up the Spanish learning curve.

These kids were just not criminals. They were in for selling hash and everyone knew they probably wouldn't be there long. A lot of prisoners were looking out for the hippies, and appreciated that I was helping them out. I guess they thought I was a good influence, being a rich smuggler with a sailing life. I was becoming a kind of favorite across the strata of the prison population.

How everyone knew so much about me still remains a mystery, it was as if everyone had read my court transcripts. Maybe the guards gossiped with the prisoners. I was the guy who got busted for smuggling marijuana while sailing around the world on a fancy yacht with his young girlfriend. This fantasy appealed to everyone, including hardened killers and terrorists.

It was during this third week that I started the Banco Del Fruita.

I was eating at the Basque table, and now Marcel was as well. I think those Basque separatists trusted us because we were *extranjeros*, foreigners. They were in prison because Spain refused to allow the Basques an autonomous province, and treated them as second-class citizens. Of course Spain wouldn't let the Basques go, because Pais de Vasco was the most productive region in the country. Franco saw the Basques as terrorists, so he tortured them, and refused them the use of their own language (which predated any living European language). The Basques saw themselves as freedom fighters in a civil war. There was a lot of bad history in this ancient conflict.

To the Basques, Marcel and I were fellow imprisoned foreigners. But, as far as I was concerned, they just liked me, and the fact that I gave them my beer at every meal.

One of the guys at the table, Izar, started giving me his vegetables and fruit when he noticed I didn't eat meat. Then, a lot of prisoners started giving me fruit at meals. Pretty soon I had most of the fruit in the cafeteria, and the guards let me take it back to my cell. I guess, because Spaniards are such carnivores, they thought I would starve without meat.

A few days later somebody down the hall of cells shouted out, "Navigante, tienes fruitas?" So I marched down to their cell to give them some oranges and apples. When I stepped in, they shut the door, and I thought, *Hold on, this might get weird!*

To my relief, they uncovered a stash of wine makings in a large bucket. I tasted some of their finished product, and it was damn strong. From then on I delivered half of all my fruit to the winery cell, and I became known as el Banco del Fruita.

Look, I am not saying there wasn't a dark side to that prison, there was. AIDS and Hepatitis were being passed around like Halloween candy. And there was violence.

One morning I awoke in the dark to a grinding noise, but didn't think much of it. When it was time to go to breakfast, Rafa wouldn't go. I gave him the *What's Up?* look. He said, "Listen. You don't hear it?" Once he called my attention to it, I recognized the noise: It was the signature sound of someone sharpening metal on a rough stone. Someone was making a knife. Even though I didn't think anyone was after me, that persistent grinding made me uneasy. No, it made me downright nervous.

Nevertheless, I went to eat, and the cafeteria had about a third of the normal *desayuno* crowd. It was the same at lunch. But that evening the cafeteria was full again, and there was a sense of relief in the air. Izar leaned over and quietly told me one of the AIDS junkies had gone to the hospital.

I never asked how all the contraband came into the prison. Every day packages would sail over the outside wall, and the shared wall to the next exercise yard. Only an idiot would touch one of those packages if it landed nearby. Some things probably came through from conjugal visits. I was careful to stay out of this prison gray area. The guards liked me and I wanted it to stay that way. I was always very polite towards them.

From the beginning, I did aerobics for thirty minutes every day, along with some fast laps around the yard. Some of the prisoners made some nasty comments about it, but I just ignored them, and as time went by they got used to my routine.

One day another prisoner took leave from his cadre of fellow Gypsies, and came over to join me. Carlos was a tall, very thin, very dark *Gitano*, with long, black, greasy hair.

We weren't friends. He would just show up at the same time each day. No talk. We really got into pushing each other, and the workouts became a lot harder. That skinny guy could outrun me every time, and we were up to fifty push-ups. He did tell me his name.

Once Carlos had joined my aerobics class no one would even look our way. The rumor was that he was convicted of four murders. Carlos had a scary presence, a kind of dark charisma. After a while, I asked what he was in for. "*Asesinato*," he replied... Murder. I couldn't resist asking what he used as a weapon.

His answer, "A knife is quiet."

CHAPTER 35

Crawling Out

ONE DAY IN the yard Marcel asked, "What's going on Navigante? You are usually pretty relaxed after your Gitano workout."

"Listen Marcel, the Green Hats only found a little weed on the boat, but there are a lot of things on that boat they didn't find. I really need to get out of here. I don't know why they haven't been back, but if they tear the boat apart, I will be in here for a looong time."

"Shit man! If you're saying what I think you are saying, you really *do* need to get out of here. What happened to the lawyer that your enemies hired? I wish I could help but I haven't heard from anyone. At least you have people on the outside. All of my guys are in jail, they're all in another prison. You're in a much better position than I'm in."

Louis, my lawyer, came for a visit that very afternoon. He was thirty-eight, just short of six feet tall, not in good shape, overweight but not obese. He was not a "slick" lawyer. In fact, he was just building his practice. He was perfect. I trusted him immediately and I was sure any judge would trust him too. There was just no guile or game in Louis Perez Galano. He even took a moment to tell me about his family. He had three children and one on the way. His only son Mauricio, or Maury, was the light of his life.

He told me up front that it was unusual for someone in my situation to be held in *this* prison, and, in fact, to be held at all. He confirmed that an informant had led the police to think that there was a lot more to this. The test report on my weed found that it was an "exceptionally strong type of marijuana." I chuckled to myself, *Well at least we know for sure we brought in some really good weed.*

This entire conversation was slow and difficult, because Louis spoke no English, and the translator he brought spoke worse English than my Spanish. Although I don't particularly recommend this method for acquiring a new language, my Spanish was improving quickly.

He brought the transcript of my testimony from my court appearance, and insisted that I read it before I said anything more about this case. Somehow, he made it clear that he wasn't willing to lie to the court. I guessed correctly that he wanted to base my defense on our being a young couple cruising around the world, who innocently bought a little too much marijuana.

He counseled me that although the Guardia Civil convinced the Berja judge they had good reason to believe there was more to my case, they didn't have any concrete evidence or they would have produced it by now. They had no witness willing to testify. The new constitution was going into effect soon, and all convictions would have to hold up to the new law. When we came before another judge, Louis assured me, the Guardia Civil wasn't going to get a conviction of possession-for-sales to stick on a *denuncia* and a small quantity of cannabis.

Louis said he would go to the judge to get me out on bail until the trial, and the boat would be enough security for bail.

There was one problem, he said. Arianna had to come back.

He was sure the judge would not understand why Arianna wouldn't come back, if we were what we said we were. Louis assured me there was no possibility that she could be arrested.

I gave him the number for the Portobello Hotel, and instructed him to pass a message to Fiona. He would have to track down Arianna in London.

CHAPTER 36

From Arianna's Journal

I had flown up to Germany, I took the train to Holland, and I stayed at Aloysius and Ilse's for a day before the weed arrived. Ilse was pregnant and really starting to show.

I was feeling nervous, full of adrenaline, but also a great sense of achievement. We had made it this far, so far so good. After all we had been through together, Ranen had always warned that the end is always the most tricky, most dangerous, the most exposed. Now it was up to Aloysius and company to go ahead with their part of the deal.

The camper came and they unloaded and weighed it without me there. Aloysius told me that he wouldn't start selling the weed until Jack got back from Thailand. This all seemed suspicious to me. I wondered what was really going on. I told myself not to be paranoid, but I was worried.

Then Annie called from Spain and said, "I have bad news. Ranen has been arrested. We have found him a lawyer and I don't think you should come back until you talk to him."

At first I didn't believe her. I thought she was joking. Then my heart sank, I was in shock, I was alone, and I didn't trust anyone. This was not at all what I was expecting.

I started asking questions. Why was Annie calling me? What did she and Paul have to do with this? How did she get this number? Kenny suddenly turns up in jail and now Paul and Annie are talking with our Dutch contacts? I was sure that they were somehow responsible. We never trusted those two.

Then Aloysius didn't want me at his house because he said the police might have followed me to Holland. He must have confirmed everything with Charles. I was all alone, in way over my head, and had no one to talk to. I was terrified to think that we were being ripped off and Ranen really was in jail.

There was nothing to do but leave for England. Fiona and David had invited me to stay with them in London, and I needed to get away from all these people in Holland. I was convinced they were trying to take advantage of my lack of experience. As much as I wanted to go to Spain to help Ranen, it made sense to take Annie's advice to talk to the lawyer first. All that mattered to me was getting Ranen out of prison, and it would not do to be imprisoned myself. I flew to London that day, still in shock, still unsure what to think, or who to believe.

I arrived at Fiona and David's apartment right off Shepherd's Bush. Those days of waiting to talk to Ranen, or his lawyer, I spent visiting the East West Center, trying to sort out my medical problems. The gynecologist in Singapore couldn't figure out why I had symptoms usually associated with women much older than I.

I found an M.D. at the Center who believed that eastern medicine sometimes offered better solutions than traditional western medicine. He was convinced our diet of tropical fruit and fish had thrown my body out of balance. He said that my symptoms, especially my skin problems, indicated that I was totally yin. Too much sugar. He put me on a strict macrobiotic diet. I was prepared to try anything and he seemed confident this would clear up all of my problems.

No coffee, tea, sweets, or anything fun, basically. Nothing but steamed veg, brown rice, and beans. Honestly, not a big problem, considering I was in London and only giving up English cuisine, arguably the worst in the world. The upside of my new clean-up diet was that I was distracted from twenty hours of worry every day. I think I was much calmer, not eating so much sugar.

Then one day Fiona came home from work to tell me "I got a call from some Spanish guy wanting to speak to you. His English was so bad I barely got his telephone number. He wants you to call tomorrow at nine I think. You can come with me and call from the hotel if you like."

I did call. The lawyer, Louis, had an interpreter to talk to me. Between the interpreter's bad English and my non-existent Spanish, Louis was able to tell me that he needed me to come back so I wouldn't look like I was hiding. This was what I wanted, to be near Ranen, so I immediately booked a flight.

Fiona did not like the idea of me returning, not at all. "Arianna, do not go back there. You have no idea if this guy you talked to is really Ranen's lawyer. How do you know it won't be the police waiting at the airport when you arrive? How can you believe any of these people? That woman Annie, who you think turned you lot in, is the one who hired this guy for fuck's sake!"

"Okay Fifi, there is some risk, but I reckon not as much as you think. Ranen must have trusted this guy. No one knows about you or the hotel but Ranen and me. Only Ranen could have given him the way to find me. But I have to say that I would go even if I didn't know that. I am getting on that plane and going back for Ranen and Sara, and that's all there is to it."

I arrived the next afternoon in Almeria and passed immigration with a crowd of British budget tourists, and I breezed through passport control. I could hear Fiona's warning whilst I scanned the crowd of tourists at the baggage claim, looking for whomever Louis sent to meet me. So far there were no obvious police, but I wasn't as good at this as was Ranen.

Finally, there was only myself and one man left. "Arianna Bell?" He asked.

"I am." I replied.

"Yo soy José, assistant to Louis, el abogado."

"Hello José, I believe I spoke to you on the telephone."

"You wish to go? Senior Perez Galano waits."

We drove into central Almeria to Louis's office in an older building, in a very old, but lovely, well-kept part of the city. We walked up to the second floor where Louis and his wife, Maria, met us at the door. After the introductions, Louis gave me a document and looked at José who said in halting English "first you read this."

The document, which was in English, was the transcript of what Ranen had said in court. He wanted me to know what Ranen had told the court, so we wouldn't contradict each other. Between Louis and José they got it across to me that they were going to get Ranen released.

Louis asked if I would like to visit Ranen at the prison! Of course, I said I would love that. Now, no matter what the danger, I was happy that I got on that plane.

When I asked if I could return to the boat, he put his wrists together as if they were handcuffed and said "Boat." Damn, the boat was impounded. Well, I had some ideas about that. I asked if he could get permission for me to go onboard to secure the boat. He thought for a moment and answered, "Si. Creo que si." I think yes.

I spent that first night with the Galano family. Louis's wife, Maria, was a gracious hostess, and even though they spoke no English, I felt not only welcome, but also quite comfortable. They were a lovely family, and the children were excited to have a visitor.

The next morning I shared a typical Spanish breakfast, tortilla and cocoa, with Maria and her happy children. Louis came to take me to see Ranen.

We drove for twenty minutes south, along the coast, through a desert, and then I saw the tall stone walls topped with barbed wire, surrounding a concrete building, looking to be a huge and forbidding fort out there by itself in the desert. From the first look at that place I said out loud, "I am going to get him out of there!"

Louis was very comforting and relaxed as he showed me where to go, and the guards and warden all showed respect for him. He seemed to take pride in being responsible for these very unusual clients.

After I arrived, they brought Ranen out to the meeting room. He looked okay, but in shock. The whole thing was very strange. We all talked about the plan to get him out, but we couldn't say very much, and we had to talk in code. Then Louis left us alone, after telling Ranen that he was going to see the judge this very day.

All alone, except for the guards, who were busy talking to Louis, Ranen wasted no time taking me into a powerful embrace.

Louis and I left the Almeria prison feeling a bit depressed. I was not feeling okay about any of this. Despite being a bit over-whelmed, I was determined to learn to speak some Spanish, to get back on the boat, and to keep Louis moving to get Ranen out of that place.

That same afternoon I found a nice little hotel and moved out of Louis and Maria's house. The next step was to get some transportation. Almerimar was over sixty kilometers from Almeria so I definitely needed to rent a car. Fortunately, it was between seasons, and cars were cheap.

It wasn't long before I was allowed to see Ranen again, this time for a contact visit. I found my own way back to the prison, and brought treats for Ranen with me. While checking in the guards took the cheese, olives, and salami, to deliver to Ranen.

I realized, as I waited, that I was the only foreigner in the waiting room. The rest were all Spanish Gypsies, many of them kids, aunts, and uncles, all visiting one or two members of the family. I was the only solo person there. All the rest were families together with their troubled looks.

An oriental prisoner, whom I presume had done most of his time and was allowed to help out, showed me where to go next. I felt he wanted to tell me something, maybe try to contact someone to get him out, but I was not in the mood to assist. We had enough on our shoulders to worry about.

He took me where everybody had to line up, myself and all the Gypsies, and one by one we were sent into a room with a prison guard. When it was my turn a female guard accompanied me into the room. I had to strip naked and was checked thoroughly, including up the vagina! It was very weird.

We were then led through a couple sections of serious metal gates, locked in and locked out, and I was led into a cell. I had never been in a cell before. I took note of how huge the room was and just a tiny, single, metal bed on one side.

Then Kenny arrived. We were so nervous and had so much to talk about that sex was not the most romantic. We were allowed an hour together, and we spent most of it chatting about what had happened, and what to do next.

It was always in the back of my mind that we were lying to everyone, including our lawyer Louis. We were not an innocent cruising couple and there was another thirty kilos of weed from Laos in a secret compartment in the boat that was now impounded. Now that Ranen had been arrested for marijuana we could be sure that we were being watched, so getting it off the boat was going to be a dangerous challenge.

The next day I went to see Louis. He had met with the judge, was working on getting Ranen out on bail, and he did get permission for me to visit the boat and make it more secure. He also called the Port Captain to inform him of my permission to go onboard.

I drove straight to the tower to find the Port Captain's office. Don Miguel, the snobby Port Captain from Mallorca, came out in person to see me. I was amazed at how kind he was. He assigned our favorite marinero, Antonio, to oversee my visit to the boat. Don Miguel seemed to be going out of his way to help me.

Antonio and I went onboard. The boat was a mess. It was obvious that people had been aboard. There were gouges in the fiberglass where someone had stolen fenders, allowing the boat to grind against the stone quay. Our "friends" Paul and Annie never bothered to take a few minutes to put out a couple of new fenders.

The boat was still unlocked, so I had Antonio wait on deck while I went below, and I quickly opened a valve in the head, which allowed water to flood into the bilge. When the water reached the floor boards, I called Antonio to come down below, and I showed him that the boat was in danger of sinking.

I pumped the boat dry, and closed and locked everything up. We then drove back to the Port Captain's office to speak to Don Miguel. I told him of the condition of the boat and he agreed that he would recommend I be allowed to live aboard the boat, to assure the safety of the vessel. This was going very well, much better than I expected.

It wasn't until much later that I learned why the arrogant, upper class Don Miguel was so helpful. It was well within living memory, when most middle and upper class people in Spain had family members imprisoned for being on the wrong end of the political spectrum. So, Ranen being in jail was not a black mark against us. It actually gave us a kind of status, being captured by the hated Guardia Civil made us members of a special club, a club whose members had been imprisoned for political crimes.

By the time I had my next meeting with Louis he had heard about the boat almost sinking, and had gained permission from the judge for me to move back on the boat. He was very proud of me for getting the locals on our side, and not just any locals, but the Mallorcan upper class Port Captain, Don Miguel Fuentes.

I moved back on the boat the next day, feeling good about myself for tricking the authorities into giving our boat back.

I saw Annie in the bar and, although she tried to hide it, she was quite surprised and not at all happy to see me, or hear that I was back on board our boat in the marina. Annie was not as good a liar as her KGB-trained husband, Paul.

They were always asking me over to their boat but I never took up the invitations I always said I was busy.

CHAPTER 37

The Last Few Weeks Inside

LIFE LOCKED DOWN **went on.**

Carlo and I were working out for two hours every day and I was spending a lot of time learning about Marcel's life as a cocaine dealer's enforcer.

Rafa and I washed our floors and generally kept our cell very clean. There was a free laundry in the prison so we had clean clothes and linen for our beds.

Marcel told me that we were lucky to be in this new, high-security prison, because the one in Malaga was one hundred years old and had bad insect problems and serious overcrowding. Almeria had separate cells with only one or two inmates per cell because of our dangerous prisoners. In Malaga he was in a dormitory with ten people.

One day I was led into a waiting room with one other prisoner, an American drug mule, and we were introduced to a member of the US consulate who wanted to know our stories so she could offer us help. We were the only two American prisoners.

I was defiant. I told her I was just fine, I had my own lawyer, and I was getting out. I didn't need help from my own government because I didn't want them digging around in a crime for which I could be prosecuted, when I got back to the States.

She became a little irate, "I drove three hours down here to help you!"

"I don't give a shit and I don't need your help. Help her," I thumbed towards the other prisoner and walked out. I was not going to be a gold star on this woman's resume and pay for it when I got back home.

Not long after, I had another visit from Louis, then a week after that he showed up with Arianna. "Now," he said, "I have what I need to get you out of here."

I was shocked and thrilled to see Arianna with her big, bright smile right there in front of me, and the instant Louis left us alone I gave her a crushing hug and kiss. This was a turning point and I knew it.

Neither of us could relax (I don't know why, after all, we were only reuniting in a foreign prison), so she whispered her very clever plan that got the court to let her back on the boat. She told me about the time she had spent with Louis and his family, and reckoned that Paul and Annie had mistakenly thought that they had hired a bad lawyer. "I thought the same thing!" We had a good laugh about that, and the picture of Annie's face when she saw Arianna, thinking they had got us out of their way for a while.

We were all feeling confident that I would be able to get out on bail.

I requested a conjugal visit with Arianna. The prison had some cells for private visits with wives and (in my case) fiancés.

One night, in the morning, long before the sun came up, a guard appeared at our cell to quietly rustle Rafa, told him to pack his things, and walked him out. Rafa carried his bundle out without a look back, and that was the last I saw of him.

On the day of Arianna's visit I brought clean sheets for the bed and thoroughly cleaned the cell. When I was finished the strong prison disinfectant left behind a sharp odor, but at least it didn't smell of the last couple who had used this venue.

I knew they would strip-search Arianna. It was winter outside, and I shuddered at how cold and damp it was in the unheated jail.

Then the guard brought her to the cell.

"Did you bring a file?" I asked.

Arianna laughed and we kissed.

It was good there was a lot to talk about at first, and enough time for her to fill me in on all that had happened while I was here, because these prison meetings were really uncomfortable and we were both nervous. I was impressed how well Arianna had held up. That she was back on the boat was a major move. That girl could keep her cool!

We talked about how to keep our stories straight. Louis was not a lawyer who would help us if he knew that we were hiding anything from him. As far as we were concerned we were not guilty because we were not importing weed into Spain, but to Holland where weed was legal. Still, he would have felt betrayed, even though we were protecting him.

After a while we felt relaxed enough to get under the blankets like we were a teenage couple greedily making out after school. Finally, we got the bed warm enough to make love. Although the sex was rushed, it was wonderful to be locked into a skin-to-skin embrace with this woman who I not only loved but who was my best friend and partner in crime.

It was a sad moment when they came to escort her out.

By that point I trusted Marcel, my English-speaking Dutch friend, and used him as an advisor. I ran down my situation with the contacts in Holland, and he told me that in Holland, no matter what was promised, a deal wasn't a deal until you were paid. He agreed that Arianna's suspicion they were going to try to rip us off was a real possibility. Marcel figured they probably wouldn't make a move until they got the second half of the cargo.

Soon after the visit with Arianna, Louis came to visit. He said that the judge was ready to release me, and because Louis had given his word that we were good, innocent people, the judge was ready to release me without paying any bail. Louis added that although we would not pay bail, he was going to have to put up Maury, his son, as security on our good character. I would be out until trial, and the worst outcome would be a fine. They should drop the charges, Louis thought, but I could get a big fine just because the Guardia Civil wanted me so badly. He switched to his serious voice and told me if we were caught lying it would go badly. That was sober advice, in view of what we were going to have to do next.

Late one night a guard walked into my cell and told me I was being released. I had almost nothing to pack, just a little bundle of clothes.

As I walked down the hall I knocked on Marcel's door and said goodbye. I stopped at Carlos's cell, he opened the door and gave me an *abrazo*, a macho hug, and wished me luck. Continuing down the corridor, most of the prisoners came out to wish me luck. When the winemakers shed tears, my guard muttered that I was a popular figure.

There were no papers to sign. Louis was waiting in an open office, where the guards gathered to say they were happy that I was being released. They actually went on to say they enjoyed knowing me, and encouraged me to keep up my exercise program!

On the ride to town, Louis again reiterated that if I ran away he had to forfeit his first and only son. He had guaranteed me personally. Of course, having my boat still impounded until trial had to be a big factor in how Louis was able to negotiate my release without bail.

Louis dropped me off at a little hotel in the Almeria center where Arianna had a room for the night. Well past midnight I woke her with a sleepy kiss reminiscent of the kisses we shared when we changed watch at sea on our long voyages. I can still remember the scent of a warm, sleeping Arianna. Like warm oatmeal. We tightly clung to each other and made love slowly with lingering kisses.

CHAPTER 38

Back to the World

FOR THE FIRST time in over a month, Arianna and I woke up smiling. Her smile said everything about her relief to have me back. Waking up together was ecstatic.

We went to breakfast at the market where we could talk without being overheard and came up with a gameplan for dealing with Paul and Annie.

Problem was we had no proof. We couldn't say for certain what they had done, or why. It made no sense that Paul worked directly with the Spanish police, he was too smart to get in bed with them. However, an anonymous phone call just to get us out of the way seemed very much his style. He loved "the game," he was good at it, and he was so arrogant he probably thought we hadn't caught on.

So we would just play along and run our own game within their game. We would keep them close, careful of what we revealed, and let them move in on our transport contacts. This time, we would be ready to cut them loose before they could injure us again, whatever it took.

We returned the rental car and took the bus back to Almerimar.

It was great to finally get back on *Saga*. I took a quick inventory, just because I could, before we stopped by to see Paul and Annie.

They were acting pleased to see me and, on some level, I think they were. I think they liked us, It just so happened we had something they needed. An intelligence agency like the KGB only hires and trains sociopaths. Dishonest people just assume everyone is playing by the same crooked rules, and take what they want to take. I'm sure it never occurred to Paul to just ask to work with us. Automatically, like instinct, he stole what he needed, and he would continue to do so if we couldn't outthink him.

They offered us dinner but now we were on a macrobiotic diet so we had tea instead, and a lot of catching up. Arianna and I easily slipped back into our roles as friendly, fellow yacht-criminals. We compartmentalized our mistrust, enjoyed their company, and spent a few hours talking about boats and traveling in Africa and Asia.

Paul offered to give us their twenty-year-old but well-running Renault 16, because they had bought a newer model. They were going all out to be helpful and seduce our trust. Or maybe they were just tired of driving us around. Either way, having a car was a huge help, and I bit my tongue when I wanted to ask where they got the money for the new Renault.

Now that I was back, Nigel set up a little workshop next to where the boat would be parked in the yard, to rebuild the engine, not even blinking an eye at the fact that I had just been released from prison.

We were going to do a major rebuild and refit, which meant that we would be in the boatyard for three months or more. I wanted to get everyone used to us being here, working on our boat, going and coming for parts and provisions from El Ejido, ten miles away. After a while, anybody who might be watching us would get so tired of our trivial activities that they would lose interest.

The second night back, concealed from prying eyes, I dumped all the guns except the S&W .38 into the water. God, how I hated watching those customized, expensive weapons disappear into the dark water.

I couldn't and wouldn't let go of my .38. It was real small, easily hidden, and especially deadly loaded with my special Hydra Shock bullets. I thought I would need it soon, to kill Paul and Annie.

If what Louis the lawyer thought was true, that the Guardia was certain we had contraband, then they would still be watching. I decided to find out for sure.

It was still winter and dark at 7:00 a.m. when we tossed a couple trash bags off the boat, full of old food cans, trash, and stinking, greasy rags we had used for cleaning the bilge. We stealthily packed them into the trunk of the car for the trip up to the dumpster.

The instant we started out of the yard, police cars appeared from three directions, blocking the road, green cops and red lights everywhere. They had us wait in the car while they tossed the trunk and unpacked the trash bags.

The greasy rags really pissed them off.

It was confirmed. The Guardia Civil *were* watching. Our "friends" *were* rats.

CHAPTER 39

Good Manners Again

FIRST THING IN the morning, Nigel, Arianna, and I guided the boat into the travel lift gantry. For the next two hours, Joaquin lifted the boat, moved it into the boatyard, and set up the jack-stands.

Normally, more than half your boat is underwater, it's rare to be able to see her entire form. *Saga* was the most regal boat in that yard.

At 1:00 p.m. Joaquin set up the small crane and we were ready to pull the engine.

I guided it out the cockpit from the engine room below, then I was on deck with a line guiding the engine away from the boat.

Nigel stood below next to the boat to guide it onto the stand we had built.

He and I built a roof over our work area once Joaquin finished with the crane. After the beating *Saga* had suffered there was a long list of repairs beyond the engine rebuild. We were out of the water. We might as well do it all.

Throughout the voyage I had kept a running mental tally of what it was costing in damage. Now we needed money.

It was time to get paid for what had been delivered to Holland. No way was I going to allow that asshole Jack to take advantage of us and steal our weed.

Even twenty-five years later I am feeling a rush of anger as I write this.

The weed still on the boat was going to stay right where it was until the police got tired of watching us. So far, they hadn't scored a single win from their tip off, and now the credibility of their informant was probably becoming suspicious. As time went on, whoever was in charge of our investigation was going to look like he was wasting money and police resources.

Meanwhile, we needed to get the court case settled, or get permission to go to Holland and get ourselves paid.

One night, out of the dark, Marcel showed up at the boat, alone and desperate.

"Listen man, they let me out three hours ago, it was a fuck up for sure. They're gonna' realize they let the wrong guy go and come looking for me! I have to get out of Spain right away. Do you have wheels? By the way, niiice fucking boat."

His only hope was, in fact, to get all the way back to Holland, the only country in Western Europe that had no extradition for drug charges. He didn't just need to get out of Spain, he also needed to get past France, and then Belgium.

Problem was, they confiscated his passport when they arrested him, and he didn't stick around to ask for it back after they released him with the wrong name.

He couldn't travel without a passport.

It was midnight, I was out on bail, and here was Marcel standing right there asking for help. I knew damn well that my attorney would not approve. Anything I did for Marcel would be a risk, from helping him escape Spain to just having him standing here on my boat.

Nevertheless, without words, Arianna and I both knew we were going to help him. What a pain in the ass, but there was no way to refuse. Fate had given him a break, and without my help he would end up back in prison for a lot of years. He had been a good friend when I needed one.

I was annoyed but resolved to organize Marcel's freedom, even if it meant driving all over Spain in that second-hand, clapped-out Renault. We left for Malaga the next morning while it was still dark and freezing on the southbound highway with no working heater. Not only did Malaga house the nearest Dutch consulate, but Marcel had already been working with an official there to try to get his case transferred to the Netherlands.

It was still dark when we found the building, we knew it wouldn't be open, but there was an emergency contact number on the hours notice. When Marcel got through to the official he had been working with, the man immediately drove to town and opened the office for us.

The officer, an older and sympathetic man, made it clear Marcel needed to get out of Spain as quickly as possible. He gave us a detailed road map, and suggested that flying out of Malaga was not a chance Marcel should take.

He added that he wouldn't lie to the Spanish police if they questioned him. "Listen Marcel," he said, "I'm stretching diplomatic boundaries as it is."

With that, he handed Marcel a brand new passport.

We were in and out of the consulate within two hours.

Wow! I thought. *There is no way the American consul would even consider doing this for an American citizen busted for coke, on the run, who wasn't rich or connected. In Malta the embassy official had complained about giving me a replacement passport, and that was a legitimate request!*

I studied the map and decided the best course for us to stay out of trouble was to drive to Andorra, a microstate on the Spanish-French border in the Pyrenees mountain range. Being winter, the passes might be closed, but even so I was prepared to walk Marcel over the border.

Winter in the mountains held no fear over me. A lifetime ago, before I stepped foot on a sailing boat and dropped off the face of the world, I could be found climbing in Yosemite, skiing, and sewing mountain gear in Telluride when I needed the cash.

We drove all day, stopping once at a magnificently elegant trucker-café for coffees, *jamón serrano*, and *manchego* cheese sandwiches made with fresh, crusty bread. In the late afternoon we arrived in Andorra, and by evening we were at a ski resort on the French border.

Luck was with Marcel. There wasn't much snow left in the mountains that March. Good thing, because we needed to hoof it across the border to avoid the French authorities.

I gave Marcel a warm jacket and hat, but he only had sneakers for shoes. Nevertheless, we plunged into the dark woods, sometimes postholing through knee-deep snow, keeping the ski slopes in sight to guide us. Some five hours later we veered back to the road.

We were in France.

The last I saw of Marcel, he had hitched a ride on a truck heading north on the N22 toward Toulouse, where he could catch a train to Amsterdam. I hiked back to the resort where Arianna was waiting. It was a damn good thing we helped Marcel without question. He ended up playing a major role in our story.

The whole affair took less than two days. No one in the boatyard even noticed we were gone. It looked like the Guardia Civil had lost interest in us. Now, I had to focus on one job, the title of the next chapter…

CHAPTER 40

Let's Get Paid!

AFTER PULLING OFF Marcel's border circumvention, I was confident the police were no longer tracking us. This was as close as we would get for a safe moment to get back to crime.

Jack owed us money, and we needed to pry it out of Aloysius before delivering the next load. In all business deals, when the work is finally done, there is no more leverage for getting paid. If all the weed was in the hands of our partners, what would stop them from refusing to pay? They would be holding all the cards in the game. So, if they wanted the rest (and they did), they had to pay for what they were already holding.

But first, I had to talk Louis into getting me released for travel within Europe. I needed my passport back. I told him I had to go north to visit my bank and make financial arrangements to pay his fees, and any fines I might end up with.

Meanwhile, Arianna and I kept a lot of irons in the fire. We tackled all the boat maintenance and repairs with high energy, did all kinds of aerobic exercise routines, sailed in all the regattas at the local yacht-racing club, and stuck to our Japanese, macrobiotic-diet health plan.

We were down to sleeping four hours a night. We didn't need much sleep, and we were becoming noticeably more powerful every day. Good thing, too, because we were into the hardest part of any smuggling project, and now we were distracted by the criminal charges. Still, the people we were up against couldn't do what we had already done. High seas, treacherous sailing, pirate attacks, illegal border crossings, foreign incarceration… we survived everything, and that put us in a league of our own. Despite all we were still up against, we weren't afraid, honestly, not even nervous. Even Paul and Annie shied away from us. We made *them* nervous.

Although he returned in just two days, it was no small task for Louis to secure my passport. He had to petition the court for my permission to leave Spain. Good thing I didn't get caught with Marcel!

The real problem was that the Guardia Civil had my passport. Giving it up meant giving up their trafficking case on me… Defeat had to be tough on the guys who, for sixty years, had total control over the people of Spain. My passport was the least of their problems, but it *was* a symbol for all of their problems.

Louis demonstrated serious legal power. He went straight to the judge and challenged the Guardia Civil. Put up or shut up, was essentially the translation of what he argued. No new evidence meant the charges needed to be reduced or dropped. It was past time to schedule a court appearance and let this innocent couple get on with their lives.

The judge was actually a member of the same yacht club we joined, and we were held in high regard by many locals, simply for having been persecuted by the Green Hats. Strange, but that was the pre-constitution climate in late-eighties Spain. He agreed with Louis, and gave me permission to travel around Europe, but, still somewhat leery of disrespecting the Guardia, kept the boat impounded as security.

Louis handed me my passport with a warning that he had personally guaranteed that we would not run, or break more laws.

We did feel bad about lying to Louis, but we were also protecting him. We really had no choice.

CHAPTER 41

The Captain Returns to Holland

WE WASTED NO time flying for Holland the day I got my passport.

When we knocked on Aloysius and Ilse's door it was after dark and no one was home. So we took a seat in the dark and waited.

An hour later, their car pulled into the driveway.

As Aloysius slipped his key into his front door, I jumped out and said BOO!

He freaked. He turned on me and punched me a few times. I can remember so clearly, because it was such a strange, surreal moment, how his punches felt like blows from a large moth.

I gave him a hug that trapped his arms, Arianna and Ilse greeted each other, and the moment passed.

They made us welcome and, just as before, put us up in their spare room. Ilse's baby was due any day, and her midwife visited every morning. We were amazed that the Dutch national healthcare paid for the midwife, who would not only deliver the baby at their home, but stay to look after the family for two weeks after the baby was born.

We were present and on hand to help when Ilse gave birth to a healthy girl.

With a new infant in the house, Arianna and I decided we needed to leave them to their new life, but we still had to force a conversation with Aloysius before we could leave. If he wasn't going to bring it up, fine, we'll do it. We needed to get paid, and make it clear that Jack had struck a deal with us, and he and Aloysius had better keep to it.

Arianna and I were always debriefing, sharing notes, and making plans together. I was careful to respect Arianna, and although I didn't include her in every decision, we were partners and I always listened to her and trusted her. We were partners but I was Captain, difficult to explain, but it worked for us.

We agreed Jack was pulling Aloysius's strings while he was (conveniently) still in Thailand, and they had hoped that I would still be in jail, so they could prey upon Arianna's youth and inexperience. Aloysius was too much of a "light weight" to cheat us, but his boss, Jack, was not only capable, but he *would* try to cheat us as a matter of principle. According to Marcel, that was just standard business for the region, and if anybody knew, it would be Marcel.

Out of respect for Ilse and her newborn, we took our business to Aloysius while he was working at the bar. We liked Aloysius, and he liked us. He wasn't the bad guy here, he was just stuck in the middle. I didn't want to lean on him too hard if I didn't have to.

I did all the talking, and everybody kept it civilized. We needed to get paid for the weed he was holding, and he needed to put down a serious deposit for the rest, or he would never see another gram. Also, Arianna was going to stay to keep an eye on *our* product, and he *would* give her as much weed as she wanted so she could help him market it. And if he didn't get busy selling it, we would do it ourselves. We were not going to wait for Jack to come back at his leisure. Pay us now or give back what belonged to us, Captain Ranen was out of prison and accepting no excuses.

Aloysius could tell that, true to my word, I was not going to leave him alone until he paid up. He reluctantly pulled together $10,000 worth of various currencies, called it an advance on what he owed us, and complained that he was unprepared.

We were pushing it to stay on at Aloysius and Ilse's house after the baby was born and after I had confronted Aloysius. Fortunately, it only took a couple days to get Arianna safely organized.

Mickey, an English regular at the bar, agreed to let Arianna stay at his house with him and his English roommate, Scott. Everyone loved Arianna (always), and Mickey was upfront with us that Aloysius was lying when he said he wasn't selling the weed until Jack returned. Turned out, Arianna filled me in later, Mickey and Scott didn't think highly of Jack. They were thrilled to run around Holland with her, from cities to festivals, checking market prices and selling our weed.

She would only get ten days to work Holland with her adopted running mates before she had to return to Almeria for my trial.

Before I left for the boat I called Marcel at the number he gave me when we parted ways, ankle deep in snow, on the highway in France.

It was a relief to hear his voice and that he had made it back without a hitch.

He asked, "So how is the business with the guys here going?"

I answered, "Pretty much as you predicted. They are trying to cheat us, but I'm making them pay up before they see the rest. The showdown will come when we give them the second and last load. Once they have it all, they're going to try to stiff us, just like you said. I'll deal with that when the time comes. I can promise this, after everything we have been through, I'll be lucky to break even on this whole project, and I will not allow anyone to push us around. You've seen me when I'm angry. Next time I won't be wearing sneakers."

CHAPTER 42

The "Lunch Trial"

WHEN I RETURNED to my boat, I started having lunch with Paul and Annie at the bar, and nightly dinners on their boat. I wanted to encourage them to continue to prove their loyalty, prove that they hadn't turned us in. More than anything, I was determined to keep them close. I believe in that old saying made famous in *The Godfather*, "Keep your friends close, but your enemies closer."

Paul tried to press me for information about when I expected Charles to bring back his camper and collect my next load. I just said I wasn't even thinking about that until after I cleared my court case.

The court date was set, but I checked in with Louis every couple days anyway, just to make sure there would be no more complications. It was April, the weather was improving, and I was anxious to get past all of this.

A couple weeks before the trial, I picked up Arianna at the Almeria Airport Bus stop in Roquetas de Mar.

The two of us spent more and more time with the local sailing boat racing crowd, and they loved us. I had spotted my judge at the yacht club bar, and he had also seen us, and knew who we were. Everybody knew us and knew our story. We were curious to find out how he would react to us when we came before him in court.

When the day of my court appointment arrived, I have to admit, I was plenty nervous. We met Louis at his office, walked to the court-house, and found our courtroom on the second floor.

The wood-paneled room looked like it had been unchanged since it was built, probably around the turn of the century. Seven rows of uncomfortable, wooden benches flanked an aisle down the middle, and the floor was muted black and grey ceramic tile, worn uneven from many years of use. The judge sat at a raised podium, facing the courtroom.

Our case was scheduled for 11:30 a.m. and we were called to stand before the judge fifteen minutes past schedule.

As soon as we stood in our place, and the judge glanced up from his files to look at us, he angrily turned on the prosecutor, "What is this tourist couple doing in my courtroom? WHY ARE THEY IN MY COURTROOM? Do you not know that I have killers, rapists, and terrorists to deal with? Why are you wasting my time? This case is adjourned, for *almuerzo*, to the Bodega Almeria." He rapped his gavel and stood.

The entire court--the bailiff, two prosecutors, a few others whose function I wasn't sure of, Louis, Arianna, and myself--followed the judge out the door, down the wide, marble staircase, and out onto the street.

A few minutes later, we all filed into the ancient darkness of a spacious Andalucían bodega. Really, it was more of a *taberna*, with a long, dark-hardwood bar, and a mezzanine encircling the large room stacked with casks of sherry. The blackened-oak beams above were hung with the hams for which Andalucia is famous. The hams, aging sherry, and wood-fired grill in the *cocina* gave this place a rich, enticing aroma of smoke, spice, and history.

The judge presided over what Louis laughingly called a "Lunch Trial." He requested the largest, round, oak table, and told each of us where to sit. On one side of the judge sat Louis, on the other side sat the prosecutors, and Arianna and myself sat directly across. The judge ordered for all of us, bottles of red wine, pitchers of sherry, platters of ham, rich cheese, grilled, fresh sardines, and tortillas Española's.

He conferred with the attorneys for a few minutes, while Arianna and I sipped wine and nibbled at our delicious appetizers, and then he turned to us and asked one question: How were we enjoying our stay in Andalucia?

CHAPTER 42

The "Lunch Trial"

WHEN I RETURNED to my boat, I started having lunch with Paul and Annie at the bar, and nightly dinners on their boat. I wanted to encourage them to continue to prove their loyalty, prove that they hadn't turned us in. More than anything, I was determined to keep them close. I believe in that old saying made famous in *The Godfather*, "Keep your friends close, but your enemies closer."

Paul tried to press me for information about when I expected Charles to bring back his camper and collect my next load. I just said I wasn't even thinking about that until after I cleared my court case.

The court date was set, but I checked in with Louis every couple days anyway, just to make sure there would be no more complications. It was April, the weather was improving, and I was anxious to get past all of this.

A couple weeks before the trial, I picked up Arianna at the Almeria Airport Bus stop in Roquetas de Mar.

The two of us spent more and more time with the local sailing boat racing crowd, and they loved us. I had spotted my judge at the yacht club bar, and he had also seen us, and knew who we were. Everybody knew us and knew our story. We were curious to find out how he would react to us when we came before him in court.

When the day of my court appointment arrived, I have to admit, I was plenty nervous. We met Louis at his office, walked to the courthouse, and found our courtroom on the second floor.

The wood-paneled room looked like it had been unchanged since it was built, probably around the turn of the century. Seven rows of uncomfortable, wooden benches flanked an aisle down the middle, and the floor was muted black and grey ceramic tile, worn uneven from many years of use. The judge sat at a raised podium, facing the courtroom.

Our case was scheduled for 11:30 a.m. and we were called to stand before the judge fifteen minutes past schedule.

As soon as we stood in our place, and the judge glanced up from his files to look at us, he angrily turned on the prosecutor, "What is this tourist couple doing in my courtroom? WHY ARE THEY IN MY COURTROOM? Do you not know that I have killers, rapists, and terrorists to deal with? Why are you wasting my time? This case is adjourned, for *almuerzo*, to the Bodega Almeria." He rapped his gavel and stood.

The entire court--the bailiff, two prosecutors, a few others whose function I wasn't sure of, Louis, Arianna, and myself--followed the judge out the door, down the wide, marble staircase, and out onto the street.

A few minutes later, we all filed into the ancient darkness of a spacious Andalucían bodega. Really, it was more of a *taberna*, with a long, dark-hardwood bar, and a mezzanine encircling the large room stacked with casks of sherry. The blackened-oak beams above were hung with the hams for which Andalucia is famous. The hams, aging sherry, and wood-fired grill in the *cocina* gave this place a rich, enticing aroma of smoke, spice, and history.

The judge presided over what Louis laughingly called a "Lunch Trial." He requested the largest, round, oak table, and told each of us where to sit. On one side of the judge sat Louis, on the other side sat the prosecutors, and Arianna and myself sat directly across. The judge ordered for all of us, bottles of red wine, pitchers of sherry, platters of ham, rich cheese, grilled, fresh sardines, and tortillas Española's.

He conferred with the attorneys for a few minutes, while Arianna and I sipped wine and nibbled at our delicious appetizers, and then he turned to us and asked one question: How were we enjoying our stay in Andalucia?

Altogether, we plowed through the meal in about an hour, all the while conversing about the food as we ate, and the wine as we drank. Spaniards do love to talk about their food and drink.

Finally, without ever another word to us about our case, the judge thanked the table and left, and most everybody else followed.

When only Arianna, myself, and Louis remained, Louis told me where I stood. The judge had decreed that I must pay a fine for possession, and the lunch bill.

After the fine, lunch, and Louis's bill, I had spent about half of the money I had brought back from Holland. Good thing I had made the trip to visit my "bank."

Despite the costs, Arianna and I were in high spirits. *Saga* was no longer impounded. I was no longer under arrest.

PART 8 – The Path Back to the Sea

CHAPTER 43

Running Around in Europe

ARIANNA AND I were too drunk to drive back to the boat, so we got a room, got drunker, and called Aloysius from the hotel to say we were ready to unload as soon as we got paid, plus an advance on the rest.

Tangled up in bed together, Arianna asked, "Why are we not selling this ourselves? Mickey watched them sell it right out of the bar. Everybody I met loves the weed, and all of them know our story."

"...Good point!" I replied, thinking it through.

"Have you ever sold your own weed before?"

"Didn't realize I never told you.

"I had to do a major, underground marketing campaign in the seventies when we were the first to bring in Colombian weed. None of the American dealers knew what Colombian Red looked like. They wouldn't touch it, even though it was *far* superior to *any* commercial weed at that time.

"They didn't want to sell our weed? Fine. We cut all ties with them and sold it ourselves. We made a killing. That weed became an underground, cult favorite. We gave away joints on the streets of San Francisco and Berkeley, and gave away thousands of tee-shirts with an elaborate stencil of guys unloading a sailing boat under the tagline, "Smoke the Best Smoke Columbian."

"Those dealers, who didn't want it to begin with, were chasing each other trying to figure out how to find us, leaving messages everywhere, begging us to come back. But they couldn't find us. We disappeared. Fuck them, if they didn't want it, they couldn't change their mind after we'd spent all the money and time on the marketing. It was fantastic weed. We didn't need them.

"Holland is tricky, because nobody in Holland imports weed. It's legal to grow, buy, and sell in Holland, so why risk it? They just grow their own. But we made history in Berkeley and San Francisco. We can do the same thing in Holland. You've started without me, and everything you've done is *exactly* how I would have done it. Fuck Jack. You're right. We don't need him."

Arianna hugged me, "Absolutely! Let's do it."

We invited Paul and Annie to come enjoy a fun, little trip with us to Malaga, and drop us off at the bus for the airport. Now it was more important than ever to keep them close. Arianna and I even exchanged *abrazos* and kisses of each cheek with them before we departed.

On our way to Amsterdam we dropped in on Aloysius at the bar, picked up a few ounces of our weed, and pressured him into giving us another cash advance. I put some of the money into printing 200 high-quality, red tee-shirts with a black design I had commissioned from Nai Harn Steve Hatchee in Phuket two years ago for just for this scenario.

It was a reboot of an ancient Harley Davidson tee-shirt design, except instead of a motorcycle, the front had a sailing boat flying off the crest of a giant wave, leaving behind a wake of skulls. In the clouds a giant cloud-face held up a cloud-hand giving the cloud-finger. The front text read "Smoke Em Til The Keels Fall Off." The back of the shirt had the winged Harley logo and read "Harley Davidson Marine... Phuket."

The late-eighties world of weed in Holland wasn't so big as you might think, and we made our mark. We went everywhere, giving away joints, telling stories, and selling tee-shirts. Over the years I have sold a couple thousand of those shirts. To this day, people still love the design.

Amsterdam loved us, our stories, and, most importantly, they loved our weed. We were well on our way to becoming well-known fixtures in the Amsterdam coffee shops. Thing was, even though we were having fun, we didn't want to sell our weed ourselves. We just wanted Jack afraid we were going to sell it all before he got a piece of it. If we had to, we could sell it ourselves, but honestly, we had other things to worry about. I had to get back to the boat.

Arianna wanted to stay on at Mickey's house and keep selling the weed. That was a good plan. She was established, making more and more friends, becoming kind of a cult hero with her crazy stories and prime buds, and her mere presence put the pressure on Jack and Aloysius. The longer she stayed, the more allies she would make on their home turf, where they had to live and do business. The longer she stayed, the harder it would be for them to rip us off.

So I booked my way back to Spain, and said *hasta luego* to Arianna. She and Mickey were heading to the next giant, outdoor Euro-rock concert to tell smuggling-sailing stories, and sell tee-shirts and weed.

I was in Spain, up to my elbows helping Nigel rebuild the boat's engine, when Charles just showed up and started pushing me around about getting the weed off the boat.

He didn't know it, but he was already working for Mr. ex-KGB. Paul had him completely seduced. Charles and I were civil to each other, but I wasn't his favorite person and the feeling was mutual. To a career-criminal like Charles, the slick, ex-spy Paul was more of a kindred spirit than the freedom-obsessed hippy, Ranen, who didn't respect wealth like he did. Charles was smart, but not nearly sophisticated enough to see Paul was pulling his strings.

Anything I told Charles would get back to Paul, and I needed to figure out how to make that work *for* us instead of against us. A plan began to percolate in my head, and I realized, once again, *I need Arianna back.*

CHAPTER 44

Smoke and Mirrors

THERE'S ONE THING I can say for jail, it sure gives you a lot of time. Time spent waiting, worrying, regretting, thinking, planning, deciding… Those winter nights I spent sleepless behind bars, I assembled the outline of a plan.

Unlike the last time we unloaded, I knew a hell of a lot more about the players, the smuggling scene in Spain, and how to fit it all together. But this time would be a lot more complicated, because now *we also* were known players. Now that Arianna was back from Holland, the plan would evolve quickly.

I laid it out with her, "We need to get the weed off the boat without Paul and Annie knowing."

"Right," Arianna cut in, "because according to Charles, Paul is brill and totally trustworthy. Charles is Paul's little soldier. Tells him everything."

"We can get Paul out of the picture…"

"Are you saying murder?" Arianna cut in again.

I laughed, "No, no, not if we don't have to. We can just move the weed off the boat without Paul knowing. And it has to be done long before the van gets here. Once the van gets here Paul is going to be on us like stink on shit."

"How are we going to get the weed off the boat without Paul and Annie, and God knows who else, seeing us do it?"

"I can distract Paul and Annie and make sure they won't see what is right in front of them. The weed has to disappear without them knowing it's gone. Everyone will expect the weed to be on the boat, but you will be babysitting the weed in Roquetas."

Arianna fixed me with a stare, "Me? Lovely. How is that going to work?"

"Simple. You are going to disappear. Everyone is going to think you left for England. Or Holland. Then we're going to make a car disappear without anyone ever knowing it was gone."

"I'm going to babysit the weed in our Renault? And it's going to disappear?"

"No, not the Renault. To make a car disappear, like magic, without anyone knowing it's gone, we're going to use two identical rental cars. Listen. There is going to be some serious risk, but if we think this through step by step, and pay attention to every detail, we can do this. We'll iron out every step of the way before we even begin."

I filled Arianna in on the rest of the plan, and when we found a hole in the plan, we filled it in together. This was the kind of covert stuff I loved to figure out, and like I already said, I had all that time in jail to begin framing it.

"...And that's how you make a car disappear without anyone knowing it's ever gone. Simple. Everything will be right under Paul's nose. While he schemes about how to screw us over, the weed will already be well across the border, safe from being intercepted by the Guardia Civil."

The fact is, if the police showed up again, it would be too obvious that it was because of our own personal Russian double-agent. It would give Paul away. He didn't have a good reason to turn us in this time, as far as I knew...

...But then, I reminded myself, there is the story of the scorpion and the frog.

A scorpion asks a frog to take him across a stream, and the frog protests, "You'll sting me and I'll die." The scorpion points out that if he stings the frog, he will drown and also die. The frog says, "Okay, that makes sense," but in the middle of the stream the scorpion stings him, and as they are drowning the frog asks, "Why did you sting me knowing we're both going to die?"

The scorpion replies, "That's my nature!"

My mistake the first time I did this was thinking Paul wouldn't turn us in if he had no reason to do so. I realized this time, and still believe after all these years, that Paul was the scorpion. He didn't need a reason, it was in his nature.

I wasn't going to make the same mistake twice. Our intuition told us not to trust Paul and Annie from day one. This time, even if the whole world tried to stop us, we would be prepared for anything. If the ocean couldn't kill us, then we sure as shit weren't going to let a scorpion do it. This time we were going to act when we were ready, and not a moment sooner.

Arianna would have to keep a very low profile in Roquetas, parking in her hotel parking lot, moving the car a few times a day, staying out of sight as much as possible, avoiding busy bars and restaurants, and dressing down. Making Arianna invisible was almost impossible. She had changed so much from that timid, reticent, young Kenya Cowgirl I hired so many years ago. She had become confident. She had a presence. Even when she was covered head-to-toe, in foul weather gear, she turned heads. Arianna had come into her own.

She would just have to play the part of a quiet tourist. That was a reasonable goal.

Another obstacle was how to stay in communication with Arianna after she went into hiding. This was a decade before cell phones. We would have to stay in contact to coordinate our timing. When we switched cars, timing would have to be perfect. Arianna and I would have to coordinate in such a way so that if somebody was following me they couldn't trace me back to Arianna. We needed to establish a code, a system for delivering secret messages, layer after layer of protection, redundancy after redundancy.

We started taking the coast road to the little tourist village Roquetas de Mar and spending time there. Going to the beach, having lunch, sitting in the sidewalk cafés having a tea, all the time closely observing the action. I wanted to make sure we were going to be the only "bad guys" doing business there. One of the dangers inherent in smuggling is "running someone else's gauntlet." If the police were watching some other group already running a scam here, we could walk into a trap set for *them*. So we observed… cops are usually obvious, if you know what to look for.

Roquetas indeed seemed to be the sleepy, little tourist town that it appeared to be, a perfect place to hide Arianna and our cargo. There were enough European tourists that Arianna wouldn't be out of place.

From the marina of Almerimar there were a couple routes to and from Roquetas, a main highway, and a coastal road with less traffic and less police patrols. The police that did patrol didn't pay any attention to the tourist rental cars driving the coast road in search of out-of-the-way restaurants and bars.

We also went shopping quite often in the city, Almeria, carefully scouting meeting spots where we would never run into Paul and Annie. They rarely went to Almeria, even when they flew out, it was from Malaga. Almeria was a bit low class for them, no fast lane scene, the shops were too conservative for Annie. We invited them to explore the Andalucían culture with us, knowing they weren't interested.

The big, covered market in Almeria, with its three-story high wrought-iron-and-glass roof, was a fascinating tour of the unique Andalucían culinary culture. The huge stalls alongside the walls were full of hanging, cured *jamón serrano*, or fragrant Spanish sausage, rounds of goat and sheep cheese, hanging peppers, ropes of garlic, and colorful fresh vegetable stands organized in circles around the center. Scattered throughout were numerous little cafés with massive granite counters, selling espresso, breakfasts, and lunches. We chose a café near one of the entrances for where we would meet every few days to go over plans or just catch up. We also chose a backup restaurant.

Arianna would catch a bus from Roquetas so she could avoid driving a car full of weed. In fact, it was just a storage container on wheels, and she would only start it to change spots in the parking lot.

We set up and practiced a series of moves for when and how we would meet, to make sure nobody was following either of us. It all sounds a bit paranoid, but I was determined to cover all the bases. I had a theory about covering bases. Before going to sea I always made sure everything I could think of was repaired or replaced. At sea things always go wrong, but so long as I left nothing undone before I left for sea, I would not be overwhelmed. We had enough bad luck on this whole trip already.

Arianna and I all the while maintained our purist lifestyle. We were looking and feeling better each day, whipping ourselves into condition to play James Bond. We played tourist, driving the roads, hanging out in the Almeria covered market, and having coffees in Roquetas, discreetly monitoring our playing field.

CHAPTER 45

Into the Fire

WE HAD A solid plan but first I had to go up to Holland to close out the books on the last load of weed, and get a big chunk of cash as deposit on the next shipment. Back in Holland, Aloysius didn't want to give any money up, but I pushed, and he ended up paying what Jack owed us, plus an advance on the rest. Sure, I knew we were going to have problems getting paid in the end, but I was feeling really powerful and confidant that I would get us paid. It helped to know that Marcel owed me. When Aloysius counted the last bill into my hand I told him to have Charles bring the van back to Spain. Then I flew back, I needed to stay close to Paul and Annie, and get them used to our watching them.

Charles showed up a few days before the camper, and like clockwork he contacted Paul and Annie the night before he checked in with us. To give Charles his due, he knew we would never do business with him again, but Paul looked like a source of hash for years to come. Charles thought he knew what he was doing, being an open book to Paul. In fact, we were counting on it. We had factored all this into the plan.

I told Paul that we needed a decent car to get Arianna to the airport, and generally attract less attention than driving that funky old Renault 16, and went out to rent my car. He only saw the one car. Arianna's we hid in Roquetas. There was no separating Charles from Paul, which was okay by me, because for now we wanted all the rats in one trap.

I drove Arianna to "the airport." From this point on she was underground. All communications between us were limited to our prearranged meeting schedule in the Almeria market, and for backup we had a series of cryptic messages I could leave at her hotel.

Charles ended up chasing women down in Marbella for the week before the transport van was due to arrive from England. A perfect opportunity to secretly offload the remainder of our cargo. So I parked the rental car directly under the aft deck of the boat, removed the trunk and interior light bulbs, and left the trunk unlocked.

I invited Paul and Annie over for an exotic, semi-macrobiotic meal that would be rich and healthy. They always accepted any invitation from me, because Paul was bored and needed intellectual stimulation.

I made a salty miso bean soup, steamed vegetables, and brown rice with lots of soy sauce. It was tasty and all very, very salty. Of course, I provided lots of strong Spanish wine to quench the thirst.

Paul and Annie worked through three bottles of wine with dinner alone. Then I opened a bottle of good Spanish brandy after dinner, and kept refilling their glasses as I plied him for stories from his life. Paul loved to talk about Paul. Between me asking for more spy tales, and his love of bragging, they nearly finished the brandy. Around two in the morning they staggered back to their boat.

I got busy opening the hidden compartment, and within thirty minutes I had the weed out, into two canvas bags, and the compartment closed, once again invisible. I climbed up the mizzen mast, hand over hand like a monkey running up a pole, to check that there were no lights on at Paul and Annie's boat. The boatyard was dark and silent, so I lowered the bags to the ground next to the car, slipped noiselessly down the ladder, and loaded the bags into the trunk.

During our dry runs, Arianna and I had determined precisely how long it would take each of us to drive to the rendezvous for the switch. I had thirty minutes to wait, watching and listening to the nighttime boatyard, and then drove out right on cue.

She arrived just as I pulled into the meeting spot off the main road. We each got out, had a passing kiss, and got in the other car. I waited for her to pull away then drove my empty car back to the boat. We had considered switching plates, but felt it wasn't worth the risk of being seen making the switch. I had been watching Paul closely, and never saw him give the car a second glance. In fact, he never got behind the car, never got a chance to read and memorize the plate.

I woke up the next morning, made a coffee con leche and toast, and examined my mind for psychic signs that Arianna had been caught. I could detect no sense of dread or panic, I felt totally relaxed. Paul and Annie didn't appear until *much* later, and in a delicate state. By noon I knew for certain that all had gone well, otherwise I would have heard from the Green Hats. Anyway, I was sure it was time for, if not good luck, then maybe... not bad luck.

Two days later I drove to Almeria for our first rendezvous. As planned, Arianna arrived just before me, and sat in a little park nearby the market so she could watch me walking toward the entrance. I slowly walked into the big, main entrance and went straight to the busy café and ordered a café con leche and a tortilla. From my seat in the corner, I could watch Arianna walk in with her shopping bag. She stopped at a few stalls and bought some fresh fruit and a loaf of bread. The plan was, if she saw that I was being followed, she wouldn't approach. If I saw that she had a tail, I would turn my cup upside down, and she wouldn't stop.

When I watched her approach I felt my heart beating at double pace. I couldn't wait to see her, to talk to her, to touch her...

But she walked by without even looking at me.

My heart sank into my stomach. What could have gone wrong?

My mind started racing at a high-speed, adrenalized pace. I was so sure I wasn't being followed. I had walked around Almeria for a half hour, watching my back, memorizing everyone on the street. None of them had followed to the market. I was panicked by the thought that she had drawn heat.

She came around again and this time sat down.

"Jesus Christ Arianna! You nearly gave me a heart attack."

She took my hand and with an Arianna-brilliant smile said, "Sorry man, I didn't see you in the corner."

We shared a meaningless conversation that had nothing to do with the plan or the electricity zapping between our eyes. I don't think I ever loved her more than at that moment. There's nothing like danger to amp up emotions.

Not long afterwards, Charles returned from Marbella with an attitude.

He became really rude and offended that I didn't trust our Russian friend, "You think Paul turned you in. You are so paranoid that you're not thinking straight. I'm wondering how safe *you* are."

"Listen Charles, I don't give a shit what you think of me. At this point, no one should know what we are doing. I know damn well that you tell Paul everything, and I don't know why. I'm not talking in front of him. If the shit hits the fan it won't be my fault."

"I don't like it that you are so insulting and mistrustful. They've helped you. Is this how you repay them?"

"Look Charles, have you asked yourself why Paul is so interested in being in the middle of our business? Maybe *you* aren't being paranoid *enough*. I'm not asking about your deal with Paul and his hash, because I don't need to know about deals I'm not involved in. And, for the record, we're friends with Paul and Annie. The less everyone knows, the better. In-group gossip can be dangerous."

"Listen man, don't tell me who I can or can't trust. You haven't said how you're going to get it off your boat without getting my drivers busted?"

"I'll tell you when it's off the boat. I'm not sharing my plans with anyone. You should be pleased that I'm being so careful. So when *does* the van arrive? I don't want to do it here in the boatyard this time. I'll deliver it to some resort on the coast."

"This time, Paul, Annie and I will be lookouts when you unload."

"You just aren't listening, are you? I'll let you know when it's time to deliver. Just let me know when you are ready."

"The van is here now. It arrived this afternoon."

"Great! Where is your car? Let's go find the van now. It's getting dark. We can load it within the hour. The weed's already off the boat and in a safe place. Not far."

The shock on that arrogant, pushy bastard's face was priceless. He thought they were going to decide how things were going to go down, but I handed him a *fait accompli,* and didn't even give him a chance to talk to the friendly Russian. Thirty minutes later the van was parked next to our storage car, I loaded the weed, and immediately they were off for the French border, on the road to Holland.

Charles was out of our lives. We were ready to take on the next phase... doing business with our Dutch "friends."

CHAPTER 46

Holland Yet Again

PAUL AND ANNIE were good sports about us tricking them, but what choice did they have? All they knew was that Charles was gone, and by the time they talked to him again, the camper would be long gone. We didn't rub their faces in our plan, didn't gloat about tricking and lying to them. I never told them that Arianna had never left. I just drove to Roquetas the next day with my traveling pack, we returned the cars at the airport, and caught a flight to Amsterdam.

Arianna turned to me, as she grabbed her pack off the carousel in Schiphol, "What do you think about going to see Satya, doesn't he live somewhere near Amsterdam? Nishela was pregnant when we met them in the Maldives, so they must have a two year old by now. I bet they went home, took a break from the sea at least for a while." I recalled that goofy, hippy Dutchman, and his Czechoslovakian refugee wife, who had been preparing to give birth in midst of a cholera epidemic.

Arianna continued, "I'm not ready yet to face that bunch of thieves who are going to try to steal our weed. Let's take a break. Satya said they have a nice house on a canal. Do you think you can find him?"

"What makes you think I can find him? I lost all his contacts the second I pushed the 'delete all' button on the electronic organizer."

"Because that's the kind of thing you can do better than anyone I've ever known. Walk into some unknown town, where you don't know the language, and find what you need. You found me, didn't you? Let's do it. It will be fun to see Satya. This'll be our first break from smuggling since London."

"Okay. Might be good to get away from it all. Clear our heads before the shit hits the fan. The town's Dordrecht, an old city up a river. I'm sure there's a train from Amsterdam station."

We caught the train and soon arrived at the much smaller, 100-year-old station. The population of Dordrecht was under 100,000 and there weren't a lot of Van Dorns in the telephone book. I just started calling, and after a few calls got through to someone who spoke English *and* knew the street Satya lived on.

We worked our way to his street, into the old part of the city, on an island between rivers of the Rhine complex. We wandered in fascination through the ancient, narrow passages, some of them laid down as far back as the 1100s. The houses in Satya's neighborhood were smaller on the street than on the succeeding floors, overhanging the street. What a perfect medieval town to film a vampire movie.

I knew the description of his house and which side of the street his house was on, because he had described how his backyard was the river. When we got where I thought was close, we started knocking on doors, it was either that or start yelling his name in the street.

A door opened, and there was Satya!

He and Nishela, who was pregnant with her second child, were blown away to see us, and warmly welcomed a couple of long-lost sailor-friends into their home. They put us up in our own tiny garret, on the fourth floor, with our own toilet, and a room with a down mattress and view of the river below.

We spent five days watching barges and ancient Dutch sailing boats on the river, and our nights drinking beers in the ancient pub, in the same neighborhood where Satya had grown up, and everyone knew each other since childhood.

In that waterfront bar, in that seaport town, we talked about boats, told our stories, and listened to the stories of three generations of sailors. Jesus, the seas were so high in that bar, you needed foul weather gear.

Satya agreed to help us refit the boat when our deal was finished. He wanted to look for a boat himself, so he was excited to travel down to Spain and hunt for a vessel while working on *Saga*. He had done some smuggling from India and was interested in getting back into the game.

Arianna and I were sitting in the bar, sharing a plate of *pomme frites*, when I wistfully remarked, "Funny. Originally, Dordrecht was where I wanted to bring the weed in. Too bad things worked out the way they did. We could've been tied up in that little harbor, right there across the canal." It's true. We could have pulled into Holland, gotten our passports stamped, tied up in that cute little harbor, unloaded right out in the open, and avoided all this mess. Maybe Paul had ended up being the villain of this story, but it all began with the Chinese. If that Chinese middleman in Thailand hadn't stalled us, just to gain face, none of this would've happened.

After five days of relaxed time with friends and endless, lazy sex, we were rested up and feeling strong. I guess we hadn't allowed ourselves the luxury of noticing how exhausted we were from these last stressful weeks. Arianna made a good call, we needed the break, and now we were ready to start winding up our business.

We caught a train to Eindhoven to find Marcel and prepare for war. He drove us over to Belgium to sample some famous Belgian beer. Over craft cherry beers, fresh on tap, we explained to Marcel the situation.

"Look, they haven't officially stolen our weed, which arrived last week, but I sense that when I go to collect they'll try something. I know for a fact that, for the second time, and against our wishes, they've weighed the weed without us present. I had to make them pay for the first half, now we have nothing to hold over their heads, and they're holding thirty kilos of our prime buds from Laos.

"It's exactly as you predicted in the slammer. A deal's not a deal until you're paid. I have no intention of letting them steal one penny from us. Christ! I fought pirates to get this weed here. As it is, even if we're paid in full, we're not going to profit. It's gonna' take every penny we make to repair the damage to my boat. If we don't get paid we won't have enough to continue sailing. We're pretty fucking committed."

"So Navigante, what exactly do you want from me?" Marcel asked, knowing that he owed us. He was only there, free in Holland, because we had helped him when he needed us.

"I want to buy a couple .45 automatic pistols, and maybe borrow a couple of your guys to help take the weed back. Thing is, Marcel, I don't want anyone killed."

"Navigante, you don't get to say you want a gang with guns but no shooting. You know as well as I do it doesn't work that way."

"Yeah, I do know that. I guess what I'm asking is, if all else fails, will you help me get it back? You know I'm no stranger to violence, you've seen it."

Arianna spoke up, "I was thinking about your lesbian, biker friends, Marcel. I got on well with Julka, and her friends. They are scary but... I think they're a little less violent than your guys. What about using *them* to send a message, and then using the more violent approach if we have to? But, I *definitely* want the .45."

Marcel countered, "Less violent? I don't think so. They loved you, and would be very pissed off if they knew you were being ripped off in their neighborhood. You may not know this, Arianna, but they are very much feared around here. Why don't you get into this, and let me know how it goes. Anyway, It'll take a day or two to come up with two automatics."

Our last stop before confronting Aloysius was to see Mickey and ask if we could stay at his house. Of course it was okay with him, it was good for his reputation to have the smugglers who brought in the "Smoke Em Til the Keels Fall Off" weed staying at his place. And he would never refuse Arianna.

We went to see Aloysius at the bar. He was nervous. I demanded money. He was more nervous. I loved it. Still, he resisted telling me where they were keeping our weed. As I expected, this wasn't going to end here.

I asked if he knew anyone who had a decent, older car that we could use. He said he could give us a low-mileage, two-door, 1983 Opel Kadett. The Opel was a cool, cool orange car with a black-vinyl top. Now we had a car!

We drove back to Eindhoven to visit the dyke bikers. Arianna knocked, and a tall, rough-looking woman, Julka, the leader of this outlaw biker club, answered the door.

She had a scary rottweiler named Spike, who let us sit down on the couch but stayed uncomfortably close. Julka had an equally rough-looking friend, who warned us not to get off the couch. Spike was trained to let strangers come in, but not let them leave. Every time we moved, Spike would bare her fangs and let loose a vicious growl. This was one intimidating household, and *we* were *friends*.

Julka warmly welcomed Arianna, and was vaguely polite to me. I wasn't getting much respect, but I could see that Marcel wasn't exaggerating the level of violence these women were capable of--so I sure as shit wasn't about to push my luck trying to coax respect out of these snarling bull moose.

At a concert earlier in the year, Julka and her gang had worked security for Mickey and Arianna while they sold weed and tee-shirts, and they clearly adored Arianna. Everyone loved Arianna.

Julka asked Arianna how the weed was selling. Back when Arianna felt Aloysius was trying to take advantage of her, she had discussed the problem with Julka, who had wanted to pay a visit to Aloysius and Ilse immediately. At the time, Arianna wanted to wait until I was out of jail.

This time, we asked Julka if she wanted to be there when we next went to visit them. Julka was jazzed that we asked. Any excuse to be a badass.

When we returned to Aloysius and Ilse's house, Julka and three of her girls pulled up next to us in the driveway on their Harley choppers.

Arianna whispered to me, "I hope this doesn't get out of hand."

"I hope it does," I replied.

I knocked on the door, and Ilse opened it holding her baby. Julka barged past Arianna and I, nearly knocking over Ilse, the baby, and Aloysius. The scary dyke had decided to take the lead.

"I hope you don't think that you can rip off Arianna and Kenny's load of weed they have sweated blood to bring to you. If anything bad happens to my very good friend Arianna, we will come here and tear this place apart, your bar, and maybe this whole fucking village. And, whoever we miss, Kenny's friend Marcel from the Eindhoven Riders will probably just kill."

I looked at Aloysius and said, "I think that about covers it. We'll be back. And thanks for the car, I love it."

Enough said. We left.

CHAPTER 47

The Showdown

IT WAS SUMMER and Euro-tourist season. Pot smokers from all over the world were in Holland to enjoy legal drugs and wild concerts. The sun was out and we had money in our pockets. We were super fit and happy and it made us powerful.

Arianna and I were good-looking, local folk heroes with fantastic stories. We never had to pay for anything. As we left a coffee shop the pretty, young woman behind the counter gave me a piece of "Space Cake." A little later we were in an Indian restaurant when the cake came on. I was totally high, and laughing so hysterically that we couldn't leave, we couldn't be out in public. Hours later the wait staff told us to leave so they could go home. We really were a couple of drunken sailors.

We were constantly hitting up Aloysius for payments. At this point we were nearly paid, except for the last $10,000, and a couple more thousand that we owed Muriel and Terry, the Australians who helped us load in Thailand. I didn't feel like we owed Terry much, he was such a lazy coward. Muriel did all the work, she deserved most of the money.

It was rainy season in Thailand and odd that Jack was still there. He would have to return sometime, Aloysius couldn't manage everything. We weren't looking forward to meeting with Jack. I remembered what an arrogant asshole he was. He would be dangerous here on his home court. There was a lot at stake for him, a lot of his people would be ready to stand for him, but a lot of people didn't like him, and every-body would be watching him.

I had been feeling so weightless and free lately, but I knew I was going to have to pull out Captain Ranen, the Badass Pirate, for the final settling up. We were dreading that meeting. Thing is, after all we had been through, Jack was just another dope dealer, a big fish in his small pond, and I wasn't afraid of him. Fuck him. Bring it on.

It was a Friday afternoon when we heard Jack was back, and we drove down from Amsterdam to confront him. We had heard from Mickey that Jack was back, and he was not pleased that we had become so popular in his little corner of Euroland.

Driving down the highway, we worked up a grievance list to get ourselves psyched for the showdown. With a bitter laugh, I blurted out a thought, "If we had filled the boat with pants, we'd have made a lot more money, and we wouldn't have to be doing any of this. Hell with it! Let's go get our money."

We walked into the bar side by side. It was mostly full of Jack's rough, close friends, some of whom we knew pretty well, as far back as Thailand when they were on *Sara*. I can imagine we made an imposing pair. My hair was pretty long now, I was wearing jeans, and a black "Deep Ocean Vessel, Pirate Vessel Sara" tank-top. I was a lot more chiseled than when last he had seen me in Thailand. Arianna was wearing a red "Smoke Em" tank-top, shorts, black high-top sneakers, and lots of sharp Somali jewelry. Arianna was also looking pretty damn ripped.

Jack was sitting on a stool at the corner of the bar. I chose a spot to stand at the bar near the door, where I could look Jack in the eye, and also see the rest of the room, a gunfighter's stance.

Jack fancied himself a bad dude. To give him his due, he was a big, self-confident guy with a deep voice, but he hadn't had to prove himself for a long time, maybe ten years or more. I had had to prove myself over and over ever since we left Thailand. He knew he couldn't bluff me, because he couldn't handle me if I called him out. Jack, whose total workout was lifting Singha beers and rolling spliffs, just couldn't intimidate the guy before him, who had been going toe to toe with stone cold Gypsy killers, a crooked police force built for a fascist regime, and months of violent Indian Ocean storms.

Jack got right into it, "So, you two have taken more money than your weed is worth," he claimed in a scathing tone. "So I think you owe me money. And I know where your boat is and that the new name is *Saga*."

"What? I'm not impressed Jack. You only know where our boat is because Charles, our transporter, works for you. If I wanted to hide, you could never find me, but I don't need to hide. I know where you live as well, and I also have some pretty dangerous friends around here who owe me favors."

I put myself right in his face, really close, "Listen to me Jack, YOU ARE NOT GOING TO CHEAT US. This may be your little palace, in which you are a little king, but you have to live here after we sail away. Your partner Aloysius made a deal, and we fulfilled our end, and you *will* fulfill your end."

I could tell by the anger on his face that Jack was about to get aggressive. "You paid Charles a stupid price to transport that weed up here, so I figure *you* owe *us* money. Aloysius has been giving you money, way too much money. Here's what I can do. We'll call it even."

"No Jack. We are not going to call it even. Your partner Aloysius made that deal with Charles. I don't have any arrangement with Charles. He's your transporter. Aloysius has been lying to us the whole time, on your orders. You thought, when I went to jail, you were going to be in a position to keep the weed, but that weed belongs to me until I'm paid in full. We have been through some serious shit with this weed and I FUCKING WELL WILL BE PAID. You *are* going to give me the ten thousand you still owe us."

"No fucking way. I'll give you eight thousand and I'll pay Muriel and Terry."

"Okay, give us the eight thousand now and we're done," I said, and soon realized why Arianna had started looking very nervously around the bar.

Jack's sharks were circling. I was so angry and focused on getting paid, that throughout this macho showdown, the thought of being careful never even occurred to me. I pushed Jack pretty loud and hard, and frankly, now that I looked around the bar, I wasn't confident about our chances of getting out with our money.

Jack counted out the cash slowly, and I could tell he was only doing it slow because he was about to call his thugs on us. I gave Arianna the *Get ready!* look, and I snatched the cash out of his hand, and we ran out the door, jumped in the car, and drove away fast. Not a very dignified exit, but better than being eaten by sharks, and… We got the money.

Driving in our sporty orange Opel our hysterical laughter flooded and faded before we even got back to the A2. I looked at Arianna and said, "I feel empty." We drove in silence for a while. "This is how it usually feels at the payoff," I added, "Let down. This whole reckless race, since Thailand, ended in Roquetas when we loaded the van. Very little of our last, dangerous year was about money. Halfway across the Indian Ocean I knew we weren't going to make enough money. It never *was* going to be enough. None of this was *really* about the money. For me it never is."

"Ranen, where are we going?"

"I have no fucking idea. We haven't had time to think what to do next, since Thailand, or maybe we never do…think about that."

Arianna answered, "Okay, actually I was asking where *we* are going. You and I. But let's find a room with a view, where we can drink champagne, look out at ships, and make love. We can worry about tomorrows, tomorrow."

"Sounds like paradise to me, but I need to work this out first. I can't help thinking about getting *Sara* ready for whatever's next. I want to refit her to cross oceans. Satya will come down to help us. After all, we're sailors aren't we?"

"But is that *all* we are, Ranen? I wonder…" she trailed off in classic British reserve, and I wasn't ready to think about where she might be going with that.

She had ended up becoming the real hero of this entire story, but this story was at an end. I was already moving on to the next. "Well, when we're back in Almerimar, and you've got one foot on *Sara*, and the other on the quay, you'll know."

Epilogue - Beyond 1989

Sara (Saga)

Satya, Arianna, and I spent the summer and all of our money getting *Sara* back to perfect yacht condition. We changed her name and registration back; I never really liked the name *Saga*. She and I had quite a few more wild adventures in transoceanic smuggling as well as a few more partners until 2002, when I sold her to a big wave surfer from Hawaii.

Paul and Annie

When we arrived back at Almerimar, Paul, Annie and their boat were gone. I had the impression that they headed for the States, where there was greater opportunity for their con scams.

Beach Rat

Still living somewhere near Santa Cruz, California with his red-headed girlfriend.

Lars and Carol

Were married in 1990, and ran the Peponi until Lars died in 2014.

Satya

Bought a steel sailing boat. Arianna and I spent a bitter, couple of winter months in a French boatyard sandblasting and painting that boat. I never ran into Satya again after he sailed away to become a smuggler.

The Characters From Holland

We never kept track of the characters from Holland, Jack, Marcel, Aloysius, Ilse, Julka, and Charles. We were all in different PPRs (planes of possible relationships).

Fiona and David

When Fiona broke up with David, I lost contact with David. My last contact with Fiona was in the early nineties when my girlfriend, Kathleen, and I visited her in London. She and her Scottish partner had a toddler son. I have since lost all contact with Fiona.

Red Sea Trader crew

The next time I was in Djibouti, shooting media for our tv show in 1998, The Red Sea Trader was gone.

Nigel and Mary

Nigel, Mary and their boat were gone when Arianna and I returned to Almerimar. I never ran into them again.

Carlos the Gitano

I cannot imagine the Spanish courts freeing Carlos, the unrepentant killer. Imagine that arrogant, scary Gypsy standing before a very proper Spanish parole board. They would be horrified to have him back on their streets.

Louis Perez Galano

Years later my partner Elizabeth and I were refused entry to the closed Port of Almeria in the first gusts of the worst European storm in fifty years. I called the port captain and insisted on being allowed "safe haven" and proceeded to raft up to some big, Basque fishing vessels who were also waiting out the storm.

Being in Almeria, I looked up Louis, and we spent an evening with he and his family. Maria cooked us dinner and introduced us to the newest Spanish flamenco music on compact discs. Their children were grown and happy.

Maria, now an elected official, became infuriated, however, when conversation turned to the Basques. "Those separatist terrorists!"

she muttered, ice in her voice. "Those murdering *coños* are the reason I am kept under 24-hour guard!" When we left they gave us one of their new flamenco discs. It was all very polite, friendly, and uncomfortable.

That is the last I heard of Louis Perez Galano, and I truly hope he never reads this book. I still cringe when I remember how much I had to lie to him to save ourselves.

Ulrica and Kurt

Kurt showed up one day at Almerimar. He was furious I hadn't told him I had been arrested. What a fool! I am amazed he couldn't see the danger in even coming near me. I think he was angry that he didn't get to sell the weed. In his defense we did just disappear on him, and who knows if things would have been different. I still think I made the correct decision.

Ranen and Arianna

I was just so focused on the game, Sara, and the sailing lifestyle, which were really one and the same, that I missed that there was a lot more on the table than that. I was just not ready to think about Arianna in any other context than friend, lover and partner in crime. After a couple more difficult but wild years, Arianna told me she was leaving. She didn't find someone else. Just left.

She said, "Look, Ranen. I want to leave you. It's not because I don't love you. I don't think I can ever love anyone as much as I love you. I just cannot live your lifestyle anymore, and I don't think any other woman can either."

Arianna

Arianna left from Ibiza to live with Fiona in London. At some point she returned to live in S. Africa on a big sailing schooner, then back to Lamu on a dhow with her husband. They had three boys who are now handsome young men.

Over the years my efforts to contact Arianna came to nothing. In the early stages of writing this, I passed a message through Lars at the Peponi. Arianna sent me an email and it turned out that she had been writing a journal of this odyssey based on her diary and recollections. She wanted her sons to know our story, and intended to let them read it when they turned thirty. She is quite happy to let me tell the story, and has graciously allowed me to use excerpts from her journal.

Ranen

I measure my life's timeline by crew and partners, and what oceans or mountains I was living in.

After Arianna I have a four woman history. Of them, only Gyslaine was another smuggler.

I married my last partner, Elizabeth, a courageous, long-distance sailor and a gifted filmmaker. Definitely a partner who would "get on that plane."

In the late-nineties we produced some cutting-edge, real-time documentary sailing videos from our voyages down the Red Sea to Djibouti, and from Venice down to Corfu.

After the turn of the century we moved to our house in the Idaho Rockies where our son, Casey, was born. I started this book for Casey who is now twelve and has helped me write this story.

There are photos, podcasts, and adventure sailing videos that can be found on my website:

asmugglersguide.com

Have questions, want to know more? Email: **ken.ranen@gmail.com**

Acknowledgements

First and foremost, I want to thank Cody McFadden, my editor in Missoula. Cody turned our memories of a great story into something a "grown up" might have written.

To my old friend and guru, Mark Mendel, who gave me a writer's residency at his well stocked house in the Berkshires. Thanks for believing in this project.

Thanks to my sister Carole who financed two years of my life so I could stop and write.

A shout out to all the girls at Move Missoula who turned me into a badass. Especially, Jenna, who wrote some of the King Neptune love scene.

The lion's share of this memoir was written at Aldea Coffee in The Armory in the sleepy town of Grand Haven Michigan, where I have been stuck for a couple of winters. Far from friends and my familiar mountains, the crew at Aldea provided high quality caffeine, friendship, and lots of feedback. I am a storyteller with limited writing experience. Every morning after dropping Casey at school I would tell part of the story to Jeremy, Andrew, or Brittany. When I could see they got it, I'd take an espresso back to my Mac and type it up. Brittany edited all of the Arianna journal pieces. After all, she is close to the age of the Arianna in the book.

Last but certainly not least, I want to thank Mark McMillin, the renaissance locksmith, who came to open my door one night, a few years ago. I was mumbling about not being used to locks. "Where were you living," he asked? I told him about my life on sailing boats for 28 years. He wanted to hear some stories and after a beer he insisted that I write a book. For the first year of my learning to write, Mark was my editor, and has been my supporter ever since.

Made in the USA
Middletown, DE
27 August 2022